GLASTONBURY

From Settlement to Suburb

fourth edition

Marjorie Grant McNulty

"Cotton Factory Village, Glastenbury"
now Cotton Hollow, South Glastonbury.
Sketch by John Warner Barber, 1836
(Connecticut Historical Society collection)

THE HISTORICAL SOCIETY OF GLASTONBURY

1995

For Henry, Anne, Sarah, Jim, Judy,
Christy and Frederick

Library of Congress Catalog Number 95-81518
ISBN 0-9610676-0-8

Contents

Maps from *Atlas of Hartford City* and *County*,
Baker and Tilden publishers, 1869.

The publication of this book was made possible through a generous donation by Katharine H. Cowles in loving memory of her father, Everett B. Hurlburt.

Preface

This history of Glastonbury is an account of the town from its beginnings to the present. Of course it is impossible in one volume to cover in full detail a span of three and a half centuries. Readers who become interested in Glastonbury's history should not hesitate to turn back to some of the earlier, and still very valuable, accounts of the town.

In 1928 the Woman's Club of Glastonbury published 400 copies of a history, *Glastonbury*, by Florence Hollister Curtis. The club reprinted the volume in 1963 (300 copies). Once again the Woman's Club came forward in 1970 to make possible the publication of *Glastonbury: From Settlement to Suburb* by underwriting the major costs of its printing, with some help from the Board of Education. In addition, members of the Woman's Club gave their time to collate and bind the pages of that paper-covered edition, which was printed on the Glastonbury High School press.

At the approach of the nation's Bicentennial in 1975 the Historical Society of Glastonbury undertook the publication of a revised and expanded second edition illustrated with photographs, and again in 1983 published an updated edition. The present fourth edition continues the account of Glastonbury's history to the mid-'90s.

Prior to Mrs. Curtis', only one book on Glastonbury's history was ever published, *Glastenbury For Two Hundred Years: A Centennial Discourse*, by the Rev. Alonzo B. Chapin, brought out in 1853 and reprinted in a bicentennial edition in 1976 under sponsorship of St. Luke's Episcopal Church, South Glastonbury. This book continues as a major source for anyone interested in Glastonbury history. Over the past 90 years or so there have been sections on Glastonbury history included in such publications as Henry R. Stiles' two-volume *Ancient Wethersfield Connecticut* and Lewis W. Ripley's account of Glastonbury in *Wethersfield and Her Daughters*. Numerous articles on various aspects of Glastonbury's history have appeared in the publications of the

Historical Society of Glastonbury, *Retrospect* and *The Publick Post*, and elsewhere. I have drawn freely on all this material, as well as on letters, diaries and manuscripts belonging to the Historical Society of Glastonbury. I have found it valuable, also, to check for authenticity with early town records and with the Colonial Records of Connecticut. Much material for the later chapters has been gleaned from annual town reports, a number of which have carried vignettes of local history.

In preparing all editions, I sought and was given information by a great many Glastonbury people, and I am grateful for their help. I am deeply indebted to the late Herbert T. Clark, whose association with the town government covered 55 years and to the late Dr. Lee J. Whittles, principal founder of the Historical Society of Glastonbury. I have missed the help of both these men, whose knowledge of local landmarks and early records of the town was great.

Doris Armstead, the Historical Society's librarian, has been very helpful to me in finding reference material. The late Barbara Robinson, who represented both the Historical Society and the Woman's Club, provided much valuable service in handling publication and marketing procedures for the earlier editions. My thanks are due, too, to Virginia Knox, Donald C. Peach, former town manager, and his assistant, Col. Anthony H. Shookus, and Dr. Hugh McG. Watson, former superintendent of schools, for their suggestions and help in supplying information for the earlier editions. I appreciate as well the help given me by other town officials with data for the 1983 edition and, more recently, officials and church secretaries who provided information for the present edition. My thanks, too, for their help and support go to Nancy Berlet, Executive Director of the Historical Society, Anne O'Connor, George B. Armstead and Tink Henderson. And most particularly, for his help, his constant encouragement and patience, I am very grateful to my husband, Professor J. Bard McNulty.

Marjorie G. McNulty

Glastonbury, Connecticut
October, 1995

Chapter I

Invitation from Wahquinnacut:
The Ancestry of Glastonbury

The long, lively river wound its sparkling way through green, forested banks and sunlit meadows, swelling gently as tides surged upwards from Long Island Sound. Adriaen Block and his Dutch crew in 1614 observed from the deck of their sailing vessel, the *Onrust* (Restless), the pleasant grassy plains of what in later years became Glastonbury, watching the curling smoke of Indian encampments along the river banks. A few miles upstream from the lovely Pyquag and Naubuc meadows they landed and took possession of the surrounding countryside in the name of Holland.

"Quinnihticut," the Indians called their river — "the long tidal river." These river Indians belonged to the great confederation known as the Algonquin. The tribe who lived below Hartford were the Wongunks, taking their name from the Indian word for "bend," in this case a section of the river at Portland. There appears to have been a much larger concentration of Indians on the Glastonbury side of the river than on the Wethersfield side. The Nayaugs of South Glastonbury, one of the most sizable of the Wongunk sub-tribes, were evidently a rather independent group until the Pequot War of 1675 forced them into closer alliance with the Wongunk family. Their neighbors to the north were the Hoccanums, a sub-tribe of the Podunks, whose main village was at South Windsor. The sachem, or leader, of the Wongunks lived across the river at Pyquag, now Wethersfield. Red Hill, high above the river stretching north for a mile or so from the rear of High Street, South Glastonbury, was perhaps one of the most important of the Wongunk villages. Its Indian inhabitants were called the "Red Hill Indians" in early records about as often as "Nayaugs."

Receding waters after the floods of 1936 and 1938, eroding the topsoil, brought to light many Indian artifacts, as well as distinct traces of campfires, from fields along the river. Random finds from Nayaug to Naubuc, particularly around the site of the old Coal Dock in South Glastonbury and the Meadow Hill farther north, produced quantities of Indian tools, projectile points, knives, fragments of pottery and even pendants for neck or ears. As many as 500 Indian artifacts were found in one pile of stones near Ferry Lane, sifted from soil as it washed away, according to Ray W. Bidwell, writing in the May 1938 issue of *Retrospect*, a journal formerly published by the Historical Society of Glastonbury. Some of the implements were fashioned of copper, which may have been found locally, although there has been speculation that the river Indians acquired the copper they used through trade with other tribes farther west. Copper was discovered very early in certain areas of the Connecticut Colony, although evidently in small amounts. There were, in fact, unprofitable efforts to mine it in Manchester, and it seems likely that if the hills in that town harbored copper it might have been found in Glastonbury as well.

It was copper that was responsible for the discovery of an important Indian find on Meadow Hill in 1971. Copper salts from beads buried with their Indian owner had soaked through the sand into the Indian's skull and, flashing green, attracted the attention of a bulldozer driver as he prepared the land for a housing complex. He thought at first the object was an Indian pot, but later suspected it was part of a skull and reported his find. The discovery brought Dr. Douglas F. Jordan, State Archaeologist and member of the Department of Archaeology at the University of Connecticut, to the spot, as well as Andrew Kowalsky, a local amateur archaeologist. According to Dr. Jordan, the presence of copper accounted for the preservation of the skull and parts of other skeletons found in several graves. Fine-crafted ornaments excavated from the graves indicated that these Indians were similar to the "Adena" type, of Ohio, who flourished from about 500 B.C. to 500 A.D.

In another part of this same Meadow Hill area (known to local archaeologists as the Hollister site, named for the land's previous owners), Andrew Kowalsky in 1965 had discovered an Indian burial site which yielded three intact skeletons. One is now in the possession of the Historical Society of Glastonbury. Dr. Jordan took part in this dig and helped to identify the remains as belonging to the Indian tribe inhabiting the area some 400 years ago, just prior to the arrival of the white settlers. The preservation of these skeletons was attributed to their being located on a well-drained, sandy rise of ground. At about the same time, charred remains of Indian artifacts and bones were found nearer the river. Because of the scattering of red ocher here, it was conjectured that these remains represented Indians of a much earlier group, possibly the "Red Paint" Indians who lived many centuries before Christ, inhabiting coastal areas from Maine to Connecticut.

Still another burial site was discovered in February 1975, farther north at the rear of the Carrier farm, when an interceptor sewer line was being laid. Again Dr. Jordan, Mr. Kowalsky, and members of the Albert Morgan Chapter of the Archaeological Society of Connecticut conducted a dig and excavated charred tools and bones of what appeared to be cremated Indians, evidence of a very early burial culture, thought to be possibly older than 1700 years. Certain fluted stone projectiles found in Glastonbury

Phillips Cave, Kongscut Mountain, East Glastonbury, site of a major Indian archaeological dig, 1957. (Photo by Eric Schade.)

many years ago and now at the University of Connecticut indicate the existence of a Paleo-Indian era 10,000 years ago.

Unlike the Indians who had roamed the Connecticut valley as nomadic hunters two or three thousand years ago, the Wongunk Indians known to the earliest white settlers here were an agricultural tribe, raising crops of corn, pumpkins, squash, beans, and sweet potatoes. They also raised tobacco, a crop which the settlers called sot-weed and, finding it had its uses, continued to raise through succeeding generations. The river Indians were great fishermen and made abundant catches of salmon and shad, using nets made of wild hemp which grew in the meadows, or crude hooks and spears. Ducks, wild geese and other waterfowl were plentiful for the Indians, as were turkeys, partridge, quail and pigeons.

Like other river tribes, the Nayaugs maintained more than one camping ground. In warm weather they set up their rounded wigwams and longhouse on the meadows near the river; when the weather began to grow cold, crops withered, and hunting-time approached, they moved back into the hills of East Glastonbury and made rock shelters in the cliff ledges their winter home. Game abounded: wolves, foxes, bear, wildcats, deer.

On Kongscut Mountain, east of Forest Lane, an archaeological find of major proportions in 1957 produced about 450 articles of Indian use— many types of arrowheads, spear points, axe and adze heads and pottery shards, some dating back more than a thousand years. Stanley Phillips, a newcomer to Glastonbury and an amateur archaeologist, discovered this Indian rock cave shelter (the site was later named for him, the Phillips site, by the Archaeological Society of Connecticut). Andrew Kowalsky had charge of the "dig" upon which members of Yale University's Department of Anthropology worked. Some of the artifacts they found are at the Historical Society Museum.

There were perhaps three or four thousand Connecticut River Indians, each neighboring tribe maintaining small villages of 100 or so, at the time of the arrival of the first white people. It is now more than 200 years since the last of the Wongunks disappeared from Glastonbury, but reminders of our Indian natives linger in the place names we still use: Nayaug, Naubuc, Wassuc, Neipsic, Minnechaug, and others. The Wongunks' culture was similar to that of the neighboring New York State Mohawks and Iroquois, for their homes, their clothes, their basket work and even their decorative designs were much alike. In one all-important respect, however, they differed from the fierce Mohawks — they were peace-loving, not warlike. Furthermore they had been weakened by a mysterious plague in 1616-17 and a smallpox epidemic in 1633 and consequently were easy prey for their warrior-neighbors. They lived in great fear of the hated Mohawks (the name meant "men-eaters") and the Pequots (meaning "destroyers").

Because of enemy raids, the Wongunks many centuries ago, it is believed, had constructed a palisaded fort at Red Hill on the river bank back of our present Stockade Road. Red Hill was an ideal place for a fort. Mohawk raiding parties arriving by canoe were sometimes surprised and driven away by great boulders and tree trunks heaved down upon them from the fort. Friendly Indians of neighboring tribes would often pass the word along when Mohawks were on the war-path. A local legend concerning the fort and a warning of enemy approach has come down through one of Glastonbury's founding families, the Welles, and was recounted by the traveling artist-historian, John Warner Barber, in 1836 in his *Historical Collections of Connecticut*. Once, when a warning was received, the story goes, a scouting party was dispatched to seek out the enemy's route of approach. While the group was gone, the tricky Mohawks approached Red Hill by a back way via the eastern hills, wading all the way down Roaring Brook to surprise and massacre their victims. The Pequots, too, who had migrated from the Hudson River region to southeastern Connecticut in 1514 and had captured land in Hartford, often made murderous raids upon the weak Red Hill people.

It was the river Indians' recurring problem of defense and their need for help which brought about the arrival of English settlers from Massachusetts Bay to Pyquag and thence across the river to Naubuc (Glastonbury) and Nayaug (South Glastonbury). The Dutch, who had left Hartford soon after arriving in 1614, had sent a few trappers and traders back up the river in 1631 to build a fort and trading post at what became known as Dutch Point, just below our Charter Oak Bridge. From these Dutch traders the Indians learned of the arrival of white men from England at Massachusetts Bay. Just possibly, the Indians reasoned, they might induce some of these new arrivals to come to Connecticut to settle and help protect them from the warring Mohawks and Pequots.

A Podunk sachem, Wahquinnacut (Bear-of-Long-River), was chosen to make the trip to the Massachusetts Bay Colony to bring word of a fertile and beautiful valley where corn could be grown in flourishing crops and beaver was abundant. Wahquinnacut brought with him a delegation including an Indian called Jack Straw, who 40 years earlier had been taken to England by Sir Walter Raleigh, had lived there some time and become familiar with the English language. With Jack Straw as interpreter, the delegation tried to persuade Governor John Winthrop to send some of his Englishmen to Connecticut. They offered "to find them corn, and give them yearly 80 skins of beaver," wrote Governor Winthrop in his journal on April 4, 1631. But Winthrop was not interested in spreading his colonists so far away from the base he was trying so hard to maintain. However, certain other men of the colony were very much interested indeed.

In the fall of 1633 John Oldham and three companions left Watertown, near Boston, and followed an old Indian trail, known later as the "Connecticut Path," to the Connecticut River, which they crossed to land on the meadows of the west bank then called Pyquag, the Indian word for "cleared land." It is said that these men planted a field of grain — rye or wheat — but at any rate they stayed long enough to be assured of the possibilities of the area, and presently, carrying some hemp which grew wild in the meadows ("much better than the English," wrote Governor Winthrop) they returned to Watertown to form a group of settlers.

Why these men should have wanted to move away from the company of neighbors and the security of an established government is an unanswered question. It might have been that they felt their own church could be organized more to their liking (for church policies were always to be an important factor in their lives); or they might have chafed under the strictness of Bay Colony rule, as many did. Or it might have been a simple land hunger, formed during their lives in England. This seems likely, for the Connecticut colonists as the years went by oftentimes reached out to expand their holdings. William Hubbard, author of *A General History*

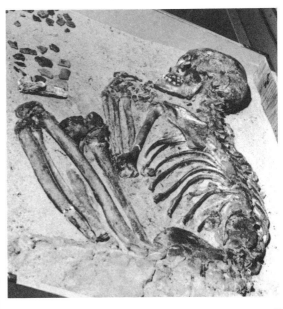

Indian skeleton, probably 400 years old, unearthed in 1965. (Photo by Duffy.)

of New England, who was born in 1621 and could remember the emigration to Connecticut, felt that Thomas Hooker's party, which left Massachusetts to found Hartford in 1636, went because of "the strong bent of their spirits to move out of the place where they were." And so might "the bent of their spirits" have inspired the group of 10 hardy adventurers who left Watertown in the spring of 1634 to found the town which later became Wethersfield.

The next summer, 1635, a few more families joined the group. But a harsh, snowbound winter was in store. By November the ships which were bringing the settlers' goods and provisions from Boston had not yet arrived and the river was frozen over. By December food was becoming scarce and it was necessary to buy what food the Indians would sell, to trap wild animals and to dig down through the snow for acorns and roots. Some of the pathetic band, accompanied by settlers from Windsor, went down the river hoping to locate the expected ship. Happily, a ship was found frozen in the ice, the *Rebecca,* which they boarded and presently, when a thaw melted the ice, they were able to maneuver the ship back to Boston. A few others managed to struggle overland back to Massachusetts, but those who stayed behind nearly starved to death that dreadful winter.

The summer of 1636 brought more families, who came along, very likley, with Thomas Hooker's group which settled Hartford, or with Dorchester people going to Windsor. Nobody knows for certain whether the Wethersfield colonists realized they did not have clear legal right to any Connecticut land when they came. Albert Van Dusen, in his story of Connecticut, states that Thomas Hooker was aware of this and delayed his journey to Hartford until he could arrange an agreement in 1636 with the holders of the Warwick patent, whose land grant from Robert, Earl of Warwick, included Connecticut.

Meanwhile the Wethersfield (or Watertown, as it was then) community was growing. By 1636 about 30 Watertown, Mass., families had migrated and others soon arrived, almost directly from England. Alone of the three towns, Hartford, Wethersfield and Windsor, Wethersfield was founded not by a church congregation but by individuals. These individuals formed what was known as a "propriety," in effect a corporation. The propriety owned the township, and the 34 proprietors, the leading men of the community, conducted the government and made divisions of the common land to all the settlers as well as to themselves.

The Wethersfield propriety considered itself only vaguely associated with the Massachusetts General Court. However, on March 3, 1636, the Massachusetts General Court established a commission giving to Connecticut settlers authority to carry on legal duties with powers wide enough to wage war. They were to call together inhabitants of the three towns to act as a General Court. In April 1636 permission was given by the church in Watertown, Mass., to seven men to establish a church of their own in their new Watertown, which presently was re-named Wythersfield (Wethersfield).

Chapter II

Crossing the River:
The Settlement of Glastonbury

The town we know now as Glastonbury had its beginnings in 1636, when the Wethersfield proprietors bought from the sachem, Sowheag, a large tract of land measuring six miles west of the river, three miles east, and six miles from north to south. No record of an Indian deed to the tract, which of course included Glastonbury, the "three miles east," has been found, but apparently there was an agreement indicating that some sort of payment had been made, for 65 years later, in 1671, certain Wethersfield and Glastonbury men paid several Indian leaders 12 yards of "trading cloth" to sign, with their marks, a confirmatory deed to the original sale. This was recorded in the Wethersfield land records and reads, in part, as follows:

". . . and six miles in length by the Riuer side on the east side of the said Conecticot Riuer, from Pewter Pott brooke, north, to the Bounds betwene Weathersfield and Middletowne, south; the said Great Riuer west, the wholle leanth to runn three large milles into the wilderness east; the which lands, as afore said, hath been quietly possessed by the English now for severall yeeres past; but, in as much as there is noe written deed found under the hand of the said Sowheag, which may be an ocasion of trouble hereafter, for the preuention of which, knowing what our predeceassers haue don, and what hee had receiued for the same; and for the consideration of twelue yards of trading cloth, giuen to us a gratuity, by Capt. Samuell Wyllys, Mr. Henry Wollcot, Mr. James Richards, Capt. Samuell Welles, Mr. Samuel Tallcot, Mr. John Chester, Mr. James Treat, in the name and behalfe, and for the use of all others, the rest of the seuerall proprietors of the said land with in the limites of the Towneship of Weathersfield, aforesaid: We, Turramugus, Sepannamaw Squaw, daughter to Sowheage; Speunno, Nabowhee, Weesumpshie, Waphanck; true heirs of and rightful sucksessers to the aforesaid Sowheage — hath fully confirmed, and doe by these presents fully and absolutely confirme the aforesaid grant made by our predeseasser, Sowheage, afore menssioned, giuen, granted, bargained, sold, alliened, enfeeoffed, sett ouer and confirmed . . . To haue and to hold all the aforesaid tract of lands, as they are bounded, with all the meaddowes, pastere, woods, under-woods, mines, mineralls, stones, qurrys, profits, comoditys, priulidges and appertinances, whatso-euer, that are or may bee to the same belonging."

The limits of the land set forth in the deed were those supplied by one of the original surveyors, George Hubbard, in a deposition made to the General Court in 1665. In the same document Hubbard testified to his personal knowledge that "Wethersfeild men gaue so much unto Sow-heag as was to his satisfaction for all their plantations lyeing on both sides the great Riuer . . ."

When the confirmatory deed was written seven years later, care was taken to spell out more explicitly a purchase price — 12 yards of trading cloth. In calling attention to the possibility that without confirmation of an earlier deed there might be "an occasion of trouble hereafter" the colonists may have been tacitly admitting to a conflict with Sowheag over the purchase. That there had been trouble with Sowheag, apparently almost immediately after the original purchase, is a matter of record. The Indian sachem complained that the settlers had not lived up to their bargain with him, that he might "sitt down with them and be protected." Wethersfield historian Sherman Adams suggested that Sowheag might have been dissatisfied with the boundaries on the east side of the river which the settlers were claiming he had agreed to. Adams based this theory on a notation in the Colonial records: In April 1639 William Good-win was asked to "put in mind" the finishing of the treaty with Sequin concerning the land "beyond the river" — Sequin being, apparently, a name for leader sometimes used in reference to Sowheag, and the "land beyond" meaning across, or on the east side. At any rate Sowheag became angry and left the area (formerly his own territory) and established a new seat in Mattabesick, now Middletown. But he remained annoyed at the Wethersfield settlers, and later on they suspected him (probably without much justification) of having abetted the Pequot Massacre of April 1637 in which six men and three women working in the Wethersfield meadows were killed and two girls, daughters of William Swayne, one of the proprietors and a first landholder of Glastonbury, were kidnapped. Governor Winthrop of Plymouth Colony noted in his journal in January 1638 that letters had been received from Connecticut men asking advice on how to treat Sowheag and the River Indians, who they suspected might try to avenge themselves for "breach of covenant." The advice, given by Massachusetts magistrates and elders, seems to warn the Connecticut settlers to guard against the possibility of another savage attack. Winthrop says "According to this advice they proceeded and made another agree-ment with the Indians of the river."

Onions became the favorite crop the settlers chose to grow in the rich, dark soil of the Wethersfield meadows, but those who crossed the river in their crude flatboats and rafts planted corn in little hillocks, as the

Indians did. Day by day through the spring and summer they made their way across the swift current to hoe and harvest and to cut hay, returning at nightfall to their homes on the river's west bank.

As more and more men were enticed by the beckoning vastness of the meadows on the east side, it became obvious that legal boundaries were necessary to separate one farm from another. In 1639 the proprietors hired two surveyors. Starting at a point a little to the north of the present East Hartford line, the surveyors laid out 34 strips of land running east from the river "three large miles into the wilderness." In order to provide farms with fishing rights, fertile meadow land, level upland and woodland, the strips were long and some quite narrow. This method of apportioning land was similar to the feudal "strip system" farm layout of England and Normandy. Known as "Naubuc Farms," the parcels varied in width from seven to 200 rods, probably according to the amount each proprietor had put up toward the original purchase price of Wethersfield. But also, according to George Hubbard in a Court deposition in 1684, the "sizers" who laid out the land took into consideration its "goodness or badness." This survey of 1639-40 was the first official survey and layout of farms in Connecticut.

The southernmost lot of Naubuc Farms ended at the mouth of Roaring Brook, which was then farther north than it is today. Below that was "ungiven" land, which had apparently been bought by the proprietors from Tarramuggus, the son of Sowheag. It remained undivided for several years. Richard Treat received an allotment of 120 acres in 1641 (later he acquired a great many more). John Hollister also received land in Nayaug; surveyors were chosen to "sett out" his lot of 50 acres in 1644. Later he bought 80 acres from Thomas Hurlbut, "a soldier," and also he acquired a one-fourth part of Matthew Mitchell's great tract of 900 acres. The Treat and Hollister farms, though they were surveyed three miles into the wilderness, were not measured from the river, according to Sherman Adams, because the river at Nayaug took a southeasterly course, but from a line drawn north and south from the mouth of Roaring Brook.

The great desire of these Englishmen to invest in land is shown by the circumstance that many of the first purchasers never occupied their farms on the east side, but later sold them to others or gave or willed them to their sons. In 1684 a second survey revealed that many of the original farms had changed hands, and the names of the new owners were those known to us as old Glastonbury names: Welles, Hale, Talcott, Goodrich, Hubbard, Kilborn, Loveland and others. Many of their descendants, as well as those of John Hollister and Richard Treat, still reside in Glastonbury. The Hale farm, widest of the 34, which more than two and a half centuries later became famous for its peaches, was bought from Clement Chaplin, a first owner-investor, by Samuel Hale and the Rev. Timothy Stevens.

Though farms were laid out, it is easy to understand why it took time for any Wethersfield people to cross the river to settle. The meadows, gay with wildflowers and fragrant with hay in the summertime, stretched upwards to thickly wooded stands of oak, chestnut, maple, elm, hickory and pine, with here and there a burned-over clearing for an Indian encampment. Beyond these, forested hills rose gradually, then steeply, with rugged outcroppings of granite ledge and shale. Way to the northeast rose Minnechaug (Berryland) Mountain, and south of Minnechaug loomed Kongscut (Goose Country). No wonder they called it a wilderness!

After a lapse of 335 years it is difficult to reconstruct with any certainty what took place and when. There is confusion about Glastonbury's first house and thus its first settler. Matthew Mitchell, whose family and livestock had been brutally attacked by Indians in Saybrook (his son-in-law was burned alive) came up the river in about 1638 to look for safer grazing grounds, settled briefly in Wethersfield and became one of the first owners of land in Glastonbury. It is believed that possibly as early as 1639 he had a herder who was the first white man to live in Glastonbury — certainly the Mitchell cattle were the first to be pastured here. Figuring in a later boundary dispute was a cow pen (also mentioned in a deed in 1641) on Mitchell's land and a "cellar hole" near it within a few rods of Roaring Brook, then called the Sturgeon River. Dr. Alonzo B. Chapin, the author of a history of Glastonbury published in 1853, believed the "cellar hole" was actually a cave where the herder lived, "cellar hole" being a common terminology for a cave at that time. But Sherman Adams speaks of the dwelling as a house. If so it must be considered the first house to be built in Glastonbury — in 1639 or 1640.

There is also a doubt as to whether it was John Hollister, Thomas Edwards or possibly Samuel Gardner who first built here in 1649. Sherman Adams felt there was evidence that both Edwards and Gardner were living in Naubuc (the Indian name for "east side") prior to 1650. Dr. Chapin considered John Hollister's tenant, Josiah Gilbert, to be Glastonbury's pioneer settler, and Dr. Lee J. Whittles, a Glastonbury historian and founder of the Historical Society of Glastonbury, found evidence suggesting that John Hollister's house was already existing in 1649, near the old Coal Dock west of Tryon Street on the banks of the Connecticut River at Nayaug ("Land of Noisy Waters").

Probably John Hollister never lived on this side of the river permanently, though when he died in Wethersfield in 1665, he left his "feather bed at Nayaug" to his son John, in addition to his Nayaug farm. Situated as the house was, so close to the river, spring freshets flooded the place badly every year. Yet the Gilberts, Josiah, his family, and his brothers Jonathan and John and later the John Hollister, Jr.'s, endured this recurring misery until early in the next century when either the whole house or part of it was moved to Tryon Street. According to one story, the house was moved east and south to a location near the Roaring Brook bridge, where it is still standing, owned by the Killam family. But according to another version, only the back ell of the original house was moved, hauled southeast to Tryon Street, where it stood for many years, eventually being used

Hollister House, Tryon Street, South Glastonbury. The town's oldest house, as it looked in 1880.

as a storage shed at the rear of the home of Theodore Pratt, a lineal descendant of John Hollister. Whether or not the Killam house was built in 1649, it is of very early construction, undoubtedly seventeenth century, and is the oldest house still standing in Glastonbury, the ancestral home of the Hollister family for many generations. The house is a two-story "lean-to", of hewn overhang construction, with uniquely carved brackets.

One of Glastonbury's cherished legends is about the first John Hollister and shows something of the character of these first settlers, as well as of the man himself. John Hollister, tall and hefty, was known as the strong man of the colony, and he had a heart to match his physique. One day, the story goes, while he was hoeing his corn in Nayaug a huge, powerfully built Indian came up to him. "You big man, me big man. We fight, see who strongest," he challenged. Mr. Hollister agreed, and they began to wrestle. Now John Hollister knew that, although the Indians were swift runners, their backs and arm muscles were not as well developed as they might have been because it was their custom to let the squaws do the heavy work. But he knew it would be unwise, and tactless, too, to win. So he tried only to tire out the Indian. It took a long time. They wrestled, then rested, wrestled again, and so on until they ended in a draw at sundown. Whereupon they sat down on a log, exchanged tokens of friendship and smoked a peace pipe.

In 1656-58 this first John Hollister demonstrated his independence of spirit by instigating a petition to the General Court asking for the dismissal of the minister of the Wethersfield church, the Rev. John Russell. The minister had excommunicated Lieutenant Hollister from church privileges, for reasons which Hollister claimed were not clear, an action which greatly excited the town, for John Hollister was much respected, a leading member of the Church and a member of the General Court. The basis for the clash between the two men was a difference in church government policy. The Wethersfield church had been drawn into what came to be known as the great "Hartford Controversy" — apparently a difference of opinion as to which should be followed, the Presbyterian system or "independent" Congregationalism. In 1659 the town bade farewell to the Rev. Mr. Russell, who with his band of followers from Hartford and Windsor as well as Wethersfield, went to Massachusetts to found the town of Hadley. John Hollister and the others who had opposed the Russell followers remained to carry on the work of the Wethersfield church.

By 1653 there were several families living on the east side of the river, and in that year the General Court gave them their first recognition as a settlement separate from Wethersfield. The inhabitants of the future Glastonbury, together with neighbors to the north, asked the Court's permission to form their own military company which would hold its drills on the east side. All young men in those days were required to hold training drills six times a year to prepare them for military defense, much as our National Guard or Army Reserves train today.

On May 18, 1653, the General Court approved this request by voting to exempt "the inhabitants of the East side of the greate Riuer from training with the Towns on the West side . . ." Thus it was the need for military defense that started Glastonbury on the road to becoming a separate town.

Almost as soon as the east side meadows began to be used by Wethersfield planters, ferries were set up to ply the river. Although the first legislative sanction of a ferry was not recorded until 1673, it is known that there must have been a Rocky Hill-Nayaug ferry in 1650. For a town meeting in Wethersfield in 1649 voted to have the selectmen "lay out a road from Mr. Nott's house to the ferry by the Rockie Hill that goes to Nayaug" — a road that was duly surveyed and laid out in 1650. One of the only two Connecticut River ferries still operating, our South Glastonbury-Rocky Hill ferry is known to be the oldest ferry in continuous operation in the United States. It did not receive official legislative recognition, however, until 1724. Many years earlier, in 1673, the General Assembly granted permission to one Richard Smith, Jr., to operate a ferry between Naubuc and Wethersfield. But it is believed that this ferry was in operation as early as the 1640s. It was the predecessor of Pratt's Ferry, which continued until the mid 1800s.

As time went by inhabitants of the river towns began to crave more land. In 1672 the General Court gave permission to both Hartford and Wethersfield to extend their boundaries five miles to the eastward "for the encouragement of the people to plant there." To this end the Wethersfield people began negotiations with the Indians, being very careful, this time, to secure a legal deed to their purchase. The wording of this deed, while even more elaborate, lengthy and repetitious than the confirmatory deed of 1671 to the first purchase, differed from the earlier deed in that it turned over the land to the "inhabitants" rather than the proprietors, a provision which later created some friction. The deed granted a tract

*South Glastonbury-Rocky Hill ferry, believed
the oldest in America in continuous operation.
(Print by Duffy from glass plate.)*

of land containing "thirty large miles square that is to say from the east
end of Wethersfield old bounds to run five large miles into the country
east and six large miles in breadth . . ." No price is mentioned; the deed
simply states "in consideration of a valuable sum to us in hand well and
truly paid," but Sherman Adams, evidently by adding up the amount of
tax money which was assessed inhabitants to pay for the land, estimated
it to be about 24 pounds sterling. Signing the deed with their marks were
Tarramuggus (at that time the sachem), Massacuppee, Wesumpshye,
One peny (Wumpene?), Nesaheeg, Seorcket and Pewampskin.

At an earlier period Tarramuggus had granted or sold 200 acres to
Thomas Edwards, and still earlier an Indian named Rechaun had given
Robert Boltwood a pond, probably Neipsic Pond, and adjoining land.
If they objected to their land being sold a second time, we have no record
of it. Connecticut Indians often sold the same land two or three times
over. This seemingly nonchalant practice may have given rise to the
expression "Indian giver." But their ideas of property-ownership were
different from those of the white men. The Indians thought they were
selling (or granting) the right to use the land, and did not understand why
the land could not be used by more than one "grantee." The name of the
Indian Tarramuggus is perpetuated in the lake at Marlborough still called
Terramuggus.

An ancient stone monument near the present Pilgrim Baptist Church
on Hebron Avenue marks the place where the 3-mile boundary ended.
From there the line went roughly southwest, crossing Buck's Corners,
then over Matson Hill, paralleling the bend of the river as it then flowed.

Some of the paved roads which wind through Glastonbury today were
once Indian trails: Hopewell Road, Chestnut Hill Road, Griswold Street,

Neipsic Road, the New London Turnpike, and others. But the one which has been our chief thoroughfare since the beginning, Main Street, was the principal Indian trail from Hartford southward along the river's east side. The Indians called this trail the "Long Path" or the "Path to Monheag." Starting in East Hartford the "Path to Monheag" followed the river southward along Meadow Hill to Roaring Brook at Nayaug, then swung east, climbing the ledges in Cotton Hollow, following the brook to Wassuc. There it was joined by a trail coming down from the Indian pool at Neipsic (a pool the Indians believed to have healing powers), turned south and east, climbing up Bare Mountain then down across a Marlborough meadow, skirting Lake Terramuggus to Colchester and on to "Monheag" (New London). Virtually the same route was followed by early inhabitants of the Connecticut River towns on their trips to New London. When the General Court in May, 1670, ordered that the "plantations . . . Shall lay out a highway, six rods wide, upon the uplands on the east side of the Great River," it was natural that the road should be sited along the Indian's "Long Path." The early route of Main Street continued over the present High Street across Roaring Brook, following Tryon Street along the river to Gildersleeve, then part of Middletown. The new "Country Road" cut through all the 3-mile farms, and to pay back the owners for the land taken, they were given an extra 20 rods at the east boundary, granted by the General Court, which seems to have overlooked the circumstance that the 20 rods, 6 miles long, had not yet been purchased from the Indians! (It was bought 3 years later, as part of the 5-mile purchase.)

Glastonbury grew slowly, household by household, during its first years. From a handful of families in the 1650s, the population gained gradually as the grass on the east side of the river seemed greener, until in 1693 there were about 34 householders here, it is estimated. There was a spurt in population at the end of King Philip's War (1675-76), the last desperate attempt of the Indians to keep the English from taking all their lands. This brief uprising put all the colonists on guard and drew young able-bodied men from all the river settlements to protect the English people in Western Massachusetts to the north and the Narragansett country to the south.

The Wongunks remained faithful to our Connecticut River settlements. But Simsbury, then a frontier town, was invaded by a band of King Philip's warriors and burned to the ground, not a house remaining. Prior to that, hostile Indians were seen skulking about the Hartford area — some were rumored to have been seen in Glastonbury — and the Standing Council ordered the settlers to make defense preparations. On October 11, 1675, the Council authorized John Hollister to "hire two or three men to fortify his house and secure his corn." They undoubtedly meant Indian helpers, as Mr. Hollister and the Indians were known to help each other with their corn-raising. The next month the Council suggested that the Nayaug Indians join with the Wongunks (referring to the tribe at Portland)

14

and, under the direction of John Hollister, build a fort either at Nayaug or at Wonggum (Portland), as they thought best. The Red Hill location was chosen and the old fort reconstructed. Under the direction of Oweneco, son of Uncas (the Mohegan sachem and the most powerful Indian in Connecticut), the Wongunks set up an outpost at the fort, sending out Indian guides and warriors to travel with colonial military expeditions to defend Massachusetts towns. Fortunately no attack was made in the Wethersfield-Glastonbury area and it was not long before the fort was again unmanned, never to be used again for defensive purposes.

One of the most remarkable Glastonbury property holders of the early colonial period was the Rev. Gershom Bulkeley. The Rev. Bulkeley was serving as Wethersfield's minister when he was appointed surgeon to the Army in King Philip's War. When he returned, wounded, after the war, he asked for dismissal from the church and evidently moved across the river to live with his daughter, Dorothy, the widow of Thomas Treat. The house where he died (in 1713) is still standing, a quaint gambrel-roofed house on Tryon Street, just below Ferry Lane. Among other bequests, he left his Negro maid, Hannah, to his daughter, Dorothy Treat, directing all future owners of Hannah to "use her well, and consider that she hath a soul to save as well as wee, and is a Christian, and therefore that they make conscience to promote her in her reading, catechism and all Christianity, that she may profit and grow in religion and godliness and attain the end of baptism to the glory of God, and this I earnestly require on her behalf, as they will answer the neglect thereof before God."

Gershom Bulkeley was undoubtedly one of the best educated men in central Connecticut at that time. A graduate of Harvard, he was not only a minister and a physician, but a lawyer, a surveyor and a linguist, being familiar with several languages including Latin, Greek and Dutch. An ardent royalist, he sided with Sir Edmund Andros and his right to seize the Connecticut Charter in 1687, and wrote many forceful essays on the subject of loyalty to the mother country, foreseeing, no doubt, the colonists' rebellion in the next century. Most famous of his tracts was entitled "Will and Doom, or the Miseries of Connecticut, by and under an Usurped and Arbitrary Power . . ." He was important in Glastonbury's history, for he was ultimately responsible for a boundary dispute in 1684 which changed the actual size of the town's area.

Mr. Bulkeley had acquired a quarter-lot resulting from a division of Matthew Mitchell's southernmost lot in Naubuc Farms. The boundary of the Mitchell lot had been set at the mouth of Sturgeon River "and so to a marked tree about the cow pens and in a straight line east . . ." But the cowpens no longer existed when the surveyors began their work at the order of the General Court, appealed to by John Hollister, who disputed this boundary So they started at the north line of the town, which in 1640 had been set at Pewter Pot Brook, and worked their way down, measuring all lots. Over the years, however, Pewter Pot had changed its course, and this pushed down all the lots a distance of 85½ rods. On

15

the basis of the surveyors' findings, Bulkeley then claimed the land south of Sturgeon River (Roaring Brook) owned by John Hollister. A suit at the General Court followed, won by Bulkeley. The long-term result of the proceedings was to deprive Glastonbury of 85½ rods of land now belonging to East Hartford.

One of the earliest settlers in South Glastonbury was Richard Treat, Jr., who received as a gift from his father about the year 1652 a farm of 900 acres in "Noyake" (Nayaug). The father, Richard the Settler, had been given this huge acreage from the town of Wethersfield, the first part of it having been granted him in 1641. That Richard Treat, Jr., was living here very early is known. An undated description of a seven-acre parcel of upland speaks of a house and barn. Both Richard Treat, Jr., and his son, also named Richard, were among the petitioners for separation from Wethersfield.

Members of the Treat family held important positions in both the political and military functions of the Colony government. Robert Treat, son of Richard the Settler and brother of Johanna Treat Hollister (wife of John Hollister) as well as of Richard Treat, Jr., served as Governor of Connecticut Colony for 15 years, from 1683 to 1698, and after that was annually elected Deputy Governor until he declined to serve further at the age of 86.

The Treats were interested in the Indians. Richard, Jr., his son Thomas and his grandson, Richard, all made efforts to Christianize the local Indians and learned to speak their language, though apparently not very fluently. Thomas, by a special resolution of the Governor and Council in March 1711 received 30 shillings from the public funds "for his extraordinary labour and science as an interpreter, and in managing the Indians who served in the expedition to Wood Creek." He had been appointed a lieutenant in the military forces when the colony first began military operations in 1703 and had gone north in the expedition against the Canadian French in 1709. A quarter of the troops sent to Wood Creek died of "camp distemper" in this expedition, including Captain Stephen Hollister of Glastonbury. Thomas Treat survived but died in 1712, his will directing his executors to see that his son Richard had a college education. Richard was graduated from Harvard College and became an itinerant minister, preaching some in Glastonbury but mainly, like his father, "laboring among the Indians." He held classes in religious instruction and presumably in English for Wongunk children for a while (until he got discouraged) and weekly meetings for adult Indians, but found that they had a "natural aversion to the humbling doctrines of Christianity." Richard died as a soldier en route to the Wolfe-Montcalm campaign in Quebec in 1759.

Despite the friendliness of the Wongunks, families in Glastonbury were always on guard against possible attack by hostile tribes. Fear of the Indians was always present. Doors and outer walls were made doubly strong. Some houses — the Benjamin Talcott house, for one, which stood opposite the present Academy School — were surrounded by palisade fences. The stockaded Talcott house, torn down in 1851, is said to have been the first house to be built here after Glastonbury became a town. Alfred E. Hollister, a Talcott descendant, who died in 1974 at the age of 103 and had lived in this house all his life, believed the ell to be the original Talcott ell, an early 18th century addition to the 17th century house. The Talcott house had been stockaded so that it could serve as a place of refuge for women and children in case of Indian attack. It may never have been used for such a purpose since there are no records of Indian hostilities against Glastonbury people. But there had been many instances of Indian attack in other towns. The Pequot massacre on the Wethersfield meadows in April 1637 was a horror persisting in the memories of several generations; so too was the burning of Simsbury in King Philip's War less than 20 years before Benjamin Talcott built his house in 1692-93. And it may be that fear of the dreaded Mohawks was passed on to the white men from the local Indians. "Watch out, or the Mohawks will get you!" was a warning mothers would sometimes give to naughty children.

Deprived of their lands, weakened by rum and subject to tuberculosis and other diseases passed on to them by the white people, the Indian families in Glastonbury gradually died off. Some moved west to join other tribes. By the time of the French and Indian War in mid-18th century, there were still a few here who fought on the side of the English.

What happened to the Wongunks? And why are there no descendants of this river Indian tribe still living in their native area? The records give a few hints. In about 1664 a tract of 300 acres on the Wongunk meadows in Portland was set off by the General Court for heirs of Sowheag. For many years the reservation was occupied by Wongunk Indians and members of their sub-tribe, the Nayaugs, but little by little the number, never great to start with, dwindled. In spite of their muscular bodies, their resistance to the Englishmen's diseases was low; they got sick, many died. Others became addicted to alcohol — beer, cider, rum. Still others wandered west to join other tribes. In 1756 when the Middletown Third Society (Portland) petitioned the General Assembly for permission to buy the reservation acres it was learned that there were only 12 or 13 descendants of the original Indian owners "and those much scattered." William Welles of Glastonbury was a member of the General Assembly's investigating committee which recommended that the acreage be broken up into building lots and sold, though the General Assembly did not approve the sale until 1765. Proceeds from the sale were to go toward the support of the remaining Indians. Portland applied to be reimbursed for support money it had paid out (70 pounds) in 1774 after the death of the last remaining Wongunk Indian, Mary (known as "Tike"), widow of Cusjoye, the last chief.

Chapter III

Cutting the Apron Strings:
Separation from Wethersfield

For nearly 50 years the east side settlement remained a part of Wethersfield, though it meant crossing the river to attend church and transact business. But it could not have been easy, and eventually the time came when the little group got together and petitioned Wethersfield for permission to be set off as a separate entity. In 1689 they asked Wethersfield for permission "to be discharged from beareing their part of the charge of publike worship here; in order to the setting up of the same amongst themselves." Wethersfield granted permission, provided "the General Court (on their application to them on said account), shall see cause to grant them on the East side of the Great River, and all the lands belonging to our Towne on that side of the River, to be a township; and the inhabitants there shal relinquish all their comon rights on this West side of the River, as inhabitants here; reserving each man's particular right here, and each person with us reserving his perticular right there, on the said east side. And also, that the inhabitants shal continue as part of said township, and shal contribute their proportion to all publike charges with us til such time as they have an allowed minister settled among them; then for their comfort and conveniency we are contented to condescend to their request that they may be a township."

It was now necessary to petition the General Court (which later became known as the General Assembly) for its permission for the east side community to be a township. Such a petition was submitted probably in February 1690, together with a document stating that a meeting house would be built on land to be given by Samuel Smith and John Hubbard (our present Green at Main and Hubbard Streets). A copy of the latter document is on file in Glastonbury's first book of records, but no petition has been found among the documents in the archives of the Connecticut State Library, although the General Court recorded that it had received such a petition.

On May 8, 1690, the Court acted favorably on the petition. Their vote has been termed by previous writers on Glastonbury history an "Act of Incorporation." Strictly speaking, however, the earliest towns in Connecticut were not "incorporated." The Connecticut State Register and Manual says that they were "implied or quasi incorporations." At any rate, the General Court gave its permission for the future Glastonbury to become a town in the following words:

"Whereas the inhabitants of the Town of Weathersfeild on the east side of Conecticot Riuer, by the consent of the inhabitants of sayd towne, did petition this Court to be a township of themselues, on the east side of Conecticut Riuer, and may haue liberty to prouide a minister for themselues, which the Towne haueing granted to their neighboures on the east side, this Court see reason to grant their petition, but aduise them to be cautious how they improue it, and that they shall pay their full proportion to all publique charge to said Weathersfeild till they shall haue a good orthodox minister settled amongst them there on the east side of Conecticutt Riuer in Weathersfeild."

As instructed under the terms of the General Court's vote, the new town was obligated to engage a minister before it could separate from Wethersfield. It took two years to acquire one. In July 1692 the Rev. Timothy Stevens, aged 26, was called as pastor of the First Society. There had

Timothy Stevens House, ca. 1693, thought to be the first parsonage.
(Photo by Duffy.)

been very few candidates available, in fact the Rev. Mr. Stevens may have been the only one. For this reason, great inducements were made to get him to come. He seems to have held back until the offers of salary and land grants were satisfactory to him and a dwelling house was promised. Even after he arrived, there was much dickering during the summer and fall until finally in October an agreement was reached. His starting salary was 60 pounds, plus 150 acres of the town's still undivided land and a homelot of six acres, with a "suitable" house built on it. In addition, certain townspeople offered to give him varying amounts of land and small sums of money. Later he acquired hundreds of acres in wide-spread parts of town, some by town grant, some by purchase. The evidence of these records and of his will points to his having been much concerned with the material things of life, as well as the spiritual. The clerics of the times, in fact, considered their services as ministers a "living" as much as a "calling," and the Rev. Timothy Stevens was no exception.

In January 1693 the town voted to build him a "girt dwelling" with a "good stack of chimnies in it" and gave him his choice of a 20-foot long house, fully completed, or a 40-foot house if he furnished the nails, glass and iron-work himself. Apparently he opted for the latter, for later that month the town voted to build a 40-foot dwelling with a stone cellar under one end and a "convenient porch", the iron work included. An attractive gambrel-roofed house, still standing in its original location on Main Street at the corner of Morgan Road, which it faces, may have been the first parsonage. Morgan Road follows the same route as a 17th century cart road to the woodlots eastward.

Timothy Stevens was one of the vital leaders of the new town. His influence was strong in the developing community where church and state were one. It is unfortunate that no sermons, diaries or letters written by this man have been found which might have revealed more about him and his flock. We know that he was married three times and had 11 children, all of whom died young except three sons, Timothy, Joseph and Benjamin, who survived their father. The first two wives, Eunice Chester and Alice Cook, died in childbirth, a common occurrence then and for many years following; the third wife, Dorothy Smithsen, survived him. The Rev. Mr. Stevens was born in 1666 in Roxbury, Mass., and was graduated in 1687 from Harvard, receiving a master's degree in 1690. He began to preach in Glastonbury in April 1690 but was not ordained until October 1693. He lived here until he died on April 14, 1726, aged 60.

He was buried in the Green Cemetery, his grave marked by a flat table stone. His will, written in his own hand and filed in the Probate Records of the Connecticut Colony, shows that he died a comparatively wealthy man for those times in the Colony. He left an estate valued at nearly 2000 pounds, including, among other legacies, a good deal of land, cattle, sheep, and "horse," much-prized books in English, Latin and Greek on such subjects as divinity, "physick" and history; a quantity of silver spoons, a silver box, several gold rings, "pistoles," trunks, a red broadcloth blanket, three silk gowns and three "petty" coats.

This will, as with others of the period, is documentary evidence of the low state held by women, who upon marriage had to lose all property rights to their husbands. Timothy in providing for his wife willed back to her her own property: "I doe give to my beloved wife all the estate that she had a good right unto before our marriage together: That is to say I give to her all the Right that I have . . . to what land she purchased at Hibron, before I was married unto her . . . I doe give to her all household stuff, that was hers before our marriage . . . I doe give to her the two cows that were hers, Lent to Isaak Hubbard . . ."

Upon Timothy Stevens' death a parish committee was appointed to find a minister to take his place. For reasons which are not clear the committee did not report or present a candidate for six months. Meanwhile supply ministers must have been occupying the "Glassenbury" pulpit.

The Rev. Jonathan Edwards, one of the most noted of all New England colonial theologians, was almost undoubtedly one of the visiting ministers who came to Glastonbury after the death of Timothy Stevens. Evidence uncovered during the summer of 1974 by the Rev. Dr. Thomas A. Schafer, professor of church history at McCormick Theological Seminary in Chicago, indicates strongly that Edwards preached in Glastonbury during the first part of the interim period between the first and second "settled" ministers. While studying and preparing for publication the manuscript sermons of Jonathan Edwards, Dr. Schafer de-coded a personal shorthand system used by Edwards in annotating sermons which he "re-preached," indicating in particular where he had preached each sermon. On six of these he had written (in shorthand) "Glassenbury." The sermons were not dated, but because of the type of ink used, the watermarks on the paper and even the kind of paper used, and taking other factors into consideration, Dr. Schafer was able to narrow down the time to May, June or July of 1726 — possibly as early as April when Timothy Stevens was suffering his final illness. There are two additional sermons which Edwards may have preached in Glastonbury. He was 23 years old at the time and a tutor (instructor) at Yale. His name was not among those presented by the committee to find a new minister when it made its first report in October of 1726. Because of parish dissension on choosing a new minister, none was called until 1728, when the Rev. Ashbel Woodbridge accepted and was ordained on October 4.

One month before the arrival of the Rev. Stevens, the General Court had officially named the new town, acting favorably on the name the inhabitants themselves had proposed. On June 22, 1692, the following vote was recorded: "This Court names the towne at Nabuck ouer against Weathersfeild. Glassenbury."

Nobody knows for sure why the name "Glastonbury" was chosen. The town was certainly named for Glastonbury, England, site of the first building erected for Christian worship in England, an abbey said to have been founded in the First Century, A.D. Very likely our ancestors hoped their new town would be a religious place worthy of the name, Glastonbury, which derives from the Anglo-Saxon for "Glistening Town." It has not been possible to trace the origins of first settlers back to Glastonbury, England, so it is probable that our town was not named out of sentiment for the home town left behind, as many New England villages were. In the 17th Century people spelled phonetically, using double consonants or extra "e's" at random. Our first citizens spelled their town's name "Glassenbury" most of the time until about 1786, when it begins to appear as "Glastenbury." In 1870 a town vote officially changed the spelling to Glastonbury, conforming to the spelling of Glastonbury, England.

The Meeting House on the Green, for which John Hubbard and Samuel Smith had given land, was a plain wooden frame building. It was completed in 1693 (probably in October). With the minister settled and the Meeting House built, the community at last considered itself a separate town and ceased to pay its "full proportion of publique charges" to Wethersfield.

The next spring the town sent its first delegate to the General Court. He was Eleazar Kimberly, whose tombstone in the old Green Cemetery states that he was the "first male child born in New Haven." Eleazar Kimberly, evidently a man of education and prestige, not only represented the town in the General Court but was also its first Town Clerk until his death in 1708 at the age of 71. From 1696 until he died he served as Secretary of the Colony. It is not certain just when Mr. Kimberly came over from Wethersfield to live in Glastonbury. He was a schoolmaster for some 25 years, teaching first on the Wethersfield side and later on the east side, and was also a lawyer. His farm in Glastonbury was that belonging to his wife, the former Mary Robbins, through inheritance — it was known as Lot No. 28 in the layout of Naubuc Farms, and was the last of the original three-mile lots to remain undivided, not being parceled off until the mid-20th century.

In 1943, the Historical Society of Glastonbury appointed a committee to determine whether the town should consider the date of its establishment as 1690, the date of the General Court's vote of permission to separate, or 1693, when the provisions of the Act were met. The opinion given by Ray W. Bidwell, spokesman for the committee, and accepted by the Society, was that it should be 1693. In part, his findings were that the townspeople themselves, as expressed in a town vote of 1714, considered this the proper date.

The question of the proper date of the town's founding came up again in 1974 when Town Clerk Edward J. Friedeberg prepared a new town seal to replace the one which had been in use for some 50 years. The old seal had carried the date May 8, 1690, the date of the General Court's vote granting separation conditional upon the settling of a minister. The Town Clerk brought the matter of the founding date before the Town Council for an official decision, and on February 26, 1974, the Council adopted a resolution confirming the date of 1693 as the correct one. "It was determined," the minutes of the Council's action stated, "that evidence points to 1693 as the date for separation of Glastonbury from Wethersfield." An investigation of the records by Town Clerk Friedeberg had corroborated the findings of the Historical Society's committee of 1943.

Although Wethersfield in granting permission to the east-siders to separate had decreed that a meeting house must first be built, the General Court had not so specified. However, a legal definition of an English town (Coke, 1628) required that "it hath . . . a church . . ." The settlers must have taken such a proviso for granted. The meeting house was important in the lives of all early American colonists. Not only did it serve as a place of worship but, being the only general gathering place for the people, it functioned also as an assembly hall for town meetings and as a news center where public notices were posted and proclamations read. Outside its doors were located the whipping post and stocks, those cruel devices of punishment. Probably our Meeting House had no bell, although Wethersfield's first meeting house did. Glastonbury inhabitants were called together for both religious and secular purposes by the beating of a drum in the various parts of the settlement. The first item in the first book of records states "Samuell Loveman begane to beet the drume the furst Sabath in Apirill: 1701 . . ."

We can only guess at the design of the first Meeting House. The congregation stood, or sat on benches, for there were no pews until 1717, when a town meeting granted Thomas Kimberly and Richard Goodrich permission to build "each of them a pue." The Meeting House burned down in 1734 (arson was suspected) and another built the next year farther south on the west side of Main Street north of the present Bartlett home, which was once Moseley's tavern. This Meeting House was demolished in 1836 when a new Congregational Church was built farther north where the present First Church stands now.

The second Meeting House, "clapboarded without and ceiled within," with "filled" walls, had pews around the outside walls and open seats or benches, also known as "slips," in the body of the church. A high pulpit covered by a sounding board stood on the west side. A seating arrangement, carefully worked out for the congregation and "dignified" by vote of the Society, designated which pews and seats came first in a descending order of importance, and who should occupy them, according to "age, state and parentage." The women were originally seated on the north side and all young unmarried people in the gallery; not until 1757 were husbands and wives allowed to sit together. A children's bench was near the pulpit. (In the 19th century the church "slips" were auctioned annually, the most important pews, apparently those closest to the pulpit, going to the highest bidders.)

Glastonbury's town meetings began in 1690, according to the First Book of Records, which was kept by Eleazar Kimberly, Samuel Smith, and other town clerks rather spasmodically over a period of 48 years in what seems to be Smith's own personal account book. Here were recorded the annual election of three townsmen or selectmen, a town treasurer and as time went on, various other town officers including haywards, fence-viewers, leather sealers, surveyors, tithingmen, listers, cordwinders, branders and gravediggers.

The voting members of the town were established according to the Fundamental Orders of the Connecticut Colony and consisted of: 'inhabitants," men over 21 or "who have bore office or have 30 pounds estate," required to take an oath of fidelity; and "freemen," admitted inhabitants who had taken the oath of fidelity, were of "peaceable and honest conversation," and were approved by the General Court to vote in elections of Deputies, or Representatives, to the General Assembly. Many men who were eligible to become freemen apparently did not bother. However, freemen's oaths were still being administered in Glastonbury until way into the 19th century. "Householders," a special category of the population, were men or women who were acknowledged heads of households and who owned a "sufficient" amount of real estate. (Women "householders" naturally could not vote.)

Before the end of the 17th century the town's population had grown to at least 50 families. We can assume this because, under colony law, when a town's population reached 50 *householders* it had to have a school, and Glastonbury voted on Christmas Day, 1699, to buy nails for a school-house. This vote seems to have set the pattern for citizen reaction to the prospect of new school construction for many future years, even centuries. For the first schoolhouse was still a-building 11 years later, in 1710. The records during the years 1699-1710 report various votes dealing with the proposed school. First it was to be built south of the Green; then it was decided to build it near the Meeting House on the Green; and after that there are a number of testy directives to the townsmen (selectmen) to get on with the building. The schoolhouse was probably completed at last in 1711. Meantime, classes were being held in people's homes. The second entry in the first book of town records concerns the hiring of Robbard Poog as schoolmaster, setting his salary at "Three pound for the first quarter and two pound for the second quarter, if the towne see fit to improve him the second quarter and keep his hors and find him bord during his keeping school." He began to teach July 7, 1701.

If there were 50 householders here by the beginning of the 18th century, it would seem that there must have been some 50 houses. As far as can be determined, only five of these 17th century houses still stand; the John Hollister, Timothy Stevens and Thomas Treat houses; the William Wickham house at 2071 Main Street, an L-shaped half-gambrel house thought to have been built about 1685; and the Amos Hollister "saltbox" on Tryon Street, South Glastonbury, dated 1693. The gambrel roof seems to have been popular in Glastonbury at that period. The Wickham house is unique in that its gambrel "turns a corner." When first constructed, the house faced south, fronting upon a roadway leading

William Wickham House, 1685, the
"gambrel that turns a corner."
(Photo by Duffy.)

east to the wood lot of the three-mile farm. In about 1716, when William Wickham deeded the house to his son John on his wedding day, another section was added which faced east upon the "country road," now Main Street. There are several 18th century houses in Glastonbury whose ells are believed to have been one or two-roomed houses of much earlier periods. Among early houses known to have existed but no longer standing were the Thomas Kimberly house "near the meadow hill," built in 1666, the Ephraim Goodrich house built in 1675 on his land not far from today's Meadow Lane, a Main Street dwelling built by John Kilborne in about 1678, and the Charles Hollister house, built about 1690 on Wassuc Road.

Houses of the early 18th century still standing include the William Miller house at 1855 Main Street, built in 1704 (this date is suggested by the date and initials W M marked on a rear doorlatch). A gambrel-roofed house, its design, particularly its width, is similar to the Treat house in South Glastonbury. Another gambrel house, dated about 1700, is a Goodrich house (probably Thomas) at 693 Main Street, South Glastonbury.

About 20 years ago Dr. Lee J. Whittles took a census of Glastonbury houses built prior to 1800 and still standing, and found 175 of them. Their number is considerably lower now. Still, few American towns the size of Glastonbury can boast as many well-preserved, treasured colonial and early federal

Welles-Shipman-Ward House, 1755, owned by the Historical Society of Glastonbury. (Photo by Duffy.)

houses. These ancient dwellings have not always been considered treasures, however. Until comparatively recent times in many of them fireplaces had been boarded up, holes for stove pipes chopped through elegant paneling, wide-board pine floors covered with linoleum, and sometimes the paneling was buried under plaster. Many of these renovations were made in the 19th century, when parlor stoves and kitchen ranges succeeded fireplaces and sensible measures were taken to promote comfort. However, even in the mid-20th century many old houses were still without central heating and had only rudimentary plumbing and electricity. The town put extremely low tax assessments on these houses.

But since mid-century, more and more people, many of them young newcomers to Glastonbury, have sought out these fine old houses and set to work restoring them, in spite of the many difficulties. Banks for a long time refused to acknowledge that unrestored, though livable, colonial houses had value enough to permit the lending of mortgages or home improvement money.

Among the earliest to recognize the value of the 18th century Colonials were Dr. and Mrs. James Ward, who in the 1930s began restoration work, which continued for many years, on the Welles-Shipman House in South Glastonbury, eventually willed to the Historical Society. Like others who

Kitchen herb garden maintained by Glastonbury
Garden Club at Welles-Shipman-Ward House.
(Photo by Richard Beatty.)

later followed their example, the Wards made interesting discoveries as their work progressed. When they uncovered the "keeping room" (or kitchen) fireplace they found it to be one of the widest in the state, measuring 9 feet 5 inches, with two rear bake ovens. This house, built by a well-to-do ship owner, has unusually fine architectural details which have been photographed and measured by the Historic American Building Survey for preservation in the historical records of the Library of Congress, and has received a citation from the Department of the Interior as being worthy of the most careful preservation.

Glastonbury's 18th century houses in general are typical of the Connecticut River valley design — symmetrical, with central chimmey, nine front windows (four in the first story, five in the second), and, often, double front doors. The placing together of two small windows in the kitchen has been called a feature of Glastonbury style.

Some of the Main Street houses have outstanding ornamentation. One is the Ebenezer Plummer house, which was moved from its original location to its present site just south of the Town Office Building in order to make room for the Main Street entrance to Douglas Road, in 1947. This fine house was built in 1747-50 by Dr. Elizur Hale, who not long before had been graduated from Yale College. The young Dr. Hale spent a great deal of money on this house, providing it with superior paneling and mold-ings, an elegant corner cupboard framed by fluted pilasters, and pedi-mented windows. Apparently he spent too much money on the house to keep it, for he sold it to a wealthy merchant, Ebenezer Plummer, lately come from Boston, for 1100 pounds.

In 1700 a strip of land a mile wide, adjoining the extra 20 rods at the three-mile boundary of the original farms layout, was set off as a public common "forever." The old name for the common, "Town Woods," was meaningful to Glastonbury residents as recently as the 1930s when the hill now known as "Apple Hill" was still being called "Town Woods Hill." Strickland Street marks roughly the eastern boundary of this public area, which was used for grazing and the cutting of timber. Running through this common was a road known as "Three Mile Road" which followed the original boundary line, meandering south over Matson Hill to the Portland line. It traversed part of today's Three Mile Road, passing through the Buck's Corners area to Woodland Street and Clark Hill Road.

At about the same time that the public common was created, the town passed its first conservation act. It voted to forbid any person from cutting any candlewood (pine) for tar or turpentine, with a penalty of 20 shillings a load and forfeit of the wood if they disobeyed. Pine at that time was valuable for export and for shipbuilders, as well as for general building uses and firewood. Nevertheless as the years went by the land was cleared of its virgin timber to provide pastures, so that most of Glastonbury's woodland today is of relatively recent growth.

The remaining four miles of land in East Farms, bought in 1673, seems to have been held by the Town "in common" for nearly a quarter-century and neither bought by individuals nor set off to them by town grant. It was fair game for squatters from Hartford and Wethersfield who came out, put up fences and cut timber. An early town committee was appointed to throw out the intruders and tear down their fences. But it was obvious that the town should parcel out the land to its inhabitants, and in 1692 the first such grant was made. Again in 1714 certain land was divided and given to "the inhabitants and householders . . . (or their heirs) . . . when this town first became a body politic, viz., when the Meeting House . . . was erected." Each was given 100 acres (except those who had previously received grants). An extra 60 acres each were given the heirs of John Hollister, Samuel Hale and Eleazar Kimberly, and to Samuel Welles, Samuel Smith and John Hubbard in recognition of their good services to the town. Another 6000 acres was parceled out to "the present inhabitants" according to their tax lists of 1713, each one's share varying according to the amount of taxes he was paying, the biggest taxpayers getting the largest share of land, certainly a case of "them that has, gits." In similar fashion, the mile of common was divided up in 1757. "Forever" had lasted 57 years!

By 1730 the population of East Farms had grown to such an extent that the families there felt the need of a meeting house of their own. There were large farms in the hills and sawmills on the streams. But the people had to drive or ride horseback many miles to church and back and they were pretty well fed up with it. A petition from 30 families for a new church society was granted by the General Court in 1731. The new society, called Eastbury, soon put up its own Meeting House (long since gone) across the street from the old burying ground which may be seen today on Manchester Road.

Nine families living in the southeastern part of Eastbury still found it difficult to get over the hills to church, which required attendance twice on Sunday and at other times called "Lecture Days." So in 1747, though the Eastbury Society objected, they were granted permission by the General Assembly, together with others from Hebron and Colchester, to form a new society called Marlborough. In 1813 the south end of John Tom Hill also became part of Marlborough, which may be considered a daughter town of Glastonbury, much as Glastonbury is a daughter of Wethersfield.

Eastbury parish had a hard time struggling along on its own. In the beginning it had trouble finding a minister. Some who were asked to come declined; several came on probation but did not stay; two died soon after coming; one had mental trouble and was not taken back when he recovered. The Rev. Isaac Chalker was Eastbury's minister for 21 years, 1744-1765. This section of the town was rugged terrain. While the First Society's lands were easily tillable, Eastbury had to contend with ledge-ridged hills and boulder-strewn forests. Still, the people accomplished wonders, and succeeding generations contrived ample pasture land with the help of oxen.

But Eastbury was marked by tragedy. It was during the brief ministry of Eastbury's second minister, the young Rev. Nehemiah Brainard, that

Holmes brothers headstone, Eastbury Cemetery, testimony to the tragedy of early epidemics. A rubbing of this stone was exhibited in Whitney Museum's "Flowering of American Folk Art," 1974. (Photo by Duffy.)

29

volunteers were called up to sail for the West Indies with a large colonial fleet to help England chase the Spanish out of the West Indies. In October 1740 the fleet set sail, but at "Dominica," they were faced with a deadly epidemic of yellow fever. It is estimated that only 100 survived out of 1000 New Englanders in the expedition. Of these, eight men from the First Society died, but 26, almost the entire young male able-bodied population of Eastbury, lost their lives. All Glastonbury was distressed, and the reaction of the families was thought to be partly responsible for the slowness of recruiting local soldiers for the Revolution later on (according to Dr. Chapin in his 1853 history). Eastbury never recovered from the blow. The area remained for the most part a sparsely-populated farm hamlet of Glastonbury township until the 20th century.

The road to Eastbury, however, was well traveled, and taverns throve along the way, as they did along other Glastonbury roads. Glastonbury was a resting place for travelers going north and south between Hartford and New London, as well as for those bound east and west, from the ferries across the river to Gilead, Hebron and Lebanon. The road now called Hebron Avenue was probably the route taken by Governor Jonathan Trumbull, Sr., to the State House in Hartford from his home in Lebanon during his long tenure from 1769 to 1784. In Revolutionary days there was much activity at Lebanon, where the Council of Safety of the Continental Congress held some 1200 meetings at the War Office, formerly Governor Trumbull's retail store. Under the direction of Trumbull, this was the northern business headquarters of the Continental forces, and its work in supplying men, money and provisions for the patriot army drew praise from Washington. With as much horseback and coach travel along the Glastonbury-Eastbury-Hebron road as there was, frequent stopping places for food for travelers and the watering of horses were necessary. There were at least two Eastbury taverns: Dr. Elizur Hale, Jr.'s house on John Tom Hill and the Treat tavern not far from the three-mile boundary.

The large, four-square Hale house in Eastbury was built by Dr. Elizur Hale for his son, Dr. Elizur, Jr., in the pre-Revolutionary period ("the house at Eastbury where my son Elizur lives was wholly built and the lower rooms finished at my expense," the elder Dr. Hale wrote in a note appended to his will, dated 1775). In addition to a medical dispensary, the ell contained a kitchen with a large fireplace harboring a great built-in iron kettle. Later on, after the period of Hale ownership of this house, the place was known as the Lee tavern, according to Florence Hollister Curtis.

James Wright in 1761 built the large central-chimney house at 1597 Hebron Avenue which was purchased in 1816 by Charles and David Treat and operated as a tavern for a good part of the 19th century. Wall stenciling decorated the entrance hall. The paneled taproom had its own entrance on the southwest corner. A list of purchases made in September 1818 for the tavern bar, found years later, included rum, cider brandy, Spanish brandy, clove water, raisins, ginger, sugar, allspice, tea, coffee, chocolate, salt fish, Long Island salt, and lamp oil.

Another 18th century house which became a tavern is the Joseph Moseley house at 1803 Main Street. It was built about 1718 by Joseph Maudsley (as the name was then spelled) following his purchase of a 553-acre tract comprising three of the original three-mile farms. The house has one of the great chimneys characteristic of colonial Glastonbury's houses, this one measuring 12 by 14 feet in the cellar. The bar room of the tavern was the southeast parlor, and, as in other taverns of the period, a second floor room could be turned into a ballroom by swinging up a panel wall hinged to the ceiling. "You will find us enjoying the pleasures of each other's company in dances as we are this evening at the usual head quarters, Capt. Moseley's," wrote Isaac Welles to his friend George Hale on September 11, 1784. From 1800 to 1840 George Moseley operated the inn, which was one of the town's chief social centers. In 1859 David Carrier acquired the house and it became the home of a Carrier descendant, Mrs. Francis W. Bartlett, and her husband.

Also once run as a tavern was the Samuel Talcott house, a "lean-to" or "saltbox" built about 1727 and torn down in 1912, which stood about where the south part of the Academy School is today. (Samuel Talcott's uncle, Joseph Talcott, was Governor of Connecticut Colony at the time this house was built.) The house was distinguished for the fact that it had in an upstairs chamber the first wallpaper used in Glastonbury. Samuel Talcott sent to London for it in 1738. Between the studs of the house were bricks which had been fired in the highway in front of the house, according to the reminiscences of a descendant, Thomas High Lord Tallcott. "All the nails, bolts, hinges and latches were forged out in a shop that stood where David Tallcott's driveway is," he wrote. Mr. Tallcott (who spelled his name with two l's, one variation of a name which had been spelled many different ways, including Tall Coat, over the centuries) was a local justice of the peace in the 19th century. "As there was no lock-up in town, I held prisoners for court at the Tallcott house," he wrote.

Thirty years after this house was built Samuel put up a similar house for his son, Samuel, which is still standing, a red "saltbox" on Manchester Road near the northbound ramp from Route 2. Like Samuel's own house, this one has handmade bricks, some with the imprint of fingers on them, between the studs. In this house was born Mary Talcott, the grandmother of Admiral Dewey, hero of the Battle of Manila in 1898.

The best known of all the Glastonbury taverns was the Welles Tavern (later known as the Welles-Chapman Tavern) which has been moved from its original location on the west side of Main Street across the street to the center redevelopment area. Now owned by the Historical Society, this building was erected in 1785 and run as a tavern by Joseph Welles until 1808, when it was bought by Azel Chapman, who kept the tavern until 1861. Welles Tavern was a Glastonbury landmark well-known to travelers, for it was the first stop of the stagecoach from Hartford to New London, a full day's journey. Henry Storrs Goslee, writing in *The Connecticut Quarterly* in 1896 about the Welles Tavern, tells of the arrival of the stagecoach, drawn by four lively horses, preceded by a resounding tally-ho. Out of the stagecoach would clamber some 15 or 20 passengers ready for a drop of rum or the toddy for which the tavern was famous. In addition to transient business, the tavern served as a center of political and social activity. It was also the location of Glastonbury's first post office, established in 1806 with Joseph Welles the first postmaster. Town boards met here, and informal, even secret, caucuses plotted the shape and direction of local government. On the second floor was the customary hinged partition which when raised formed a sizable ballroom. After 1859 the Hartford, Providence and Fishkill railroad and packet steamboats gave too much competition to the rough turnpike stagecoach, and tavern business was greatly cut down.

In South Glastonbury there were two taverns of note. The Elijah Miller tavern dating from 1802, located at 1155 Main Street, was first used by travelers journeying from the Nayaug ferry to New London by way of what is now Chestnut Hill Road. Later, after the turnpike to New London opened (in the early 1800s) the stages followed a new route and left the Miller tavern without much business and it soon closed. This tavern, also, had swinging wood partitions which would convert the entire front of the second story to a ballroom.

The other well-known hostelry in South Glastonbury was the Bates Tavern on High Street. This mid-18th century house was built by David Hollister, who used the southeast front room as a public taproom. The Bates family acquired the house in about 1828 and it continued in use as a tavern, or, in its later years as a hotel-boarding house, until the early 20th century. William Bates, last of the tavern keepers, later became the manager of the Murray Hill Hotel in New York. Miss Christine Bates was the last member of the family to run the "hotel." There are some older residents today who remember hearing about the excellent table Miss Bates set: snowy white linen damask and "solid" silver, unusual in a country boarding-house, and delicious food.

All of these taverns, and perhaps others as well, flourished at one time or another in Glastonbury. The older ones survived the Revolutionary War and the onset of that war, with all that meant of shortages resulting from British embargoes and soaring costs due in part to taxes imposed in London. But survive they did, and many played host to the men who were soon to engage in the American struggle for freedom.

Chapter IV

The Struggle for National Independence: Glastonbury in the Revolution

British taxes were a subject familiar to Glastonbury long before the start of the American Revolution. Shipbuilders and owners, seamen, shopkeepers, and customers had been aware of customs duties — very restrictive ones — on foreign imports which had been imposd by England on the colonies since the 1600s. Some of these duties had been more honored in the breach, such as the one on molasses, a principal import which often came in barrels assembled in the West Indies from Glastonbury red oak hoops and staves sent down for that purpose. The townspeople continued to think of themselves as loyal British subjects. If one can judge by existing town records, they did not show much resentment over the Revenue Act enacted by Parliament in 1764, levying additional duties on foreign imports. And local men had served their mother country in the French-Canadian campaigns and an ill-fated expedition to "the Havannah."

But when Parliament in 1767 passed the Townshend Acts, extending customs duties from foreign (that is, not English) imports to include English products, Glastonbury, like most other towns in the colony, supported resistance measures. The chief proposal was a plan to refuse British imports. On August 27, 1770, the town voted to send Jonathan Welles and Ebenezer Plummer as representatives to a meeting of business interests at New Haven to consider action in favor of a non-importation agreement. Jonathan Welles, like his father, Thomas, before him, was one of the most influential men in town. He was one of the town's two Representatives to the General Assembly and served altogether for 14 years. It was natural that Ebenezer Plummer, Glastonbury's leading merchant, should have been chosen to represent the town at a meeting of business men. He had a large part in running the community during pre-war and war years. Starting in 1773 he served for a decade as Representative to the Assembly, some of the time along with Jonathan Welles.

Welles and Plummer were instructed in forceful terms to hold out for banning all commercial transactions with England until the Townshend Acts should be repealed. Expressing dismay at New York's ignoring of the Agreement, the instructions also advised the representatives to suggest a policy of no trade with that neighboring colony. "You will not fail, gentlemen, to exert yourselves, that resolutions of this kind be come into, and whatever else the friends of the liberties of this Colony with whom you may have the honor to consult, shall judge expedient at this important crisis, for the security of all our invaluable rights and privileges to us, and transmitting down the same to our unborn posterity." The town then appointed an inspection committee of three to see that no goods were imported into Glastonbury from New York until the Revenue Acts were repealed.

Before the end of the year, Parliament did indeed repeal the Townshend Acts, and the non-importation agreement was lifted. This meant that Glastonbury ships, as well as others, were free to resume their sea trade. And so there was a brief spell of prosperity for two or three years. Thus we find nothing in the town records during this period to indicate a further surge of anti-British feeling. But it was the lull before the storm. The only imported item on which the Townshend duty had not been repealed was tea. In May 1773 Parliament legalized an arrangement which made it no longer possible for tea to be smuggled into our ports from Dutch sources, and the British East India Tea Company then began to send ships loaded with tea to the colonies. But the Boston "Sons of Liberty" (patriots inspired by Samuel Adams) by dumping tea into the harbor one night touched off a series of events which led directly to the Revolution.

The Boston Tea Party needled Parliament into passing a series of laws called the Coercive Acts, first of which was the Boston Port Act, blockading the Boston port until it should pay for the destroyed tea. When news of the Boston Port Act reached the Hartford area, all the surrounding communities were inflamed with indignation. June 1, 1774, when the blockade went into effect, became a day of mourning in Hartford. Bells began to toll early in the morning and continued all day. The Town House was hung with black, the shops were all shut and windows were draped with black.

In Glastonbury a town meeting was called on June 23, with Elizur Talcott as chairman, for the purpose first of all of putting into the official record the town's firm resolve to support Boston and the entire patriot effort to resist the tyranny of Britain. And, just as important, to name a Committee of Correspondence as requested by Samuel Adams, and to set in motion a contribution of aid, both money and provisions, for the distressed city of Boston.

The first resolution was the following:

"Voted: That it is the opinion of this meeting that the act of Parliament imposing a duty on tea exported to America, for the purpose of raising a revenue, is subversive of the rights and liberties of the British Americans, unconstitutional and oppressive. And we consider the late act of Parliament for blocking up the port of Boston, and others that are pending with respect to the province of Massachusetts Bay, designed not only to enslave that province, but as we hold our liberties and privileges on the same footing with them, of all the English colonies in America.

"We, therefore, are resolved to exert to the utmost of our power, in every lawful way, to oppose, resist, and if possible, defeat the designs of our enemies to enslave us. And we are of opinion that the safest and most effectual method to obtain a repeal of those rights and privileges, will be universal agreement of all the colonies, that all commercial connections with Great Britain and the West Indies be withheld. And as we are informed that a General Congress of all the colonies is proposed, we are of opinion that such a Congress would be very expedient, and that (that) is the most probable method to cement the colonies together in a firm union, on which (under God), our only security depends. And when this Congress shall convene, (which we hope will be as soon as possible) we shall be ready to adopt any measure which shall be thought by them to be the most effectual to obtain relief from the burdens of which we so justly complain."

Such a Congress was indeed set up. It held its first meeting at Philadelphia six weeks later, on September 5. Known as the First Continental Congress, it became the federal government of a nation at war.

The town meeting's second resolution set up the following Committee of Correspondence, a group of the town's leading and perhaps most learned men: Col. Elizur Talcott, William Welles, Capt. Elisha Hollister, Ebenezer Plummer, Isaac Moseley, Thomas Kimberly and Josiah Hale. The committee's duties were to receive and answer letters and promote and send contributions to Boston. Its first action was to send the following letter to Boston:

"Glassenbury in Connecticutt, 23d June, 1774
"Gentlemen —

We cannot but deeply simpathize with you under the gloomy prospects which at present are before you, on account of those oppresive acts of Parliament which have lately been passed, respecting Boston in particular, and the province of Massachusetts Bay in general. Especially when we consider that our liberties and privileges are so nearly and indissolubly connected with yours, that an encroachment upon one at least, destroys the security of the other. It seems the Parliament of Great Britain are determined to reduce America to a state of vassalage, and unless we all unite in the common cause, they will undoubtedly accomplish their design. We are surprised to find so many of the merchants in Boston courting favor of the tools of the ministry, and heaping encomiums on the Enemy to liberty, that traitor to his country, and abettor, if not author of all these evils to America. However we hope the spirit of liberty is not yet entirely fled from Boston, but that you will yet hold out, and to the last resist and oppose those who are striving to enslave America. You may depend on us, and we believe all Connecticut almost to a man, to stand by you and assist you in this defense of our invaluable rights and privileges, even to the sacrificing of our lives and fortunes, in so good a cause. You will see the determinations and resolves of this Town, which we have enclosed. A subscription is set on foot for the relief of the poor in Boston, and what money or provisions shall be collected, we shall forward as soon as possible. We are informed that your house of Representatives have appointed a time, for the meeting of the general congress, in which we hope all the colonies will concur, and that a nonimportation and nonexportation agreement, will be immediately come into, which we doubt not will procure the desired effect; and notwithstanding the gloomy aspect of things at present, we cannot but look forward with fond hopes and pleasing expectations, to that glorious era, when America in spite of all the efforts of her enemies to the contrary, shall rise superior to all opposition, overcome oppression, be a refuge for the oppressed, a nurse of liberty, a scourge to Tyranny, and the envy of the world — then (if you stand firm and unshaken amidst the storm of ministerial vengeance) shall it be told to your everlasting honor, that Boston stood foremost in the cause of liberty, when the greatest power on Earth was striving to divest them of it, and by their noble efforts, joined with the united virtue of her sister Colonies, they overcame, and thereby transmitted to posterity, those invaluable rights and privileges, which their forefathers purchased with their blood — and now Gentlemen relying on your steadiness and firmness in the common cause, we subscribe yr most obdt Humble Servants

Elizur Talcott
William Welles
Eben'r Plummer
Isaac Moseley
Josiah Hale

Committee."

(The curious implication that Boston city slickers were "courting favor of the tools of the ministry" may have referred to several Tory merchants who were playing along with General Gage, the Massachusetts governor, in his attempts to prevent sedition.)

This letter sent by the Committee of Correspondence may have been composed by Ebenezer Plummer, as the original was owned by his grandson, George Plummer, who lent it for publication in Dr. Chapin's history of Glastonbury.

A unique document once possessed by the late Mr. and Mrs. John Lambert is the only other known surviving paper drawn by the Glastonbury Committee of Correspondence. An appeal to townspeople to turn in to the authorities any tea they might have in their possession, the undated document was obviously motivated by the high resentment people held over the tax on tea. Probably the notice was posted up on the town (bulletin) board.

"Advertisement

This is to notify all the Inhabitants of the Town of Glastonbury that at a Meeting of the Committee of Correspondence for this Town on the 8th day of March Instant: it was thought advisable by them in Order that all Temtation to break through the Association of the Continental Congress should be removed from the People of this Town; that all the Tea remaining on the Hands of any Person in this Town should be collected together and storred in some safe Place there to remain until the Acts of Parliament mentioned in the Association aforesaid, are repealed and all Persons that have in their Possession any Tea are hereby desired to deliver the same to the Committee of Correspondence and Inspection for this Town by the First Day of April next, and every Person is desired to write his or her Name on the same together with the Quantity therein contained. — and those Persons that will not comply with this request may be expected to be accounted Enemies to their Country, and will be dealt with accordingly. Elizur Talcott, William Welles, Elijah Hollister, Elijah Smith, Josiah Hale, Thomas Kimberly: Committee."

Glastonbury patriots had been aware for some time that the touchy situation in the Boston area might mushroom into a full-fledged clash. When the British soldiers fired on the line of farmer-patriots at Lexington April 19, 1775, word spread fast — that is, for those days. On April 20, Silas Deane, Wethersfield member of the Continental Congress, received a letter informing him of the Lexington incident. He tended to disbelieve it, but the next day, a Friday, it was confirmed and he had the drums beat "To Arms." On Saturday, 100 Wethersfield troops crossed the river en route to Boston.

This action must have been known to Glastonbury men, so that it was an uneasy congregation which attended church on Sunday morning. They could not have been much surprised when, dramatically, a call for help was received from Boston in the midst of the Rev. John Eells' sermon. As Mrs. Florence Hollister Curtis told the story, hoofbeats of a galloping horseman were heard approaching the church. He drew up outside, burst into the room, and in a husky whisper asked the tithing man seated near the door to call outside Ebenezer Plummer and his committee. To them he gave his message: "War has begun! Our men have been fired upon at Lexington and at Concord. Send help at once."

Mr. Plummer passed on this urgent request to the Rev. Eells, who announced the news to his congregation, advised them to go home and prepare for a march to war, then quietly gave a benediction. The dusty postrider was already on his way to the little church at Eastbury. Here the Rev. Eells' cousin, the Rev. James Eells, announced the same stirring news to his congregation. Outside the churches there was great excitement. Train band members gathered round their captains, little boys cheered and women wept. All that night candles flickered and Betty lamps burned as families worked to get their menfolk ready for a march to Boston, fitted out as required by the companies of militia.

At daybreak a band of 59 men led by Captain Elizur Hubbard started off for Boston. They were the following: Stephen Goodrich, Benjamin Stevens, lieutenants; Thomas Hollister, ensign; Aaron Hubbard, Meletiah Nye, Israel Hollister, George Stocking, Samuel Bidwell, sergeants; Jonathan Treat, David Hollister, drummers; David Nye, fifer; and Joseph Hubbard, John Andrews, David Andrews, Levi Brooks, Jonah Chapman, David Cole, Samuel Dealing, John Eddy, Abraham Fox, David Fox, Simeon Fox, Asa Goodale, George Goodrich, Israel Goodrich, William Hildrith, Elisha How(e), Aaron Hollister, John How(e), Jr., Benjamin House, Jonathan Hall (i.e., Hale), Jr., Joseph Lamb, George Stocking, Sr., Samuel Well(e)s, Jr., Gad Loveland, James Maden, Alexander McDowell, Samuel Nowiden, Jonathan Strickland, Benjamin Howard, Samuel House, Stephen Shipman, Jr., Jonathan Stevens, Asaph Smith, Moses Scott, Joseph Scott, Samuel Taylor, Joseph Temple, William Talmage, George Talcott, Jonathan Talcott, John Wickham, James Wire (Weir), Elias Wares, Jonathan Weaver, Elizur Brooks and John Case, all privates; and Howell Woodbridge, commissary.

The patriotic volunteers, on this first call-up of the Revolutionary War, never reached the field of battle. After about two days' march along muddy overgrown cartroads, they were only as far as Stafford Springs when they were met by a courier bringing news that the British had retreated back into Boston. Captain Hubbard, reasoning that help at this particular time was no longer necessary, gave the order to return to Glastonbury.

Captain Jonathan Hale,
Revolutionary soldier, died at
Jamaica Plain, Roxbury,
Massachusetts, March 7, 1776.
(Photo courtesy Donald B. Reid.)

The group arrived back on Thursday, having been in service only four days. Yet all of them knew that at any time they might be off again and this time would be pitting their patriot strength against the well-trained forces of the British.

In less than two weeks, volunteers marched once more to the Boston area. Glastonbury men were in the group quartered at Roxbury when on June 17 the drums beat out a call to arms. It was the first great battle of the war, the Battle of Bunker Hill.

The soldiers belonged to the Sixth Connecticut (Militia) Regiment, which included men from Wethersfield, Middletown and Kensington parish as well as Glastonbury. They were clad in uniforms "wholly blue turned up with red," some of them probably made by Asa Talcott in his tailors' and saddlery shop in the front yard of his home on the "country road." The men must have had a distinctive appearance, for many of the patriot soldiers wore mufti from start to finish of the Revolutionary War. The Sixth Regiment Company was quartered at Roxbury, Mass., where a church was their barracks.

In July 1775 the militia company was adopted as a Continental regiment, and reorganized for duty in 1776. Militiamen volunteered for periods of three months, while enlistment in the Continental Army was for three years. The changeover from militia (which included local trained bands like Glastonbury's) to continental status was not particularly pleasing to the men. A letter home from Captain John Chester of Wethersfield, the commanding officer of the regiment, comments on the poor state of the commissary: "Our position is not a fifth part so good as when we lived from our own colony provisions. I care not how much of a Continental war it is, but I pray for Connecticut provisions . . . Half the time no sauce, no milk . . .The Congress allows us no butter, chocolate, or coffee, or sugar, which our Colony allowed us. The pork is thin, poor, flabby stuff . . ." One can imagine that the provisions got much worse as time went on.

Captain Jonathan Hale of the 4th Company, Sixth Regiment, sent by Connecticut to the siege of Boston in 1776, was killed on March 7 on Jamaica Plain, 10 days before the British evacuated Boston on March 17, 1776. His son, Jonathan, Jr., who had marched off for the Battle of Lexington in 1775 and remained on duty with his regiment guarding the lines, returned sick to Glastonbury in September 1776, and died a few days later, on October 1. Jonathan, Jr., aged 31 and apparently not married, had made his will on the very day he died. In it there is mention of a Negro servant, Newport, doubtless the same Newport who was bequeathed in the will of his grandfather to Jonathan's father, the Captain Jonathan who was killed at Jamaica Plain.

The Sixth Company of the Sixth Regiment appears to have been largely composed of Glastonbury men, commanded by Lieutenant Stephen Andrews. The company took part in the Long Island, New York, and White Plains battles in August and September 1776. A payroll for this company listing 59 Glastonbury men and the amounts they received is among the documents of the Historical Society of Glastonbury. The troop was made up, in addition to Lieutenant Andrews, of four sergeants, four corporals, a drummer boy, a fifer, and 48 privates. Each man was given 19 shillings 8 pence for "travil money." "Sauce money," or board, averaged two pounds 11 shillings per soldier, and wages were less than three pounds for a month's service. It was in this New York campaign that many of our local patriot soldiers were taken prisoner by the British. More than a few of these died in captivity, on their way home, or after they got home, from disease they had contracted while prisoners. A Glastonbury boy who escaped from a British vessel near the West Indies arrived home safely and well, according to a story told by Florence Hollister Curtis in her history, *Glastonbury*. James MacLean, she said, escaped by swimming in the shadow of the vessel to shore. From there he booked passage to Charleston, S. C., and walked home, a distance of some 600 miles. Then he promptly re-enlisted.

Glastonbury was an important supplier to the Revolutionary War effort. Its largest industry at this period was a gunpowder factory located on the north bank of Roaring Brook in South Glastonbury, at Cotton Hollow, run by George Stocking, Sr., and his sons. The Stocking mill was one of the few powder plants in New England which helped to supply ammunition for General Washington's Army. That it managed to do so was a tribute to the courage of one of the unsung heroines of the Revolution, Eunice Cobb Stocking.

On August 23, 1777, a fire broke out in the Stocking factory and touched off an explosion which destroyed the mill and killed six men. Mrs. Stocking had driven a load of gunpowder to the outskirts of Boston and was returning when, going through Bolton Notch, 15 miles from home, she felt the ground tremble and saw a cloud of black smoke to the west. Horrified, for there was no mistaking what had happened, she urged her horse on homewards as fast as he could make it. Her loss was great. Killed in the explosion were her husband and three of her sons, George, Jr., Hezekiah and Nathaniel. The only remaining son, Elisha, had been sent on an errand and escaped the explosion.

Mrs. Stocking was endowed with great courage. She enlisted the financial help of Howell Woodbridge, built the factory up again and continued to supply gunpowder for the Army until the end of the war. The Daughters of the American Revolution have honored the memory of Eunice Cobb Stocking by giving her name to its Glastonbury chapter. When the war was over, Mrs. Stocking took on the operation of the former Bidwell grist mill across the brook from the powder mill, which her husband had bought before his tragic death.

In 1774 the town had bought two half-barrels of gunpowder from the Stocking mill for the militia. Two years later, in January 1776, the town voted to buy 300 weight of powder for the defense of the town. It was a precautionary measure which never became necessary to put into effect as the British never ventured as far up the river as Glastonbury.

Nevertheless, it was urgent that every citizen be ready to defend his home and his country, and with this in mind, the town in September 1776 appointed a committee "to inspect each able bodied man in this Town and see whether each man is equipped with a good gun . . ." The committee appointed were Joseph Moseley, Thomas Kimberly, Eleazer Wright, Elijah Hollister, Benjamin Hodge, Joseph Goodale, Nehemiah Strickland, Thomas Hunt and Nathan Dickinson. The committee was to warn every man without a gun in workable condition to get it fixed within one week. If he was too poor to have it fixed, then the town was to do it for him. However, if the owner should be unable to pay back the town for the repair job within six months, then the gun was to be kept "for the benefit of the town."

Very likely the gun, if it had to be fixed, was repaired at the little water-powered gunsmith's shop which stood near Flat Brook, a tributary of Roaring Brook, in Dark Hollow about two miles below Buck's Corners. This gun shop manufactured muskets during the Revolution, and even after the war was over continued to turn out firearms for the federal government. Run by the Colton family, who also kept the Tollgate and tavern just above on the old New London Turnpike, the shop at one time housed a turning lathe for making four-poster bedsteads, and probably wooden chairs and other articles as well.

By 1777 the town was striving hard to provide its soldiers with clothing and camping necessities, as directed by the State. At town meeting the selectmen were ordered to borrow 30 pounds to buy "tents, pots, bowls, canteens, lead, etc." and to lay a tax to cover this expense. In March a committee was appointed to see that the families of enlisted soldiers had provisions, and in September (preceding the order of the General Assembly, which in turn was following the directive of the Continental Congress) the town set about providing "shirts, frocks, shews and overhalls" for its soldiers. The selectmen were also ordered to send two loads of provisions to Boston and to purchase two loads of salt to be sold "for the benefit of the soldiers in the army from this Town." (Salt was very scarce, owing to the stopping of sea trade with the West Indies, as of September 1774, but it was something everyone needed as it was the chief means of preserving meat and fish.)

In the spring of 1777, all Glastonbury buzzed with excitement when a group of Yale students arrived to hold classes here. For some months, the Yale administration, facing wartime shortages, had had problems trying to provide adequate food for the students. In late March, President Naphtili Daggett decided to disperse the student body to several inland towns until provisions were more plentiful. There was also some concern that New Haven might be invaded by the British. Glastonbury was one of several towns which issued invitations. Probably the invitation came from William Welles, who had been a Yale tutor. William's son, William, Jr., and his nephew, George, were members of the sophomore class at the time.

*Samuel Talcott House, 1727-1912, where
Academy School now stands. Yale students,
including Noah Webster, boarded here in 1777-78.*

Under the supervision of Professor Nehemiah Strong and the Rev. Joseph Buckminster, a tutor, the Yale sophomores and juniors were sent to Glastonbury. Seniors went to Wethersfield and freshmen to Farmington. Classes began about April 30, being held at the home of William Welles, and continued (except for vacations) until late in June of the following year.

The students boarded with local residents, several of them staying at the home of Asa Talcott, which stood about where the Academy School is today. Among the boarders at Asa Talcott's was Noah Webster, whose Dictionary and Blue-backed Speller later became best sellers. Noah, who was already noting events of the day in the diary he kept for many years, does not say much about his sojourn in Glastonbury, but he does give one sidelight on local wartime privations with this comment: "At one time food was so scarce that the farmers cut cornstalks and crushed them in cidermills, and then boiled the juice down to a syrup as a substitute for sugar."

Yale-in-Glastonbury underwent a town-gown controversy during its short existence. The students formed a drama group and rehearsed the play, *Tancred and Sigismunda,* hoping to put on a performance for a local audience. But the sober-minded Glastonbury villagers, still under the domination of the Puritan church, would have none of it. Anything having to do with the theater was considered immoral. Not to be cheated of their efforts, the group hired the State House in Hartford the following May and put the play on there. It was apparently the first dramatic production ever given in Hartford.

George and William Welles, Jr., and their fellow students had been back in New Haven about a year when, during the night of July 4, 1779, about 2000 British troops under General Tryon landed in the harbor and swarmed the streets, looting and plundering. A hastily-organized company of Yale students, under George's command, joining with local volunteers, unsuccessfully attempted to defend the town. Fortunately the British departed without burning New Haven. George was the son of John Welles, owner of the Welles-Shipman-Ward House, now the property of the Historical Society of Glastonbury.

During the course of the war, Glastonbury's taxes went up steadily, reaching two shillings and sixpence on one pound's assessment, the equivalent of an assessment of 125 mills. The soldiers' wages paid by the State were small, and the town at various times voted extra pay for its soldiers as an inducement for enlistment. The measure was obviously successful, for at various times nearly every able-bodied man of fighting age was in the service. Tradition has it that barracks for recruits were erected in the meadows (perhaps for training). It was also said that during the periods of greatest battle urgency, Glastonbury crops were sown and harvested almost entirely by women.

George Welles, Yale senior, drilling students he mustered to defend New Haven, July 1779. Watercolor sketch by St. John Honeywood, then a Yale freshman. (Photo courtesy Connecticut Historical Society with permission of owner, Mrs. Frank Mauran.)

Dr. Whittles found that 369 Glastonbury men served in the Militia or Continental Army. Of the total who went to war, 31 are known to have died either in battle or later of wounds or disease, some having been stricken while prisoners. One man (Alexander McDowell) was hanged at Hartford for desertion. Altogether, a larger percentage (23 per cent) of the town's population served in this war, and a larger percentage gave their lives, than in any other war to date.

From the records, it appears that Glastonbury men fought in the Boston area, at Ticonderoga, in Benedict Arnold's Quebec campaign, in the battles of Long Island, New York and White Plains, at West Point, at Germantown, Pa., and in Rhode Island, and probably they served in other battle areas as well.

The service of Benoni Buck of Buck's Corners to his country's cause might be given a special place in the records of Glastonbury's participation in the Revolution. Benoni Buck, aged 16, in 1781 was chosen to drive a load of salt beef and gunpowder by oxteam from Glastonbury to Washington's troops in Pennsylvania. Starting out at the end of August, he joined an oxwagon team at New Haven and slowly made his way south. By the time the convoy reached the battle area, Washington had Cornwallis bottled up at Yorktown. Although he was not a soldier, Benoni joined the battle, armed with a musket he had picked up from a dead soldier. Probably no one knew or cared that he was an 'irregular," fighting in mufti among the tattered troops. He stuck with it until on October 17 Cornwallis sent out the white flag. Then Benoni put down his gun, retrieved his oxen and slowly made his way back to Buck's Corners.

The final vote clearing up the business of the Revolution was taken in 1783, the year the war officially ended. At this town meeting a committee was appointed "to look up all the powder and ball, guns and cartouche boxes, fines and forfeitures paid to the commanding officers, & all other things that belonged to this town and have been receipted out since the present War."

Thomas H. L. Talcott holding musket carried by Asa Talcott in Battle of Saratoga, 1777. Wallpaper, the first in Glastonbury, was imported from England, 1738.

Chapter V

Wheels of Progress:
The Beginnings of Glastonbury Industry

From the end of the Revolution to the beginning of the Civil War Glastonbury's population increased by nearly 50 per cent (2346 to 3363). There was a good reason: Industry was humming. Nineteenth century Glastonbury saw the rise and growth of shipbuilding, as well as the manufacture of textiles, forged iron, glass, hats, cast metal goods, clapboards, barrels, cigars, soap and leather.

Glastonbury fortunately had plenty of water power to keep mill wheels turning. Roaring Brook flowed through the southeast part of town in a long, curving, tumbling, splashing rush from its source in the eastern hills to the Connecticut River at Nayaug, fed along the way by little tributaries. Salmon Brook, smaller but lively, followed a similar east-west course through the north part of town from the top of Minnechaug Mountain down through the plains to empty into the river at Naubuc. Other brooks paralleled the two major streams through central Glastonbury. All had their quota of saw mills and grist mills powered by water wheels.

Industry got its start here with saw mills. The General Court in 1667 granted permission to Thomas Harris of Hartford to build a saw mill on a stream, probably Salmon Brook, "beyond the three-mile lots and to have forty acres of land for the convenience of timber and the like." It is not entirely clear why the Court felt it had a right to convey land which presumably the Indians still owned, since the 5-mile purchase (known as the Great Indian Purchase) was not made until 1673. In any case, other mills soon followed on the various streams. Water-powered mills were an important element in the life of the people not only of colonial times but for two centuries until the industrial revolution, occurring later in this country than in England, introduced the steam engine. William Blodgett's map of Connecticut in 1791, marking the locations of industries and churches, showed that in Glastonbury there were then three saw mills on Roaring Brook in Buckingham, one saw mill on Salmon Brook, two saw

Dam on Roaring Brook at Manchester and Quarry Roads, site of water-powered mills from 1712-1914. (Photo by Duffy.)

mills on Hubbard Brook, one saw mill on Roaring Brook in South Glastonbury, two grist mills on Roaring Brook in Buckingham, one furnace on Roaring Brook in South Glastonbury, one grist mill on Holland Brook and one grist mill on Roaring Brook in South Glastonbury. In addition, according to Herbert T. Clark's article in *Retrospect* on "Early Industries Along Roaring Brook," there was a saw mill on the Connecticut River bank near Log Landing, there were three saw mills on Roaring Brook in South Glastonbury (the Hollister-Welles saw mill in Nayaug, the Talcott saw mill approaching Cotton Hollow, and the Bidwell saw mill in Cotton Hollow). And there were three grist mills (the Great Grist Mill of Nayaug, with bake shop and oven, erected about 1760, the Bidwell grist mill later run by Mrs. Eunice Stocking in Cotton Hollow, and, upstream, Timothy Easton's grist mill, for which the land was leased for 999 years). There was also an early grist mill on Salmon Brook and a grist mill on Hubbard Brook. Doubtless there were others, in addition to Blodgett's list, on other streams in the town.

The first saw mills produced clapboards and pipestaves, not only for local building but for export downriver to New York, to the colonies to the south and to the West Indies. With these products, and tar distilled from pinewood, providing salable cargoes, shipping became Glastonbury's first real industry. Shipbuilding, with its needs not only for saw mills but also for forges, supply stores and sail making, as well as for seamen, gave employment to many fathers and sons of the town for a long span of years.

There were difficulties in carrying on sea trade, however, one of them being English restrictions on trade within the colonies, and another being the excise duties imposed by the Connecticut Colony itself, to build up the colonial treasury. The duty that affected Glastonbury shipping the most was that on lumber, the town's chief export. Such an excise tax was first levied in 1714; in 1747 a heavy duty was put on "all staves, headings, ship-timber, planks and bark shipped from this to neighboring colonies." A much earlier tax had imposed an import duty on wine and rum brought back from the West Indies. Further fretting shipping interests was a tax of 15 shillings per ton assessed in 1726 on the cargo of vessels. This Act created the temptation to underrate a ship's cargo capacity when it was registered. The actual size of vessels built in Glastonbury may often have been greater than recorded.

Dependent as they were upon prevailing winds and the trickiness of navigating ships over the numerous sandbars in the river, the ships sometimes took a long time to get from Glastonbury to the Sound and even longer to come upriver against the current. Because of these problems, the ships were small, generally sloops, schooners or brigs of not more than 200 tons "burden," or capacity. (The *Mayflower* was recorded as being 120 tons burden; Glastonbury vessels would have been of similar size or smaller.)

Shipping started at an early period in the Connecticut Colony. Samuel Smith, who gave land for Glastonbury's first Meeting House, was part owner of what may have been the first ship in the Colony, the *Tryall*, built at Wethersfield in 1649. The Rev. Gershom Bulkeley was an early exporter of timber and beaver and deerskins.

Because of a series of mishaps — fire which destroyed the Royal Customs House (where colonial ship records were kept) in Benedict Arnold's raid on New London in the Revolution; ship registration records mysteriously missing from the Middletown Customs House for the periods 1776-1804 and 1810-24; and the apparent discarding of records formerly at the Middletown Customs House when the old State Street post office in Hartford was demolished in 1934 — Glastonbury's ship records are incomplete. But from various sources (account books or bills of lading) enough is known to give some picture of Glastonbury in sailing days.

The earliest mention of a Glastonbury mariner seems to be that in a diary kept by Thomas Tryon. Thomas mentions going to New York with his brother, David, who lived in Glastonbury, to pilot a sloop that David had bought there, returning on November 3, 1709. Another early local mariner was John Talcott, who served as captain of the transport *Gull*, which carried troops to Fort Louisburg, Cape Breton, in the English-French campaign of 1745.

Altogether, until steamboats substantially succeeded sailing vessels in the mid 1870s, several hundred ships were built and launched from Glastonbury yards. The first shipyard in Glastonbury was that known as the Naubuc Shipyard, located at the south end of Keeney Cove near the old Pratt's Ferry. The site is now under water. Another yard was at Log Landing, South Glastonbury, on the river bank between Pease Lane and the old Coal Dock. It was so named because of the logs which were floated down the river and guided into the shipyard by a log boom. Still another was the Tryon shipyard farther down the river, south of the present marina, in the area known for years as Tryontown.

Thomas Welles' shipyard at Log Landing was established before the middle of the 18th century and continued under his son, John, and his grandsons, John, Jr., George and Ashbel, until at least 1784. During this period the yard launched many vessels; did a brisk trade with other colonies and the West Indies; and during the Revolution sent out privateers under "letters of marque" issued by the General Assembly. An early record of the exasperation caused by efforts to comply with colonial shipping laws is that of a petition brought to the General Court by Thomas Welles and Elizur Talcott in May 1748. The petition advised the Court that these men "are building a schooner and are obliged to get cables and anchors outside of the colony . . . As they suppose the law is not intended to prevent shipbuilding they ask abatement of duty on cables and anchors bought at Boston." Welles and Talcott were probably seeking relief from a recently enacted five per cent "ad valorem" tax on goods imported from other colonies. There were exemptions of various goods including "train oil," whalebone, rice, window glass and lumber as well as cast, bar and slit iron, but evidently not cables and anchors. If the men had imported those items directly from England, there would have been no duty.

Though England's war with Spain in 1762-63 somewhat deterred the coastal sea trade, the Welles shipyard still flourished, and John Welles made plans to expand its operations by setting up another shipyard in Philadelphia. He went to that city in 1764 and negotiated for land, but the yard was never built because on the trip John caught cold and died.

During the Revolution, ocean trade came to a stop. Embargoes enacted by the General Assembly prevented our ships from leaving Connecticut waters, with certain exceptions: to deliver supplies to the patriot army, and to procure salt. Among shipowners who were given permission by the General Assembly to go for salt was John Welles, Jr., who in June, 1777, was allowed "to transport by water to the port of Dartmouth, in Mass., 30 barrels of pork, 7 of beef, 6 of flour, and 100 pounds of flax to procure salt for our inhabitants."

The Welles shipyard kept busy during the years of the Revolution. It turned out three sturdy oak vessels specifically for privateers to sail the seas in pursuit of British ships for prizes — a wartime practice allowed by the Continental Congress. They were the *Delight,* a schooner built in 1778 with four guns, carrying a crew of 40; the *Hero,* a sloop built in 1778, mounted with two guns and manned by a crew of 16; and the ship *Hunter,* commissioned in 1781, with a battery of 18 guns and a crew of 100 men. Several Glastonbury men invested in these privateers, but evidently the investment turned out to be poor. Gains were few, losses were high, according to the local historian, Herbert T. Clark. Two of the Welles vessels brought in prizes. The *Delight* captured a British sloop and a schooner and sent them in to Fairfield for "libel." The Welles company was per-

Unloading coal at Phelps coal dock,
Naubuc, about 1900.

mitted to keep the cargoes and probably the vessels as well, turning over the seamen on them for imprisonment. The *Hunter,* largest of the three privateers, captured the British brig *Resolution* after a lively engagement, and brought the ship, which carried a large cargo of turpentine and rice, into New London as a prize.

When John Welles, Jr., sent the firm into bankruptcy about 1784, apparently due to the failure of his Revolutionary privateering as well as the embargo against shipping, he lost his home, now known as the Welles-Shipman-Ward House, to two creditors, Stephen Shipman, Jr. and Nathaniel Talcott, Jr. His brothers, George and Ashbel, left Glastonbury for Baltimore to find new fields of enterprise. But George returned home, resumed the shipping business, and sent down to Baltimore for Ashbel to sell cargoes of farm produce and lumber. Soon the brothers went into the business of horse-trading, sending down to Maryland finely-bred Connecticut horses.

Roswell Hollister owned and operated a shipyard at Log Landing from 1795 to about 1820 (his most active period as a shipbuilder), turning out some "100 sail of vessels," wrote a Hollister descendant, I. N. Hollister, to a relative, Mrs. Florence Hollister Curtis. The Hollister shipyard built ships for Hartford businessmen as well as certain Glastonbury investors, including Howell Woodbridge, Pardon Brown and Elias Kellogg. Like the Welles ships, Hollister's vessels carried on West Indies trade, carrying down chiefly agricultural products and bringing back sugar, molasses and rum. It is said that he had three captains (one was Sampson Horton, whose descendants still live in Nayaug) who took out ships and sailed them until they were sold. In 1830 Roswell Hollister built a brig, the *Nestor,* for his son, Elijah. The young captain sailed south but was never heard from, until, months later, wreckage off the Carolinas was identified as coming from the *Nestor.* Hollister's son-in-law, Jedediah Post, brought home from the wreck a copper spike which is now in the Historical Society's Museum.

Ship launchings were festive occasions, drawing thousands of cheering spectators from surrounding towns as well as local folk, and often were followed by dances in the ballrooms of the town's taverns. There is mention in Alonzo Chapin's history of Glastonbury of one such launching on October 30, 1794, which drew a crowd of 3000 persons, about 700 more than the town's total population at that time. The ship was probably the *Confederacy,* one of the largest ever launched from Glastonbury, of 459 tons "burden."

At the Naubuc shipyard the brothers Samuel and Joseph Welles were partners in a lively shipbuilding and West Indies trade at about the same period as the Hollister shipyard. Some of the details of this business are available from the account books which Samuel methodically kept. On May 31, 1786, he recorded that he and Benjamin House had chartered half the sloop *Betsy* to George and Ashbel Welles for the transport of livestock. The sloop "now lying in the harbor of New London is bound for Tobago or some other island in the West Indies," he wrote. On June 26 he reported carrying cash down to New London, apparently to finance this same trip, and listed the cargo as follows, carefully giving identification to each of the horses: "1 E. Talcott horse, 1 Miller mare, 1 Wickham mare, 1 small bay stallion, 1 large Goshen stallion, 1 light sorrel stallion, 1 old blind mare." This particular cargo also included 7 oxen, 13,750 feet of white pine board and 105 feet of red oak hoops and staves.

Samuel Welles' account book for 1802-3 records the sale of the ship *John Morgan* to Isaac Thibbe of New York for $13,500 in May 1802. Among the many vessels built at the Naubuc shipyard was probably the *Exact,* a schooner referred to in the State of Washington as "Seattle's Mayflower" because it transported the first settlers to that area. It is known that the *Exact* was built at Glastonbury in 1830 and sold in 1841 to George Folger, Levi Starbuck and Henry Coffin of Nantucket.

The father of Glastonbury's famous son Gideon Welles (Secretary of the Navy under Lincoln), Samuel Welles was a man for all seasons. He was, possibly, typical of many able, versatile men of the 19th century who could and did turn their hands successfully to a variety of endeavors. Not only a shipbuilder, Samuel was also, like most Glastonbury men, a farmer, operated a small factory (the Eagle Woolen Mill in Addison), and in effect was a banker, lending money and profiting from interest. His account books show that he also collected board money from the sailors who ate at his home. He and his brother Joseph, who ran the Welles Tavern, were cousins of the South Glastonbury Welleses, and, like them, descendants of an early colonial governor, Thomas Welles.

The shipping industry enlivened the village of South Glastonbury, filling the air with the rhythm of hand saws and the thump of caulking mallets. Vying with the thunder of Roaring Brook, the ring of anvils and the boom of the trip hammer resounded down the hemlock-fringed gorge of Cotton Hollow from the South Glastonbury Anchor Works.

Iron ore had been discovered in the swamps of northwestern Connecticut in the 18th century. Soon forges began to appear along the banks of Connecticut streams. The earliest water-powered forge in Glastonbury was Talcott Camp and Company, which in 1780 was hammering out iron shovels and other farm implements at a place on Roaring Brook known as Cranberry Bog, upstream from the gunpowder factory in Cotton Hollow. Farther up the brook was another forge operated by Robert Hunt who had come here, it is thought, from iron ore country at South Canaan, where his family had an anchor works. In 1841 Jedediah Post, son-in-law of Roswell Hollister, acquired the anchor works from Hunt. Twenty years later he engaged George Pratt, of Hanover, Mass., to operate the foundry, and under his direction the South Glastonbury Anchor Works, familiarly called Pratt's Forge, became one of the town's best known industries. It turned out mammoth anchors, "3900 pounders," for oceangoing vessels out of New York, as well as smaller anchors for the many vessels launched from Connecticut River shipyards. The forge closed down in 1891. The sylvan site once occupied by the old anchor works is today part of a 51-acre

*Pratt's Forge, 1880. The site is now part of
Cotton Hollow Nature Preserve.*

preserve given to the town by public-spirited citizens in 1964. Hardly anyone in town now, except the old-timers, would recognize the name "Forge Hill" as belonging to the uphill section of Hopewell Road which borders the Cotton Hollow Nature Preserve.

Farther upstream on Roaring Brook, in Hopewell, was another early forge. The dense black clouds of smoke from the hardwood charcoal that fired this forge gave the area its name: "Smut." This lovely spot and its pond with the unlovely name was given to the town by the J. T. Slocumb Company as an open space preservation area in 1967.

On the bank of the Connecticut River, a forge operated by Thomas and Joseph Stevens was put out of business when neighbors complained that such a noisy occupation did not belong "in the center of a village." The forge stood not far from the Main Street home of Zephaniah Smith, father of the famous Smith Sisters. Zephaniah brought suit in 1814 against the Stevenses for damages caused by "the amount of water used to run the bellows and hammer (which) injured his land by holding back the water thereon." Mr. Smith did not use the term "environmental impact" in his complaint, but he made his point just the same, and the forge was closed down.

But another industry with severe "environmental impact" throve for many years in Glastonbury. Back in the hills above "Smut" were charcoal pits where soot-blackened "burners" kept watch day and night over the

Fifty-foot Cotton Hollow dam supplied water power for mills as early as 1814.

fires that produced charcoal, a fuel much in demand for industries and particularly iron forges, for the coal gave an intense heat. One of these pits was located on Matson Hill. There was another on Mott Hill and others on the wooded hillsides leading to Marlborough. Still others were located to the northwest, on Minnechaug Mountain. The production of charcoal was at one time one of Glastonbury's principal industries; in 1845 it was listed as the sixth largest item of produce here, being surpassed only by the production of hay, leather, Indian corn, potatoes and rye, in that order. Great quantities of hardwood were used in making charcoal, particularly birch and chestnut. But it is now some 60 years since the pervading, pungent smell of the burning wood and the thin, wavering columns of smoke reminded residents of the "money crop" being readied for harvesting in the hills. No longer do the high black charcoal carts lumber northwards to Colt's Patent Firearms Company as they once did. Around 1910 the industry began to peter out. There were various reasons for this, one being imports of charcoal from Canada. The devastating chestnut blight, a fungus disease brought into America from Asia around 1904, which gradually killed off all of the many chestnut trees in Glastonbury (as well as almost everywhere else in the country) may have been responsible, too, for the decline of the charcoal industry. Glastonbury had been noted for its chestnut trees, many of which were five or six feet in diameter.

Roaring Brook in about 1814 attracted one of the largest cotton mills in Hartford County — the Hartford Manufacturing Company. It was a picturesque mill in a picturesque site still known as Cotton Hollow. Built of native stone, the factory was six stories high, contoured to the various levels of the ledgy hillside. John Warner Barber, the traveling artist, in 1836 caught the beauty of the soaring stone building, tall-windowed and lofty as a castle in its leafy bower. Even today, artists wander down the Cotton Hollow Road to sketch the granite ruins of this monument to the bygone industrial busy-ness which once enlivened the banks of lovely Roaring Brook.

The Hartford Manufacturing Company stood near the site of the old Stocking gunpowder mill which had exploded during the Revolution. The company management had been drawn to the area because of a great stone dam, 50 feet high, its location still discernable. This dam had been built by Pardon Brown, whose father-in-law, Col. Howell Woodbridge, owned land there. Pardon Brown, in the belief that Cotton Hollow had a great manufacturing future, built a brick mill on the brookside, where he made cotton sheeting. The tremendous force of the impounded water turned a wheel, supplying power for Brown's mill with ample power to spare for the larger mill erected just above by the Hartford Manufacturing Company. Cotton Mill workers lived in a little community on both sides of Roaring Brook, occupying company-owned houses. They even had their own school and store. The great stone dam created behind it a long and very deep pond, nestled in the gorge of the brook. How the mothers must have worried, knowing that their small fry were frolicking in these entrancing waters of a summer's day or trying out their up-curled skates in the frosty winter!

Farther up Roaring Brook near the intersection of Hopewell Road and Matson Hill Road a 20-acre site was bought by Amos and Sprowell Dean, of Great Barrington, Mass., in 1838 for a small mill for the manufacture of wool and cotton into twine, yarn and cloth, the chief product being "all-wool satinets." Martin and Horatio Hollister, of the same family which had maintained a little clothing and carding shop for many years on Roaring Brook in Nayaug, had their eye on Dean's mill, and when the opportunity came in 1848 organized the Naog Manufacturing Company and bought out the Deans. The Hollisters continued the output of wool satinets until 1860, when Franklin Glazier joined Martin Hollister in operating the mill. During the Civil War the mill produced cloth for soldiers' uniforms. The Hopewell mill turned out woolen cloth for nearly a century, the Glazier Manufacturing Company being the final owners. By the turn of the century it was producing woolen goods for ladies' garments, "flannels, meltons, broadcloths, auto kerseys, pedestrian cloths, golf and bicycle goods and serges." It did a large business, too, in "smoking jacket, raglan and rainy-day cloths." From 1865 to 1895 the mill was continually being expanded, including the addition of a five-story building, a Morse elevator, a fire tank tower and finally a reading, music and game room for employees. But the depression of the 1930s and the competition of cheap labor in the South combined to put the old woolen mill out of business permanently. After a succession of subsequent enterprises, the J. T. Slocumb Company took the mill over in the second half of the 20th century, producing small tools for the aircraft industry.

Above the Hopewell woolen mill, the Hartford Manufacturing Company bought the site of the old forge at Smut and constructed two mills about mid-century which later were taken over by the Plunkett and Wyllys Company of Manchester for the manufacture of twine and cotton. Various companies (the best known called the Wassuc Manufacturing Company) continued this operation through most of the 19th century.

The Wassuc area farther east near the old New London Turnpike was the site of an early glass works. In 1816 the Glastenbury Glass Factory Company organized by a few enterprising townsmen began the manufacture of free-blown glass bottles. Olive-green and olive-amber, the graceful bottles, swirled and ribbed, were much like those produced in the Pitkin and Mather glass factories in neighboring Orford Parish (later named Manchester). In 1962 the imminent relocation of Route 2 prompted a group of amateur archaeologists led by Dr. Kenneth M. Wilson, then of Sturbridge Village but presently director of the Corning Glass Museum, to unearth the remains of the glass works on the property of Mrs. Josie Lavalette. Many shards and pieces of this interesting old glass were found, as well as remnants of the old melting pots. The glass factory was short-lived. Unfortunately, it had started operations at a bad time, shortly after the War of 1812, when a business depression gripped American industry.

Glazier Manufacturing Company, Hopewell, 1900,
site of woolen mills since 1836.
J. T. Slocomb Company now occupies this site.

This circumstance, and the difficulty of obtaining skilled glassworkers, made the going tough, and after about 20 years the factory closed down.

Farther east on Ash Swamp Brook, a tributary of Roaring Brook, Elisha Treat was given permission by the town in 1769 to build a "lineet" mill. This mill, known to residents of the area as "the oil mill" (it was probably linseed oil) was in operation for a long time, possibly even supplying oil to the J. B. Williams Company for making soap in its early days and to the David Hubbard tannery, predecessor of Roser's Tannery. Those who brave the hazards of thorny underbrush and rattlesnakes may still observe the remnants of a stone dam four feet high and some 35 feet long, and a line of stones which may have been part of the oil mill's foundation.

A more widely-known local industry was Goslee's Hoe and Farm Implement factory on Old Hebron Road, which might have been in operation as early as 1836. In the latter part of the century Ozias Goslee acquired many U.S. patents for his farm implement inventions, including what he called "tobacco hoes." The Goslee horse-drawn cultivator was said to be the first of its kind. Among the best known of the tools made by the Goslee shop was a three-pronged "marker" which made holes for seeds. In its latter years the mill was run by steam.

Not far from this factory was one of the largest blacksmith's shops for many miles around. It was a three-forge shop, unusual for a town of

Glastonbury's population but possibly evidence that the Hebron road was quite heavily traveled.

Farther north, near the junction of Weir Street and Ash Swamp Road, was one of Glastonbury's earliest carding and spinning mills, that run by Elijah Covell. The Covell family were the builders of the large, native "dressed" stone house at that intersection. According to Alvah Russell of the Historical Society of Glastonbury, an authority on old houses and the materials and manner of their construction, the Covell house was the only one in Glastonbury to be "finished" with doors and window frames of black walnut.

Eastbury Pond (now a pool) was at one time a reservoir supplying water power for the Roaring Brook Manufacturing Company, producing cotton and wool satinets. This firm built a substantial stone mill at that location about 1840. Edwin Crosby and Sereno Hubbard were running the factory in 1862, and some time soon after the Civil War it became the Crosby Manufacturing Company. In its manufacture of wool the factory needed some shoddy (reprocessed wool) which it used together with virgin wool. It bought some but needed more, so it established a mill for the purpose of producing shoddy, farther north on Roaring Brook. Over a period of 65 years men from the Crosby factory would go to the shoddy mill to grind woolen waste of different colors into a dark blue product from which a woolen yarn was spun. In 1906 Angus Park acquired the Crosby Manufacturing Company and, since the new operation did not use shoddy, work at the shoddy mill ceased. Presently the mill was made into a tenement, its nearby pond being used by neighborhood boys as a swimming hole. A Manchester company harvested ice there until the advent of electric refrigeration. The shoddy mill area is now a town nature preserve.

Although when Angus Park bought the Crosby mill it was run by steam, a waterwheel remained in the finishing room. For years the water which originally turned the wheel, flowing from a flume leading from nearby Eastbury Pond, kept East Glastonbury's one hydrant operative. House fires might have devastated that rural center if it had not been for the Angus Park hydrant, its fire hose and its firemen who were the mill workers. But it was a fire which finally spelled doom to the factory. The Angus Park company was sold at auction in 1939. In December 1941 a spectacular fire — said to be the worst in Glastonbury since 1888, bringing out fire companies even from Hartford — burned down the main part of the mill. The Peerless Woodworking Company now occupies one part that did not burn. Quality Name Plate, Inc., in the 1950s bought the dye house, garage, machine shop, weave shed and storehouse.

Salmon Brook had its share of industries from the 17th to the 20th centuries. Along the upper reaches of the stream, there were several active operations, including a still, a felt hat factory begun by Stephen Hurlburt who invented and patented the machinery he used, and Jared Strickland's casting works, which turned out plows and household implements includ-

Fire destroys much of Angus Park woolen mill, December 1941.

ing a hand coffee mill. Near Keeney Street (then North Street), there was a cooperage producing barrel staves.

Soon after the Revolution, Fraray Hale and partners had a clothing and fulling mill in the area known as Addison. Fraray Hale, Samuel Welles and others organized the Eagle Manufacturing Company in 1822 and built another mill for the production of woolen goods. It failed in 1848 and in 1855 the plant was bought by the Glastenbury Knitting Company. This firm made good warm underwear, including men's camel hair drawers, boasting in ads that they did not shrink! The Addison section was named for a president of this company, Addison L. Clark, and a post office established there, since discontinued.

Many 19th century industries grew up on sites that at first had been saw or grist mills. So it was with the woodenware shop of Oswin Welles on Salmon Brook in Naubuc, site of the earlier Welles saw mill. From about 1801 to 1820 he turned out all kinds of wooden kitchenware; then he converted his business to a cigar manufactory, using tobacco grown in the Welles fields. Tobacco growing and cigar making became a prosperous enterprise for Oswin Welles. He set up tobacco packaging plants in other

Elijah Covell House, 1835.
One of several 19th-century East
Glastonbury native stone houses.
(Photo by Duffy.)

towns and had a store in Hartford. But in 1846 the site of the cigar works plus 18 acres was acquired by Frederick Curtis, who established the Curtisville Manufacturing Company for the production of German silver and fine silver-plated ware.

The Curtisville factory is believed to have made the first German silver in the country, German silver being a silver-white alloy of copper, zinc and nickel. Table holloware of German silver became extremely popular in the 19th century. Examples of some of the Curtisville products, including some elegant plated-silver pieces, are on display at the Historical Society museum. A little community known as Curtisville sprang up in the Naubuc Avenue vicinity of the factory. It continued to be known by that name for many years, and even had its own post office and general store. Many of the houses were factory workers' homes.

During the Civil War the Curtisville Company sold out to the Connecticut Arms and Manufacturing Company, and Curtisville's name was changed to Naubuc. The new firm, mainly a war industry, produced rifles and pistols for the Grand Army of the Republic. Shortly after the war, a mortgage was foreclosed, the plant was re-organized again, this time as the American Sterling Company, and went back to making silverware. In 1880 James B. and William Williams bought the factory. As the Williams Brothers Manufacturing Company, this firm produced many types of silver plated and German silver flatware, particularly knives, which had a wide market in American cities.

One of Glastonbury's most successful industries begun in pre-Civil War days was the J. B. Williams Company, soap manufacturers. It started in a small way but grew to such proportions that it really put Glastonbury on the world map. James B. Williams in 1840 had a drug business in Manchester, but on the side he experimented with chemical formulas for shaving soap. When he produced a formula which satisfied him he moved his business to Glastonbury, taking over Hubbard's grist mill on the present Williams Street. Two years later he was joined by his brother, William Stuart Williams, and together they built up what is believed to be the first shaving soap manufactory in the world. Though shaving soap was their first product, ink and shoe-blacking were also made in the early days. (Further details of the progress of the J. B. Williams Company will be discussed in a later chapter, along with accounts of other industries which flourished in post-Civil War days.)

An early local enterprise which grew and prospered, bringing world-wide recognition to a Glastonbury factory, was leather tanning. The first tanner of Glastonbury pigskin of whom there is a record was David Hubbard. His tanning mill, located on Hubbard Brook near the old J. B. Williams Company, was probably not erected until after 1783, when the town first allowed its people to operate mills without permission. This practice of forbidding milling operations without town approval was in effect a precursor of zoning regulations. Even after permission was no longer required, it was evidently still necessary for the operators to agree not to infringe on the rights of their neighbors. But one thing all of the waterpowered industries overlooked from the beginning was the fact that they were polluting the streams. Not until well into the 20th century, when their attention was pointedly called to this problem by the State Water Commission, was any notice taken of the seriousness of the matter.

David Hubbard went out of the tanning business in the early 19th century, but his brother Edward, in company with Isaac Broadhead, established a tannery on the old New London Turnpike in 1854. After Edward died, Isaac Broadhead continued the business of tanning pigskin leather for a decade or so. (The tannery's subsequent purchase by Herman Roser will be discussed in a later chapter.)

By the start of the Civil War, Glastonbury had become a partly industrial town, in contrast to its original solely agricultural status. Through the mid-decades of the 1800s it grew, and construction of all sorts to provide for the influx of population got under way.

Chapter VI

Spirit and Mind:
The Growth of Churches and Schools

Early in the century, population growth began to be noticeable in South Glastonbury, where the cotton mill on Roaring Brook was drawing workers, and soon the town needed new churches and schools. The mill had started operations about 1814. South Glastonbury residents at that time were still driving their wagons nearly three miles to church; years went by before a church was built within their own area. It was the Methodists who first acted on the need for a South Glastonbury parish.

Though other Protestant sects were being organized in other Connecticut towns, Glastonbury as late as 1790 still had Congregational churches only, the First Society and Eastbury. The first new sect to be established in Glastonbury was the Methodist. In 1793 a Methodist preaching circuit was organized in New London and Methodist preachers on horseback traveled as far north as Eastbury, preaching to the people there in houses, barns and open fields.

Eastbury Methodists organized a parish in 1796, though not until 1810 was a church building erected there, in Wassuc near the little red schoolhouse, now a dwelling. Figuring prominently in the history of the Eastbury Methodists was their first preacher, the Rev. Jeremiah Stocking. Jeremiah because of poor health had been advised by his doctor to take a job as post rider. In 1799 he began carrying the Connecticut Courant to Saybrook (and later the mail as well). It must have been the right prescription, for Father Stocking kept it up for 25 years, preaching as well and building up his congregation. A new church on Manchester Road, built 1847, burned in 1885, but was rebuilt in 1886.

The Methodists organized a South Glastonbury parish in 1828 and built a handsome red brick church on High Street — now the South Glastonbury Library. In 1962-63 the Asbury Methodist Church was built on Buttonball Lane.

At about the same time the Methodists were getting established, some Glastonbury families (most of them from the south end) began holding private services in the Episcopal faith. Episcopalians had not had an easy time during the Revolution, as they were suspected of being Loyalists. The Glastonbury group took longer to set up their parishes than those in some other Connecticut towns. But in 1806, 51 families formed an Episcopal Society and began holding services in a schoolhouse which stood on the east side of Main Street across from the Old Church Cemetery (near the present American Legion Hall). The Old Church Cemetery got its name from the church the Episcopal Society began constructing near it in 1813. The church was called simply the "Episcopal Church" until 1821, when members voted to call it "St. Luke's." It took a long time for the church to be built. Subscriptions toward doing the interior were still being taken in 1821, and it was not consecrated until 1831. Within a few years the parish decided to build a new church farther south, where population and church membership were continuing to grow.

Meanwhile the First Society (Congregational) was considering dividing into two parishes. In 1836, 14 members of the First Society formed an "Ecclesiastical Society by the name of the Congregational Society in South Glastonbury." The next fall 39 members left the First Church to join the new one. A large white clapboarded church was built on High Street near the corner of Main. In 1965 the church building was lifted up and turned around to face Main Street, with a large addition for parish rooms built on to the rear, facing High Street.

Hammers and saws pounded and buzzed for months on end as the new Congregational Church and neighboring St. Luke's Church on Main Street just below High, went up at almost the same time, 1837-38. St. Luke's was a substantial brick structure with a neo-classical facade, in outward design more like the Congregational churches of the period than the gothic-style Episcopal.

During that same year a new church for the First Society was being built farther north on Main Street at the site of the present First Church. The Society had decided that its old meeting house, built in 1735 after the earliest meeting house on the Green had burned down, was no longer adequate for the thriving parish. The 102-year-old structure was sold for $106 to John Moseley and Normand Hubbard and taken down. The new church, with tower, bell and clock, was dedicated in December 1837. It burned to the ground in 1866 (the ashes were sold for $7 to John Moseley), but the next year a new, larger one was built to take its place. Yet again the First Church suffered disaster when in 1938 it was demolished by the hurricane. Once more a new church went up on the old site.

The Congregational Society of Eastbury, which had split off from the First Society in 1731, by the early 1800s began to chafe at the inconvenience of having its meeting house so far from the center of the parish. It did not seem likely that the congregation could raise the necessary building funds themselves, so in 1806 the Society petitioned the General Assembly for a lottery to raise $2000. The petition was granted in May of that year for a lottery in conjunction with the Milford Episcopal Society, which also had sought a lottery for the same purpose and for a similar amount. As required, Eastbury parish chose two prominent Glastonbury businessmen, Samuel Welles and Pardon Brown (both from the First Society) as managers. According to the scanty remaining records of this enterprise, the managers tried hard to make a go of it, but the times, as they said, were "dull," and tickets sold on credit were never paid for. Eastbury had to wait until 1819 for its new church. Wherever the needed funds came from, it was not from a lottery.

The Society sold its church on Manchester Road and built a new one at the corner of Hebron Avenue and Weir Street. Records say that it had paper curtains (ahead of its time by about 150 years) until equipped with blinds in 1850. But by the mid 1860s Eastbury, seat of a thriving textile mill, needed a larger church. In 1866 construction began on a church building next door to the old one. The builder was Albert Barrows, who at that very time was also building the new First Church on Main Street. The parish of Eastbury changed its name to the "East Glastonbury Congregational Society" in 1862, but in 1873 it was changed once more to "Buckingham." The little village had petitioned the federal government in 1867 to name its post office "Buckingham" to honor the then Governor of Connecticut, William A. Buckingham, who held office during the Civil War. The Buckingham Congregational Church, like the First Church, was demolished by the 1938 hurricane. By that time, the parish was smaller than it had been in 1866, and the new church which went up on that same site was not as large as its predecessor.

St. Luke's Episcopal parish in South Glastonbury got nearly a half-century's head start on the organization of an Episcopal church in the north end. St. James parish was organized about 1857, though for some time prior to that services were being held in homes or halls. The cornerstone of St. James Church was laid in 1859. Inlaid in the tower was a piece of the foundation stone of one of Connecticut's earliest Episcopal parishes, St. Peter's in Hebron, built in 1735. The tower was the only part of this first St. James Church to survive a fire which destroyed the building on Sunday, February 14, 1904. A new one was built immediately of brownstone from the Portland quarries, on much the same lines as the first, somewhat reminiscent of many of the old parish churches of England.

The spiritual needs of the people were uppermost in their whole life outlook, but schooling, perhaps prompted by colony law, ran a close second. By the end of the Revolution, Glastonbury had six schools in the First Society and four in Eastbury. These had been established one by one throughout the 18th century.

In 1731 the schools had come under the supervision of the ecclesiastical societies. But they were financed partly by an appropriation from the State, with the remaining costs paid half by a local property tax and half by an assessment for each child between the ages of 6 and 12, whether they attended school or not. This assessment was often paid in wood for the schoolhouse stoves; as the town records quaintly put it, "Wood levied on children's heads."

When the school system passed from church supervision to the town by state law in 1795, there were seven public schools in the First Society. These schools were: "That by Mr. Alger's (Hopewell); by Mr. Taylor's ("South Part"); Mr. Woodbridge's ("South Village"); by Mr. Gideon Hale's ("Centre"); by Mr. Griswold's (Green); by Mr. Welles ("North Glastenbury"); by Mr. Smith's ("Pratt's Ferry"). A Nayaug district came into being in 1808. Interestingly, the location called "Centre" was about where the Glastonbury Expressway presently ends, Mr. Gideon Hale's being the large 18th Century colonial house at 1401 Main Street. The "North Glastenbury" site was at what we call the Center today. Records list the locations of the four Eastbury schools at that time as "South School," "Middle South," "North School" and "East School."

With the separation of Church and State, legally accomplished by the Constitution of 1818, the school-governing units of the ecclesiastical societies became "school societies," which had charge of the town cemeteries as well. The first local tax levy for town support of schools, to supplant the earlier method which included partial payment on "children's heads," was made in 1800. But the State did not make the school tax mandatory until 1854. Two years later by legislative act the school societies were divided into 17 districts (an 18th was shortly added). The districts were autonomous, each one having corporate power to own and maintain the school buildings and to hire and fire teachers. These districts managed Glastonbury schools until 1909.

The early schools were in session a minimum of four months a year by state law. The children were needed at home the rest of the time for farm work and help with the constant spinning, weaving, soap and candle-making and other tasks vital to survival. It was 1865 before the State lengthened the mandatory time for keeping school to six months of the year. Official "school visitors" dropped in to observe how things were going twice each term. Their reports were often critical, not only of the condition of the school buildings but of the teachers, who were generally young and untrained. There was a frequent teacher turnover; often the teachers would stay for only one term.

Readin', writin', and 'rithmetic were about all that was taught at first. As the 19th century got under way, "declamation and dialogues" and probably a little geography were added to the curriculum. In 1820, however, a curious ruling was made by one of the school societies, cutting out of the curriculum grammar and geography, but leaving in literature, religion, morals and manners, spelling, reading and writing. The Rev. Alonzo B. Chapin, in his history written in 1853, says that "the object of this measure was to raise the standards of education by compelling children to attend the High School or Academy."

In mentioning the "High School or Academy" (there was no public high school) Dr. Chapin must have been referring to the Academy on the Green, built about 1798, which was considered one of the best schools in the Hartford area and attracted students from surrounding towns. And

Neipsic School, about 1900; now East Glastonbury Public Library. Miss Eva Crosby is teacher.

he may have referred as well to the Glastenbury Seminary, a private school underwritten by a few public-spirited men in 1792 and built sometime between then and 1796 on Main Street, South Glastonbury, between the Welles-Shipman-Ward House and the former Pratt homestead on the corner of Main and Hopewell Road. Land for this school was donated by Stephen Shipman, Jr., who probably took boarders for the school in his home next door.

The Glastenbury Seminary flourished until about the year 1845, when it was destroyed by fire and not rebuilt. It began as a "grammar" school similar to other old New England grammar schools, featuring Latin and Greek, English literature, natural philosophy and algebra. By 1840, the curriculum also included chemistry, astronomy, trigonometry, surveying, and navigation, the latter subject being of practical local interest. Teaching there in the early 1830s was Elihu Burritt, the famous "learned blacksmith" of New Britain, who, it was said, knew 50 languages (including dialects), but whose powerful blacksmith's arms helped in keeping discipline, according to the reminiscences of one of his pupils, Henry T. Welles.

The school produced Glastonbury's first newspaper, a 4-page student publication called "The Tyro's Casket." It included verse, editorials (not political, by policy), and humor, poking fun at such things as women's fashions and tea-drinking. The first issue mentioned the beautiful view from the knoll (next the Welles-Shipman-Ward House) down over the meadows to the hills across the river! Many such beautiful views from the cleared Glastonbury hills across the pastures of the 19th century have been hidden behind trees for a century.

The Tyro's Casket mentions that Noah Webster, the famed author of Webster's Dictionary and the Blue-Backed Speller, was once a teacher at the Glastenbury Seminary. A search for further evidence that Noah Webster taught at this school has not been fruitful. He did indeed once teach in Glastonbury — in fact his first job after graduating from Yale in 1778 was teaching school in this town for the winter term of 1778-79, so he says in his diary. He was no stranger to Glastonbury, for he had been a Yale student here during the Revolution. But the Seminary was not built until 1792, and by that time Noah was practicing law in Hartford and was a member of Hartford's Common Council. Perhaps the editor of Tyro's Casket got his information by vague hearsay.

South Glastonbury was the seat of another private school which came into being in 1862. This was Academy Hall, founded as the South Glastenbury Academy School by a group of south-end citizens who met to draft a constitution and put up stock in October 1860. The stockholders bought the old abandoned Episcopal Church near the cemetery for $200 and moved it down Main Street to a new location on the southwest corner of the present Stockade Road. Classes beyond the grade school level began in 1862 and continued until 1884. It was a spacious two-story building and served as a social center for south end community affairs for many years before and after the school ended its days. Two major events took place at Academy Hall: The organization of the Connecticut State Grange on June 24, 1885, and the 100th anniversary celebration of Columbia Lodge No. 25, A.F. & A.M., on May 18, 1893.

Academy Hall in South Glastonbury served as Glastonbury's only high school until 1869, when several Glastonbury citizens, among them

Originally St. Luke's Church, this building was moved in 1861 from site near Old Church Cemetery, to location near present corner of Main Street and Stockade Road, where, as Academy Hall, it stood for more than 70 years.

the Williams family, organized a stock company for the purpose of building and maintaining a high school. The Glastonbury Academy, as it was called, was built on the site of the present Academy School. It opened in 1870 with a student body of "gentlemen, 43; ladies, 50." In no sense a public high school, as we understand the term today (tuition was charged), it ran into financial problems after 20 years, and townspeople were appealed to for support. The response was "adequate" and in 1890 the school was re-organized as the Glastonbury Free Academy, a Resolution of Incorporation being voted by the State Legislature in 1893. The resolution set up an unusual self-perpetuating board to govern the Free Academy. It consisted of 11 corporators, who were to name their own successors, together with the pastors of the then-existing churches. The Board of Incorporators continues to this very day, made up of sons or other descendants of the original incorporators where possible (otherwise descendants of old Glastonbury families) and the pastors of churches extant in 1893.

Among the teachers at Glastonbury Free Academy at one time (1890-94) was one of Glastonbury's best-known native daughters, Miss Mary Kingsbury, who went on to become the first public school librarian in the country — at Erasmus Hall Academy, Brooklyn, a New York City public high school.

Entrance examinations were required for admission to this first town-run high school. Of the 51 who applied for the "Introductory Year," 41 were admitted. The total enrollment of 110 included those who had been attending the Academy. The first class to graduate (June 1903) numbered 14. Miss Amy Killam, who had grown up in the ancient Hollister house on Tryon Street, was valedictorian, and Miss Mary K. (Minnie) Curran was salutatorian and class president. Miss Curran went on to teach school in Glastonbury for 43 years, most of them in the old Matson Hill School.

In 1902 Glastonbury voted to establish a high school. The Free Academy building was transferred to the town for this purpose, together with the income from the Academy's invested funds. At the same time the Free Academy Corporation voted to augment its membership by including elected representatives from the town (six at first, but at some point over the years this number was narrowed to three). Even though the town ceased to use the Free Academy building as a school, and demolished it in 1960, the Free Academy board has continued to disburse annual funds for one particular purpose: to buy books for the high and junior high schools, though not for the elementary schools, since it was the high school level which first was served by the old Free Academy.

In spite of the establishment of a local high school, a number of Glastonbury families sent their children, particularly their sons, to the new Hartford High School which had been built in 1882-83, supplanting one which had burned down, the Hopkins Grammar School founded in 1638. Hartford High School was then one of the most highly rated schools in the country, and for many years leading families in surrounding areas

Glastonbury Free Academy,
built 1870 on site of
present Academy School.

sent their children to it. To prepare Glastonbury children for entrance there, Miss Jennie Pratt maintained a private school in the red Wells house at the corner of High and Main Streets, South Glastonbury, from 1884 (the year Academy Hall, South Glastonbury, closed down) through 1893, when she began to teach at Hartford High.

Although public high schools had come into existence in America in the mid-1800s, only a fraction of the adolescent population was enrolled. Even by 1900, only 11 per cent of the country's teen-agers were taking advantage of this opportunity to extend their education beyond grade school. Glastonbury's enrollment record may have been better than most.

A tragic incident marred the opening of Glastonbury High School's first year. A fatal football accident so shocked the school's administration that the result was the banning of football as a GHS sport for the next 64 years. Charles Raze Gager, who had graduated in June from the Free Academy, while attending a football game between Glastonbury and East Hartford High Schools in East Hartford on September 27, 1902, was drafted as a substitute although he had never played the game before. During a scrimmage his neck was broken and he died two weeks later. Not until 1966 was football again allowed as a sport on the Glastonbury High curriculum.

Chapter VII

Simple Pleasures and Complex Issues:
The Coming of the Civil War

The diaries of Joseph Wright, farmer, Yale graduate, deacon of the First Church, and owner of Wright's Island, kept faithfully over a quarter-century, 1837-1863, reflect a Glastonbury which might have been pictured by Currier and Ives.

Deacon Wright lived in the red brick house still standing at the corner of Main Street and Meadow Lane. In the summer, he and his family moved down across the meadows to an ancient farmhouse which had been occupied by generations of Wrights on a wide promontory of land extending into the Connecticut River, known as Wright's Island. It had been a true island, once a habitat of Indians, in Glastonbury's earliest days, river channels flowing on both sides. But gradually the east side had filled in and the island eroded; the diaries tell sadly of its gradual disappearance.

Spring planting, fall harvesting, family gatherings at Thanksgiving, winter sleigh rides, floods, the passage of stately steamboats up and down the river — all are described in Deacon Wright's diaries. It was a pleasant, peaceful rural existence. Yet in the diaries there is an uneasy sense of something wrong, a problem that will not go away and must be faced: slavery, and all its implications for a free and pious people. The problem gnawed away, decade by decade, until at last it burst into the open, culminating in the Civil War.

Meanwhile, life in Glastonbury flowed familiarly on from generation to generation, as gently as the river bordering the meadows. There was plenty to do on the farms. And shad fishing, since early colonial days a principal springtime activity, continued to thrive. Joseph Wright and his partners often caught in their nets over a thousand of the silvery fish in one day, when the run was good.

Produce was loaded on vessels bound for New York (Wright sent potatoes, chiefly). Pork was butchered and salted down for winter dinner tables. In August boys and girls went whortleberrying (huckleberrying) on Minnechaug Mountain. North, south and east the anvils of blacksmith shops rang out with the forging of horseshoes. Living conditions had changed very little in the past century. The dirt roads were dusty in summer, snowbound in winter, and rutted much of the rest of the time. Water was hauled up in buckets from "dug" wells; there were outside "privies" only; houses were as cold in winter as ever; and lighting continued to be by candlelight or oil lamps.

Church bells called everyone to Sunday services, and many who went stood up, confessed their sins and announced that they had found their Lord. Deacon Wright mentions in diary after diary the names of townspeople who had become "saved" in this manner. It was a period of widespread religious revival, reflecting, perhaps, a reaction from the religious let-down after the Revolution 50 years earlier. Visiting preachers often occupied the pulpits of the Congregational churches. Deacon Wright had been instrumental in organizing the Glastonbury Sunday School Society in 1819. The Society embraced both Congregationalists and Episcopalians, holding Sunday School classes for four hours every Sunday in various schoolhouses. This early try for ecumenical unity was not successful. After two years the classes had to be discontinued due to conflicts in religious thinking. Deacon Wright then organized a Congregational Sunday School (still continuing) which held its first classes at the old Meeting House. Later in the century the Sunday School gave monthly concerts in a small building known as the Conference House, which stood south of the new First Church. Years later the Conference House was moved farther south and across the street to its present location as a dwelling just below the old Goodrich home, bordering Hubbard Brook near the Green.

There were signs that Deacon Wright and other leading citizens were interested in up-grading the level of cultivation in town. In 1837, Wright and a group of 22 friends organized a library. Meeting at the Deacon's home, the original subscribers included names of many old Glastonbury families: Hale, Plummer, Moseley, Hubbard, Talcott and others. Unfortunately the library lasted only three years. Glastonbury bookworms had to make do with the old custom of book-borrowing between neighbors for another 50 years or so before a successful attempt at organizing a public library was made.

Deacon Wright's library was not the first to be organized in town, however. Surely one of the earliest lending libraries in the state was that started by Dr. Asaph Coleman and 27 Glastonbury men in 1803. A small "Libra Constitution and Subscription," now owned by the Historical Society, outlines the library's policy and lists the following titles in its possession: "Seabrook platform; Church & state a political union; William Brown oration July 4th 1799; Asahel Morse oration July 5th 1802; Ecclesiastical oppressions; Strongbox dissenters; Cucumber oration; Hale storm history (2 copies); Observations of the Importance of the American Revolution by Richard Price; and 'Hudson and Goodin paper (Connecticut

Horse and buggy days, East Glastonbury.
Flora Clark and C. A. L. Morgan in 1889. (Print by Duffy from glass plate.)

Courant) for our information.'" Nothing more is known about this first Glastonbury library; it was probably short-lived, very likely because of a shortage of books!

Dr. Coleman, one of Glastonbury's most distinguished citizens of the Revolution and post-Revolution periods, had served as a surgeon in the war. At that time he became interested in combatting smallpox, always the dread disease of the colonists. He persuaded the town fathers to let him try inoculation, along with Dr. Elizur Hale. The town had a hard time making a decision to grant this permission, first voting "yes", then rescinding, but finally agreeing. Dr. Coleman then built a small hospital, evidently for this special purpose, on his land somewhere between Knob Hill and Apple Hill. He also built a "pest house" where the worst small-pox cases were kept. He must have had some success with inoculation, for the town never withdrew its permission. Coleman Road, which runs through his former property, was named for him. His medicinal herb garden is thought to have been off Coleman Road.

In the days when every household was self-sufficient to a large degree, growing its own food, spinning its own wool and flax for clothes, trading produce to pay the doctor and buy necessary household items, the problem of caring for the poor could not have been as great as it became in later years, when the economy of the town changed from agricultural to suburban. Yet from the time of the first settlement, there were those who were too ill, too mentally-disturbed or perhaps too shiftless to work, but could not be left to starve.

One of the earliest town regulations concerns a money-raising device for the support of the poor, the payment of fines by persons disorderly in town meetings: "At a town meeting in Glassenbury December the 22d

1703: Voted . . . that if any person or persons shall presume to Come into town meetings and there debate about their own private affairs, or fall into other Impertinent and disorderly discourse thereby disturbing the Carrying on of the Affairs of the towne that are in agitation: being Convicted thereof before the Selectmen then in being, he shall forfeit the Sume of one Shilling cash, one halfe to the Complainor that Shall prosecute to effect and the other halfe to the poor of the towne: Voted." Law and order were of primary importance in running the town, it is plain to see from this early precursor of Robert's Rules of Order.

For nearly two centuries, the indigent poor and suffering were under the paternalistic care of the selectmen. Poor people were boarded out under contract with the town for many years. The record of a town meeting on December 1789 seems to imply that bids were sought for these contracts: "Dec 1789 Voted the Selectmen appoint time & place & see who will keep the poor of this town the cheapest as they did the last year."

This practice continued throughout most of the 19th century. An inventory of clothing brought with one woman when she went to board with other paupers at the home of Daniel Andrus (Andrews) in South Glastonbury in 1830 shows that, poor as she was, she brought with her: "2 bonnets, 1 Vandike (shoulder cape), 2 woolen frocks — one new, the other old — 2 callico frocks, 4 petticoats, 2 new cotton shirts, 1 night gown, 1 cotton mantle, 2 caps, 2 shawls, 2 handkerchiefs, 2 new woolen aprons, 3 old aprons, 3 pair stockings, 1 pr. mittens, 1 work pocket, 1 pr. new shoes, 1 pr. cloth shoes, 1 pr. old shoes, 1 pr. mits." Apparently persons who boarded the poor also sometimes kept wrongdoers confined in their homes. A town contract with Daniel Andrus and Ashbel Alger shows that they agreed to build "suitable places or cells to receive such persons as may from time to time be sent there by proper Authority, for Correction or to be put to hard labour . . ."

As the century drew to a close, the town established an almshouse, the first one being the McLean farm on Chestnut Hill (since burned down). Later almshouses were the old Goodrich house on the northeast corner of Foote Road and Main and the former Stevenson house across the street on Still Hill. In about 1895 the town bought the present Town Farm, the Still Hill Boarding Home, at 634 Main Street.

One of the significant achievements of the mid-1800s was the building of a Town House where town meetings could be conducted. Town meetings, once a secular function of parishes, had been held in the various churches, mainly in the First Church. The Town Clerk's office was in his home, court was held in the local Justice's home, and town boards met at taverns, usually Welles (later Chapman's) Tavern in the Center or Bates Tavern on High Street, South Glastonbury.

In 1839 the town voted to build a Town House. As in the case of school construction, there was divided opinion on where to build it, the south end people holding out for their part of town. It very nearly was built at Buck's Corners, considered the geographical center of town. The vote was close, but the location on the Green at Hubbard Street was finally decided upon, and the handsome red brick structure was begun at once by Parley Bidwell, who had built the Methodist Church on High Street in 1828.

Voters came to the Town House to cast their votes, but the building contained no official space for town offices. It must be assumed that selectmen, town clerk, "listers," tax collectors and other town officials continued to enact the town's business from their homes (or in some cases from the public rooms of local taverns) until 1881, when a brick Town Records Building was constructed at the Center, its site now a parking space. The Town House occasionally served as a place for social gatherings. At one period popular country dances, with prompter, fiddler, and sometimes a whole band, were held there. By town vote in 1960, the old Town Hall was leased to the Historical Society of Glastonbury (which had been organized in 1936) for a term of 99 years.

Political parties in Glastonbury as elsewhere in the state were rudimentary until the broadening of the franchise accomplished by the adoption of a state constitution in 1818. The constitution revised suffrage requirements to admit as voters males, regardless of church affiliation, 21 years of age with six months residence, having a freehold estate worth seven dollars a year, or having given military services or paid taxes within the year. From the time of Glastonbury's founding in 1693 through the establishment of a federal government after the Revolution, political offices were pretty much held by members of the "ruling" families. Time after time Glastonbury sent to the General Assembly Hales, Goodriches, Welleses, Talcotts, Smiths, Hubbards and Kimberlys. Candidates were nominated in town meetings, it is true, but these meetings usually ratified the choices made by small groups of leaders in private conference.

The total number of Glastonbury votes for Governor as recorded with the Secretary of the State for the election of, for instance, 1820 was 192, only about six per cent of the total population of 3114 for that year. Assuming that the statistics on file are correct, in 1824 only 85 Glastonbury people voted for Governor, and in 1827 only 123. Of course the franchise was pretty limited, but it would seem that Glastonbury citizens at that period were not much involved in politics. Still, the federal government was young; the American political situation was in its infancy. In 1830 Gideon Welles and Alexander Hollister each received one vote for Lieutenant Governor — probably what we today would call a "write-in." By 1851 the total number of votes cast had jumped close to 400, and from 1837 on to the Civil War we have the personal notations of Deacon Joseph Wright to bring us a clearer picture of what went on in Glastonbury politically.

Wright was a Whig and as such recorded some anti-Democratic sentiment. In February 1838 he made note of a "great Whig State Convention at Hartford," to which the Glastonbury delegates were Pardon Brown and S. Hubbard. At the local "electors meeting" that April there were 511 voters at the polls, Wright recorded. "On the first ballot for Representa-

tives Ezra Dayton (Loco Foco) had 286 votes — G. Plummer (Whig) 191 —H. Turner (Conservative), 21 — and three scattering — majority for Dayton, 64." The next day Wright reported W. W. Ellsworth, the Whig candidate, elected Governor. "Three quarters of the members of the Legislature are Whigs," he wrote happily. "This will be the death of Loco Focoism in Conn."

In Glastonbury it would seem that the Democrats in general were known as Loco Focos, since according to the Wright journals elections appeared to be between the Locos and the Whigs. In 1840 Wright reported a "division in the loco focos on account of the Town House which was built this summer, the S. Glastenbury locos being adverse to building on the 'Green' though the town had voted two years ago to place it there . . ." He further reported the ousting of a long-term Town Clerk, Gideon Welles' brother Thaddeus, who must have been a Loco Foco. Said Wright: "At the town meeting today the S. G. Locos put up Henry Dayton for Town Clerk instead of Thad Welles, the Whigs uniting with them to put him in. This was a kind of triumph on the part of the locos, and a signal defeat of the Welles tyranny."

Although according to the Columbia Encyclopedia the Loco Focos "petered out after a few years," the name seems to have stuck to Glastonbury Democrats for a long time. One of Deacon Wright's last entries, that for electors meeting on April 7, 1862, reports that "We (meaning

Republicans) have one Rep. — the Locos one." A possible reason for the longevity of the Locos in Glastonbury and in fact the strength of the Democrats, which was equal to that of the Republicans, was that during this period the town had become more industrialized.

Another political group which became very active in the East in mid-century were the "Know-Nothings," a formidable group which followed in the wake of the Native American party of the 1840s. The Native Americans came into being through animosity aroused by Democratic bribing of Irish-Catholic immigrants. Glastonbury had its quota of "Know-Nothings." Wrote Joseph Wright on April 2, 1855: "Electors meeting. Elected J. B. Holmes and Aaron Kinne, a Whig and a Democratic Know-Nothing."

One of the first meetings to be held in the Town House was on the subject of "liquor licenses." Temperance was a heated issue of the day. The question of the granting of liquor licenses to tavern-keepers was optional in Connecticut towns. Great efforts were made to prevent the sale of liquor in Glastonbury over a great many years, but apparently in years when the town went dry it was hard to control the liquor traffic. There was a Glastonbury organization called the Friends of Temperance which held many meetings planning ways to get men to stop drinking, and listening to outside speakers, sometimes "reformed drunkards." Deacon Wright and his friends regularly made formal calls on local tavern-keepers to plead with them to obey the ordinance forbidding the sale of spirits. In South Glastonbury Deacon Oliver Hale and Reuben Shipman were successful in their efforts to get Josiah Strickland to give up his grog shop. After numerous pleas, Mr. Strickland finally acquiesced, perhaps persuaded as well by public sentiment. But he was not happy about it and once told Deacon Hale, "You have taken $300 out of my pocket."

Among the most active forces for social change, not only in the town but in the state, was a remarkable Glastonbury family noted for its intellectual brilliance. This was the family of Hannah and Zephaniah Hollister Smith. The Smiths would have been an outstanding family in any society in any era. Hannah, daughter of a Yale graduate, was a linguist, a mathematician, an astronomer and a poet. Zephaniah, himself a Yale graduate, had been a minister in Newtown (he was a Glastonbury native) but had become convinced that to accept money for preaching was to make merchandise of the gospel, a doctrine of the Sandemanian Sect. He got into a controversy over his beliefs with his pastorate, excommunicated the whole congregation and was in turn dismissed by them. Smith gave up the ministry, went to Eastbury and ran a country store while studying law. When he had become a full-fledged lawyer, he bought the old Eleazar Kimberly house, still standing at 1625 Main Street, north of Smith Brook.

The Smiths had five unusual daughters to whom they gave unusual names: Hancy Zephina, Cyrinthia Sacretia, Laurilla Aleroyla, Julia Evelina and Abby Hadassah. The daughters were as brilliant and as rugged individualists as their parents. They were inventive (Hancy's device for shoeing cattle was used by local blacksmiths); mechanical (Hancy built a boat she sailed on the river, and turned out a piano keyboard made of wood); poetic (they wrote verses and hymns); artistic (Laurilla's water-color sketchbook of her neighbors' homes is a treasured possession of the Historical Society); and politically active (they campaigned for woman's rights decades before woman suffrage became a nation-wide issue.)

Like their father, the Smith sisters, though deeply religious, were scornful of a paid clergy and seldom went to church. Instead on Sundays they read the Bible at home. As an intellectual exercise at one period they held weekly meetings with a friend, Emily Moseley, comparing the King James version with the original Hebrew and Greek in an effort to determine the literal meaning of the Biblical words.

Julia, who was the classics scholar of the family (she taught at the Emma Willard School at Troy at one time) became so interested in the Bible-comparison project that she set to work writing her own translations of the Bible. All in all, she made five translations: two from the Greek, two from Hebrew and one from the Latin. In 1876 at the age of 84 she published one of these translations. The Historical Society of Glastonbury has several of these unique Bibles, now collectors' items, said to be the only translation ever produced by a woman. The Society also owns Emily Moseley's Bible, which is liberally annotated with margin notes on changes in wording.

Julia's chief object, as expressed in her *Preface,* was to produce a com-pletely literal translation "giving no ideas of my own . . . while King James's translators have wholly differed from this rule." She appears to have been a very self-assured person for she goes on to explain: "It may be thought by the public in general, that I have great confidence in my-self, in not conferring with the learned in so great a work, but as there is but one book in the Hebrew Tongue, and I have defined it word for word, I do not see how anybody can know more about it than I do. It being a dead language no improvements can be made upon it."

The rules of Hebrew grammar are not, of course, the same as the rules of English, particularly in regard to the tenses of verbs. But Julia was not about to adapt what she took to be God's language to the rules of English. "If I did not follow the tenses as they are," she wrote in the preface to her translation, "I myself should be the judge, and man must not be trusted with regard to the Word of God." That her own translation was so obscure in places as to be hardly intelligible did not faze her. "There must be something hidden that we must search out, and not hold to the outward, for the 'letter kills but the Spirit gives life.' " The extent to which the spirit gave life may be judged from the following passage from the Twenty-Third Psalm — first the King James version, then Julia's rendering of the same passage:

King James: Thou preparest a table before me in the presence of mine enemies: thou anointest my head with oil; my cup runneth over.

Julia Smith: Thou wilt set in order a table before me in front of mine enemies: thou madest fat mine head with oil; my cup being satisfied with drink.

Emily Moseley, who had been a friend of the Smith sisters for many years and who had studied various versions of the Bible with them, was one of the most independent and outspoken women of her day, particularly on the subject of religion. It was shocking to the town when Miss Moseley, a member of one of the leading, most respected and oldest families in town, was excommunicated from the First Church Society in September 1844 for her non-conforming religious beliefs. One of her "sins," apparently, was knitting on Sunday.

Wrote Mrs. John Howard Hale (wife of the man who became known as the "peach king") to a friend in 1904: "I was acquainted with both Julia and Abby (Smith). The friend who studied with them was Mr. Hale's maiden aunt. A very close friend, one of the most unselfish women I ever knew, always expressing love and helpfulness, a wonderful Bible student — but she would knit mittens for the poor on *Sunday* and had a very broad religious thought — so much so that she was excommunicated from the Congregational Church in Glastonbury for "Denying the Sanctity of the Sabbath of the Decalogue."

The incident shows not only how relatively broad-minded Emily Moseley was, but also how narrow was the view of the churchmen of those days. In his diary entry for that September Sunday, Joseph Wright reported that Miss Moseley was excommunicated for "abstaining from the communion and publick worship and for holding such errors as . . . the sabbath is no better than any other day, there is no obligation on christians to send missionaries abroad or to labor for the conversion of sinners, the bible is all that is needed to guide us to heaven, etc. We were all shocked to see to what lengths she had gone in her delusions."

It was Julia and Abby, the two youngest, who achieved fame as the "Smith Sisters" through their valiant championing of woman's rights in a tax fight with the Town of Glastonbury. Julia was 77 and Abby, 72, when in 1869 they first objected to discrimination against them by the town tax collector. Again in 1872-73 the Smith sisters claimed that the town had increased the property taxes of widows and unmarried women but not of men. Getting nowhere by appealing to the town, the sisters in some indignation turned to the woman suffrage movement, which was getting started about that time. Abby attended the first Woman's Congress in New York in October 1873 and came home inspired to defy the Town of Glastonbury.

On election day in November, the two prim, black-clad women entered the Town House and asked the moderator for permission to speak. He refused; they left. But outside the door someone offered the use of an oxcart as a platform. Abby jumped up on it and produced from her reticule a speech previously prepared for just such an opportunity. It was a protest against the taxation of unfranchised women (and must surely

The Smith sisters, early champions of women's rights. Julia, left, and Abby.

have included the famous quotation "no taxation without representation"). Her audience consisted of men, most of whom responded with guffaws. From that day on, the Smith sisters refused to pay their property taxes.

The next May the courageous sisters presented the following petition to the State Legislature asking that women be exempt from taxation until they should be given the vote:

> To the Honorable General Assembly of the State of Connecticut.
> The petition of citizens of the State of Connecticut who believe in the propriety and duty of rendering equal and exact justice to all persons. Your petitioners would respectfully represent that in as much as it is a fundamental principle of our government that "taxation without representation is tyranny" and as the women of this State are denied the privilege of voting — the only method by which representation is or can be assured — the observance of justice toward them requires that they should be exempted from taxation. We would, therefore, respectfully ask the passage of a law exempting the property of women from taxation so long as they shall be denied the privilege of the ballot.

By thus standing up for their rights, Abby and Julia not only put the town on the spot but gave it notority. Reporters from as far away as Boston came to Glastonbury to cover the story of the two old ladies whose cows were seized and sold at auction in lieu of taxes. Seizure of personal property was legal, but one year the tax collector seized land instead of cows and sold it privately instead of at auction ($4000 worth of land for $60, it was said). The Smith sisters sued the town in the local Justice's

Court and won, but the town appealed and the appeals judge reversed the decision, in favor of the town. At this point the Springfield *Republican* started a defense fund for the Smith sisters. They appealed to a higher court and won their case at last.

Despite their age and the difficulties of stagecoach travel, Abby and Julia traveled over the country addressing woman suffrage meetings. Several times they petitioned the State Legislature for the right to vote, and Abby, shortly before she died at 77, spoke for woman suffrage before a committee of the United States Senate. Left alone after Abby's death, Julia at age 87 married Amos Parker, a New Hampshire judge whom she knew only through correspondence. It was a mistake, she soon found out. When she died in Hartford seven years later, she left a note asking to be buried in the Glastonbury family plot with her maiden name on the headstone. Her funeral was conducted by a layman, and Isabella Beecher Hooker, the famous suffragist, offered a prayer.

When the Smith sisters were young ladies, the Smith home had been the scene of numerous meetings promoting the abolition of slavery. Mrs. Smith was deeply interested in abolition and enlisted scores of her friends to join the crusade. She and her daughters circulated in Glastonbury what is believed to be the first anti-slavery petition to be sent to Congress. About 40 Glastonbury women signed the petition, which former President John Quincy Adams presented to Congress. The ladies' petition is good evidence that anti-slavery feeling began early in Glastonbury.

By 1850 there were strong anti-slavery sentiments in town. At first it was not so much directed against the southern slaveholders as it was towards the expansion of slavery to the new western territories. Many Glastonbury people, according to Deacon Wright's journals, felt, like others elsewhere, that slavery should be contained where it was and not be allowed to spread. "A most iniquitous scheme," Deacon Wright called the passage of the Kansas-Nebraska Bill, designed to open those territories to slavery.

Glastonbury had once had slaves, and more than one might think, since the town was never a wealthy community. The Colonial Records reveal that Glastonbury in 1774 had 79 Blacks in a total population of 1992 (about 4 per cent, or one Black to 25 Whites). Glastonbury slaves, like those of other New England villages, were not only farm hands and domestic workers but worked in the village industries and shipping and shipbuilding trades. In the early days, the First Society seated slaves in a special place in the meeting house — a little platform in a rear corner. All early New England churches seated Negroes in a segregated place, and sometimes put small boys, the bane of the congregation, with them.

As early as 1711, the Connecticut Colony had passed a law freeing slaves on condition that if they became paupers, their former owners would support them. In 1783, all children born of Negro slaves became free at age 25. In 1792, all healthy slaves under 45 were freed; and in 1840 all Connecticut slaves were set free. But even before the passage of the 1783 law, Glastonbury was acting to free its slaves. Filed in the town records are manumissions of slaves, legally recorded by their owners. The following is a sample of such a manumission:

"Glastenbury Feby 16th 1781. This may Certify to all whom it may concern that We the Subcribers Benjamin Stevens & Samuel Smith Jun. of Glastenbury in New England do Give Freedom to Cuff Acklens a Negro Servant country born — twenty one Years of age — We further Certify that the above said Cuff Acklens is a Free Citizen of the United States of America in Witness whereunto we have set our hands and Seales this 16th Day of February A.D. 1781."

Glastonbury's freed slaves built themselves little cabins along what is now Chestnut Hill Road, which then became known as "Nigger Lane." In some cases, at least, the town bought the land for these cabins; there were deeds recorded for six half-acre parcels on a back road no longer existing, running from Main Street to Coleman Road. A town vote on December 10, 1787, illustrates the concern Glastonbury had for its freed slaves: "Voted the selectmen do what they think proper for Prince Simbo & his family in finding a place for him to set his House."

Runaway slaves from the South for years filtered through Connecticut on their way northward to freedom. During the decade preceding the Civil War they came in ever-increasing numbers, though it is likely not many passed through Glastonbury, since the central route of the underground railway appears to have been on the other side of the river.

By 1856 Glastonbury people were greatly aroused over the slavery question, and many local voters joined the ranks of the new anti-slavery party, the Republicans, after its organization from the ranks of the old Whig party, the Prohibitionists and the Free-Soilers. But there was still a large body of Democrats here; this was considered a Peace party and its members maintained a policy of silence on the great question of the day, slavery. Glastonbury was split nearly evenly in the election for Governor in 1859. William H. Buckingham, the Republican candidate, got 346 votes here; his opponent, James Pratt, got 337. Again in 1863, while the war was raging, Glastonbury gave Buckingham 322 votes and the Democratic candidate, Seymour, 297. The closeness of this vote does not mean that nearly half of Glastonbury was in favor of slavery. Rather, it probably reflects party loyalty.

Young Republicans were particularly active in the campaign for Lincoln and Hamlin in 1860. Joseph Wright tells of the formation in Glastonbury of a company of "Wide-Awakes," an organization of youthful Republicans throughout the country set up to campaign for Lincoln. "They are disciplined like soldiers wearing caps and carrying torches on a pole over their heads," wrote Wright. "The company for this town paraded through the street last night (September 5, 1860) about 60 and made an exciting appearance."

The firing of the guns at Fort Sumter on April 12, 1861, was as shocking to the people of Glastonbury as the shots at Lexington had been in

April of 1775. And, as then, the immediate local response was a chain-reaction of fervent patriotism. The Stars and Stripes were flourished from many a farmhouse window or porch, and from the church spires too.

When President Lincoln issued a call for volunteers, 10 Glastonbury men immediately signed up. They were Robert McManus, James Adams, John Daniels, Harvey Taylor, William Abbey, Samuel Dickinson, William Gordon, Edward Risley, Burgess Hale and Walter Lord.

A pathetic appeal for money with which to finance the war effort went out from the state government. Banks in Hartford and other cities responded with sizable loans, and private citizens came forward, too, with sums of money, large and small. Among them were some Glastonbury men, including James B. and William S. Williams, Isaac W. Plummer, Thaddeus Welles and Benjamin Taylor, whose group promissory note is among the documents collection of the Historical Society. The local sums were to be expended by the War Committee which had been appointed by the town to obtain enlistments and to organize a company of 9-months' volunteers. This committee was composed of Edwin Crosby, Isaac Plummer and James B. Williams.

When the first flush of enthusiastic patriotism wore off, there was a slump in filling volunteer quotas. The town had voted initially for payment of a bounty of $10 to each volunteer, $6 a month to the wives or mothers dependent on them and $3 per month to each dependent child, brother or sister. But these payments had to be increased substantially as time went on — at one time bounty payments of $500 to each volunteer were voted by the town. Even so, many families suffered hardships while their breadwinners were off at the battle lines, for the meager paychecks the soldiers received from the federal government were often many months late in coming.

When it became obvious that volunteers alone could not provide the needed manpower for the Union side, President Lincoln put into effect the Conscription Act of March 1863, the first draft. The Democrats, in the midst of a heated election compaign, called this "military dictatorship," and in Connecticut the Conscription Act was used as propaganda by the Democrats in their effort to unseat the Republican Governor Buckingham in the May election. They fully expected to elect their peace candidate, Thomas H. Seymour, but Buckingham won by a slim margin. He was then accused by the defeated party of furloughing soldiers to get their votes at home, and this accusation is borne out by a letter from Henry Goodrich, a Glastonbury volunteer, in the Historical Society's documents collection. Mr. Goodrich also mentions in this letter that the "Copperheads" were working the same game to get votes for Seymour.

"Buckingham Legion, Co.D., 20th Regt., C.V.
"Camp near Stafford G.H. Va. Apr. 11 1863
"Dear Father - - - - I hav been expecting I should get home to vote but the plan was all knocked in head it was to hav three go from each Co. one of the officers come to me about a week ago took me one side and asked

me if I wanted to go home and vote for B. I told him yes, I would like to go first rate, he wanted me to keep dark about it, he said plan was to send three from each Co. and if it would work, I could go. I should be the second anyhow. Tom Francis was anxious to go and had been trying to get a furlough for a long time so as he was an old man and quite an old gaffer Capt. Post let him go and that is (all) they would let go from our Co. I suppose it was because there has been so many home from our Co. but they did not let three go from any. They started yesterday morning so you see I got cheated out of that. It was no great disappointment because I did not think it would work from the start. If we had a Democratic administration and they wanted to carry the election as bad as the Rep do now they would hav let half of the Regt gone home. I hear that the Copperheads have taken every man out of the Hospital that was able to go and sent them home to vote for S. I hear Frank Hurlbut, Frank Sage & a Cromwell chap has gone all from Co. D. They are all good for S. It seems strange to me that the Copperheads can do Just as they are a mind to right around Washington and in sight of a Republican administration. I do not care much if Old Abe cannot see an inch from his nose (and I believe he never has) he ought to be turned out and someone put in his place that can. I think it would be about as well to Let Politicks drop and put this rebellion down. It has been a political (game?) all the way through if old Abe gone along and had not tried to please all partys my opinion he would hav done a good deal better. I guess I have written politicks enough for once . . . .

Your son
Henry."

Conscription got duly under way in Glastonbury as in all Union towns, though it did not work as our draft does now, for it was possible for men to hire substitutes to go in their stead. The Historical Society has records of some Glastonbury men who did just that.

Statistics on the town's participation in the Civil War, reported by town officials, are as follows: War expenses, $50,035.94. Number of men furnished, 393, as follows: Three months' volunteers, 10; nine months' volunteers, 62; three years' volunteers, 159; re-enlisted veterans, 28; three years' recruits, 74; three years' substitutes, 46; surgeons, 3; lieutenant regular army, 1; navy, 10. The bounties paid by the town ranged from $10 to $500 per man. Appropriations were also made for the mothers and infant brothers and sisters of volunteers. There were killed in battle, 16; died in service (including three at Andersonville Prison) 16. The town furnished 1 lieutenant-colonel, 4 captains, 2 lieutenants, 3 surgeons, 1 lieutenant in the regular Army and 3 warrant officers in the Navy.

The highest-ranking officer sent by Glastonbury was Lieut. Col. Daniel H. Stevens. The other commissioned officers were: Capt. Charles H. Talcott, Capt. William W. Abbey, Second Lieut. Benjamin F. Turner, all of the 25th Regiment, Capt. Robert G. Welles of the 10th Regular Infantry and Capt. Alpheus D. Clark of Co.D, 122nd Regiment. Capt. Welles, son of Thaddeus Welles, Town Clerk for many years, and nephew of Gideon Welles, was severely wounded at Gettysburg and died in Glastonbury in 1866. Capt. Clark, who had been a member of the "Fighting Fourteenth" (14th Conn. V.I.) was promoted to lead the 122nd, U.S. Colored Infantry, in January 1865. A chief contribution of the town to the Civil War effort was its most famous son, Gideon Welles, who served in Lincoln's wartime Cabinet as Secretary of the Navy. Gideon Welles was a descendant of one of the town's founding families. His Glastonbury forefather, Samuel, was a grandson of an early Connecticut governor, Thomas Welles. The Fundamental Orders of Connecticut, drawn up in 1638, are said to be in this governor's handwriting.

Gideon Welles,
Secretary of the Navy
in Abraham Lincoln's cabinet.

The Glastonbury Welleses were a leading family in the history of Connecticut, succeeding generations of Welles men holding important offices in both town and state. Gideon Welles carried on the family tradition of involvement in public matters when he first entered politics as Glastonbury's tax collector and from that post went to the General Assembly. He was one of the founders of the Republican party in Connecticut, worked for Lincoln's election and was appointed by Lincoln as Secretary of the Navy. He held the post for 8 years, through the Civil War, carrying on after Lincoln's assassination during the terrible period of reconstruction until the inauguration of President Grant in 1869.

It was an important job and a difficult one, as the war rolled on, for the members of Lincoln's Cabinet (and Johnson's after him) were often at odds, and decisions were not made easily. Gideon Welles, who had confidence in the new iron-clad Monitor-type warships, brought the United States Navy to a peak of excellence it had never previously known. He had a rather special knowledge of ships and ship-building, acquired first-hand when he was a boy underfoot at his father's Glastonbury shipyard. In 1967, Glastonbury honored the memory of its famous son, Gideon Welles, by naming a new junior high school for him. His birthplace, a large white house which had been built for his father and mother, Samuel and Ann Hale Welles, in 1782 and had been a Glastonbury landmark for nearly 200 years, stands again at the corner of Main Street and Hebron Avenue, returned to a site approximately at its original location in 1974.

When the Civil War was over, Glastonbury settled down into a long era of conservatism, going about its business with characteristic caution, seemingly bypassed by the mainstream of change beginning to affect American life.

Chapter VIII

From Steam to Electricity:
Post-Civil War Growth

The post-Civil War period was a time of industrial expansion in the North, accelerated by the rapid extension of railroads. But for many years Glastonbury continued to think in terms of wooden ships and horse-drawn wagons. Not until the turn of the 20th century did the town begin to grow as much as the rest of the country was growing.

On June 1, 1867, a special town meeting was called to alert the townspeople to the dangers of river navigation implied in a legislative proposal to span the river with two railroad bridges. In later years, Glastonbury would make a belated try to route a railroad through town. But now it was alarmed by the spectre of an iron horse riding roughshod across the river to block the passage of tall-masted schooners, a railroad carrying to market the very goods and produce which had always been the backbone of river shipping.

Summoning up its most talented sources of literary persuasion, the town meeting adopted the following resolution:

"Whereas, it is proposed to build two bridges across our great natural thoroughfare, the Connecticut River, the one at Middletown and the other at Lyme, therefore (be it) Resolved unanimously by the inhabitants of the Town of Glastonbury . . . that the construction and erection of such bridges . . . , by establishing the pernicious precedent that communities have no rights as against the persevering onslaughts of chartered monopolies, by impeding and obstructing the natural flow of commerce in the channel which it has occupied for nearly 250 years, and by adding greatly to the difficulties of navigation, would be an outrage upon rights and privileges more ancient and sacred than those vested by any mere legislative charter, as well as in the highest degree prejudicial to the interests of our town and of all other communities similarly situated, and a distinct blow to our prosperity as connected with the free use of the river Resolved, that we protest in the strongest terms against a consummation so fraught with injury to a large section of our State, and, as we believe, finally advantageous to none, and earnestly request our Legislature and our Governor not to approve measures so suicidal in their effect upon the general welfare, both directly and as precedents which may be hereafter followed. Resolved: That our Representatives are hereby instructed and our Senator requested, to use all honorable means to protect the Commerce of the Connecticut Valley by defeating the attempt to bridge the river below the city of Hartford."

Glastonbury was not alone in its alarm at the prospect of ruined shipping. The controversy raged for months in the legislative halls until finally in 1868 the Middletown railroad bridge was chartered. There was reason for the dismay of the townspeople. Not specifically because of the bridge, but because of railroad competition, shipping rapidly declined, and in 1876 the last Glastonbury-built vessel — a barge — slid off the ways of the Hollister shipyard at Log Landing.

From the town's beginning, the river had been almost the sole means of transporting its products to market. First they went by sail and then, when daily steamboat runs to New York began in 1825, goods were shipped by steamboat as well. Sometimes as many as six packets a day would glide up and down the tidal Connecticut, carrying passengers as well as produce and manufactured goods.

The river was important to Glastonbury, and not only as a means of livelihood. Many years earlier, when the town was set off from Wethersfield in 1690, the river was made the boundary line between the towns.

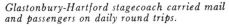

Glastonbury-Hartford stagecoach carried mail and passengers on daily round trips.

The Hartford, *shown at Glastonbury, 1927.*
The last of many steamboats from Hartford to
New York, 1840 to 1931.

For countless ages the Connecticut had meandered in a shifting serpentine course, the channel running sometimes more toward the east, sometimes further to the west. When the Legislature set the river as a boundary, the stream happened to be running in a fairly direct line through the eastern part of the meadows. Eighty years later the river had shifted its course so greatly to the westward that the General Assembly in order to return lost land to Wethersfield in 1770 reestablished the boundary, bringing the line back to its original position. In 1792 at the request of James Wright, the Legislature again altered the boundary to place that part of Wright's Island then owned by the Wright family within the town of Glastonbury, instead of partly in both towns.

Boundary disputes have always been a touchy point between neighbors, but disagreement over the line between Wethersfield and Glastonbury stirred up real bitterness between the two closely-related towns which otherwise had co-existed peacefully for years. By 1870 the course of the river had altered the size, shape and location of Wright's Island to such a degree that this part of the boundary line between the two towns had become uncertain. Now, a hundred years hence, it is not easy to understand why the relatively small amount of meadow land involved should have seemed important enough to have caused a fight between the two towns. Yet fight they did. Wethersfield sought to establish a new mutually-agreeable line with Glastonbury through "perambulations." Glastonbury refused and instead petitioned the Legislature to make the river as it then flowed the line. There then began a long period of legislative deliberation (Glastonbury petitioned the Legislature five times) and court litigation (instigated by Wethersfield), one of the legal problems being that the Wright's Island boundary change had not been clearly defined. The boundary line was finally laid out, defined by "courses and distances" by legislative surveyors and agreed to by both towns, in 1874. The final line had given to Wethersfield a small amount of land on the east side of the river at Glastonbury's north end.

When the railroad barons invaded Connecticut in the 1840s and many miles of railroad track began to criss-cross the state, Glastonbury was bypassed. It seems to have been of no particular concern to the town then, for at this period water resources were drawing industry. Even after steam began to replace water power in many of the state's larger industries, Glastonbury brooks attracted small enterprises which used water power in their actual manufacturing processes.

One of these was paper-making. In 1865 the Roaring Brook Paper Manufacturing Company converted an ancient saw mill on Roaring Brook south of Buck's Corners into a paper mill for making "binders' board" for book covers. Run by the Clark and Loveland families, this mill made book covers for some of Mark Twain's early books. (Paper Mill Hill, below Buck's Corners past the mill, was a favorite wintertime sliding place for youngsters on "pig-stickers.") The Roaring Brook Manufacturing Company was the first of several paper mills to try their luck in Glastonbury, all manufacturing binders' board.

In 1876 the Case Brothers of Manchester purchased an old grist mill on Salmon Brook below Addison and constructed a small factory where they made binders board (later selling out to F. B. Clark). It was destroyed by fire in 1893 but was rebuilt on the same site. Still later in the century, John W. Purtill took over the burned-out twine mill of the Wassuc Company at Smut and began the manufacture of paper. But paper-making was a hazardous operation. Fire was a constant threat and there was no adequate fire brigade for protection. When the Smut mill again burned, the Purtill company moved downstream to the old stone mill in Cotton Hollow which had been vacated by the Hartford Manufacturing Company and succeeding owners. This they enlarged, housing their workers in the same little community which had formerly been composed of cotton mill

Sliding down Paper Mill Hill, near New London Turnpike. Wall painting in house at Buck's Corners, by local artist, Charles Grimmons. (Photo by Duffy.)

Glastonbury steamboat dock at Naubuc, 1890.

workers. Once more fire consumed the ill-fated paper mill — in 1920 when there was still no fire company — and this time the mill closed its doors for good.

P. H. Goodrich founded the Riverside Manufacturing Company in 1884, making binders board, at a site not far from the steamship dock in Naubuc. The Goodrich plant as well as the former Case Brothers mill were also plagued by fires and did not last long; but the Goodriches had another string to their bow — a coal supply firm which had its own dock on the Connecticut River.

Another industry which needed soft water for its processing was tanning. Leather tanning was one of Glastonbury's oldest industries; several early tanners set up shop along Hubbard Brook, which had its source in Neipsic. Herman Roser, arriving in the 1880s from Germany, where his ancestors had long operated a tannery, picked Glastonbury as the site for a tannery he had come to America to establish, and in 1886 bought the Isaac Broadhead plant on the old New London Turnpike. One of the reasons for his choice was the quality of the water he could pipe down from the old Neipsic pools, located in the present Williams Park area, which were famous for an old Indian legend that the clear, sparkling water had miraculous healing power. Later, long before pollution became a major issue, Roser's Tannery installed a water purification system to return the water "as pure as before it was used."

Mr. Roser built the tannery up into a plant known world-wide as a producer of quality pigskin. In time his two oldest sons, John and Martin, joined him in the family business. Another son, Conrad, died as a young man while serving as Glastonbury's representative to the General Assembly; and John's son-in-law, Roger Bestor, while he was president of the tannery, died in 1968. Martin's son, David, joined the family firm in the mid-50s.

Roser pigskin was used for all manner of fine leather goods. In early days it was used largely for such things as saddles, horse collars, whip handles and puttees as well as for bookbinding. Pierce-Arrow limousines had upholstery made of Roser pigskin. (At one time Ford cars had woolen upholstery manufactured by the Glazier Manufacturing Company in Hopewell.) In more modern times, Roser's chief outlets were "personal" leather goods such as luggage, belts, wallets, briefcases and fine shoes.

One of the last shipments of Glastonbury-made goods to be sent down-river by sailboat was feldspar. A product native to Glastonbury, feldspar is an off-white crystalline mineral which, when decomposed by weathering, forms a clay used in the manufacture of ceramics. George S. Andrews discovered this substance in the great granite outcroppings on his farm just north of the Portland town line, and realized its potentialities for industrial use. He set up a small mill near his quarries about 1870 (the first feldspar mill in Connecticut) and began the grinding of the rock into powder which he sold to makers of pottery, glass and soap. Ox teams carting the spar to the Andrews' dock at the river used a road specially built for the purpose, called Old Maid's Lane for the Tryon sisters who lived there.

Ten years later Andrews sold his quarries to Joshua and William P. Huspband. The Huspbands bought for their spar operation the Hollister grist mill on Roaring Brook, which had been moved from its original location at the Nayaug Bridge when an abnormally high flood in 1869 swept away its underpinnings. The new site of the grist mill was on the east side of the stream farther down the brook about opposite the barn-

Howe's spar mill, 1904, High Street at Roaring Brook. Site was earlier that of Hollister's grist mill.

yard of the ancient Hollister home. The huge millstones which had ground grain for Glastonbury people for two centuries proved ideal for the crushing of spar, and the grain elevator was just as efficient for spar as it had been for wheat, rye, oats and corn.

After several changes of ownership, Louis W. Howe took over the spar mill in 1905. Under his direction, the feldspar operation became the largest in Connecticut. Over a period of 23 years he mined, milled and shipped 100,000 tons of feldspar to be used in the manufacture of such diverse products as bathtubs, fine china and false teeth.

Perhaps the greatest fighters for business enterprise in Glastonbury were John H. Hale and his brother, George H. Hale. Against great odds — fickle weather, transportation difficulties and lack of money — the Hale brothers built up an enormously successful peach-growing business and led the way for other industrialists to reach out for wider markets.

The Hale brothers started their fruit business as boys in 1866 with a small strawberry bed planted on a sandy hillside on the 200-year-old Hale farm. During the next 10 years they achieved a modest success with berries, but one day they took a long, calculating look at a few old native seedling peach trees straggling along a fence row in what is now the Overlook section of town.

The peach was one of the fruits that had been abandoned in New England because of a disease, the "yellows," and the heavy winter frosts which often killed off the trees before they could reach a bearing age. But the Hales decided to try their luck with peaches (the market in New England was wide open) and planted their first orchard with several varieties which would ripen after the New Jersey and Delaware crops were out of the market. Over several years they planted three orchards, but each winter the crops were killed by extreme changes in weather. Meanwhile the berry plantation was carrying the farm, on which a church society held a mortgage of $2000.

One year a great freeze in May totally ruined a strawberry crop estimated to have been worth about $5000. The brothers were not unduly discouraged, knowing that the peach crop seemed to be untouched by frost, but the church committee holding the mortgage felt otherwise. It "waited on" the Hales and gave them until October to pay up. In the summer the first real peach crop was marketed at last with gratifying results (profits of $9000) and in September the Hales took great satisfaction in paying off the mortgage in full. The church society committee had failed to understand the potential of the Hale operation.

In time the business prospered beyond even the Hales' expectations. They augmented their Glastonbury holdings by buying land in Seymour and in Fort Valley, Georgia, eventually owning 2000 acres in Connecticut and 1000 in Georgia — orchards containing 350,000 peach trees. This was the first Glastonbury industry to establish a branch outside the state. Among the many varieties of peaches they produced was their own special Hale Peach, still marketed today, a large luscious rosy specimen they developed from one of the old peach seedlings ("grandfather's") the brothers had found growing in the fence row.

By the 1900s, Hale peaches were being shipped all over the country. John Howard Hale was a pioneer in marketing produce on a nationwide scale. An enterprising businessman, he reached out for new markets by sending samples of his fruit across the country, by advertising and by mailing detailed, informative catalogs. He came to be widely known as the Peach King, a well-deserved title.

Though J. H. Hale himself had never continued his education beyond grade school, he was largely responsible for the establishment of Storrs

Hale's peaches in packing shed, about 1900. (Print by Duffy from glass plate.)

Agricultural College which later became the University of Connecticut. As a representative from Glastonbury to the General Assembly, he pushed through a bill which transferred land grant funds from Yale to Storrs, and in 1888 became a trustee of the college. In 1885, he helped organize the Glastonbury Grange, and later that year spearheaded the formation of a Connecticut State Grange at a meeting held at the old Academy Hall then located on Main Street at Stockade Road.

One of the problems the Hales and other Glastonbury businessmen had to face was the lack of a railroad going through town. In the 1880s the Hale brothers, the J. B. Williams Company, P. H. Goodrich and William E. Gates called a meeting to interest the town in sponsoring a project to get a railroad routed through Glastonbury. The project fell through, however. Another failure was an effort in 1890 to run a horse railroad through here from Manchester to Portland.

Early in the 1900s, when electricity was just coming into use, a group of local businessmen headed by Lewis Ripley and including J. H. Hale and James B. and Samuel H. Williams, conceived the idea of building a Glastonbury electric power plant, making use of the town's good water power. Planning to locate the plant at what is now the Coldbrook Reservoir of the Metropolitan District Commission, the men formed the Glastonbury Power Company and sought financial backing. With the electric power the plant would generate, the company planned to run an electric railway (trolley) from the South Glastonbury steamboat dock to South Manchester, there to connect with the tracks of the Hartford, Manchester & Rockville Tramway Company. The route would have taken it through Cotton Hollow, crossing Hopewell Road near the Glazier mill, through the valley past Purtill's mill at Smut and thence through East Glastonbury to Manchester. It would have been a boon to the mills, for horse-drawn teams had a tough time managing the steep grades from East Glastonbury and Hopewell to the dock. The General Assembly was petitioned in 1904 for a charter, but the project did not materialize, mainly for financial reasons.

An ambitious transportation scheme was that of the Norwich, Colchester and Hartford Traction Company, which in 1910 bought up rights-of-way through Glastonbury extending south and east from the East Hartford town line at Great Swamp Road, planning to run a *trackless* trolley route apparently all the way to the shore. Cars, powered by electric

First trolley to Glastonbury, on the day it arrived: March 26, 1892. (Photo from a glass negative.)

overhead trolley wires, were to run on a hard-surfaced roadbed. The road-bed was graded from the East Hartford town line to Addison Pond. In sections of Addison traces of this old route may still be seen. Wells A. Strickland, then a selectman, evidently was the Glastonbury representative of this corporation. But the project was abandoned for lack of capital.

However, in 1892 an electric trolley line had gone into service from Church Corners in East Hartford to Hubbard Brook. The next year it was extended to Roaring Brook in South Glastonbury. Old-timers will remember the pleasant, woodsy Brookside Park located on an island connected to the south bank of Roaring Brook at the end of the trolley line. Families and young people would ride out from Hartford on the breezy open trolleys for a summer day's outing at this bosky dell.

The Hales made a special arrangement with the Hartford Street Railway to put in a switch fronting their farm and to fit up three freight cars exclusively for their use. Every day in the peach season the cars were loaded with fruit and sent off to market. Glastonbury factories, as well, were making profitable use of the trolley line. About 1908 a special line for freight was put through to the J. B. Williams factory. And special freight cars for the Hopewell woolen mill went down to South Glastonbury whenever a full load of freight was ready for shipping. Trolley tracks were laid down Water Street about 1915 so that feldspar could be shipped from the Howe spar mill. The Glastonbury trolley line was discontinued for passengers in 1928, but diesel cars for freight still lumbered down Main Street and into the J. B. Williams loading yard until the 1950s. Meanwhile the Hartford-to-New York steamboat made daily stops at both Glastonbury and South Glastonbury, and local industries continued the ancient practice of shipping their goods by water until the "Hartford" and the "Middletown" stopped their runs in 1931. (The old docks were located in Glastonbury west of Naubuc Avenue at about the point where that street curves north, and in South Glastonbury south of Ferry Lane.)

The first public utility to reach Glastonbury was the telephone. All things considered, it came pretty early — in 1883. The line was hooked up with the Hartford system. In 1904 Glastonbury got its own telephone exchange and "hello girls," located in the old Conference House just north of the Green and Hubbard Brook. By that time Glastonbury had 101 telephones.

The first street lights in town were kerosene lanterns strung on wires across Main Street between Salmon Brook and Hubbard Brook. They were in service only a few years, being supplanted by electric lights in about 1913, when the East Haddam Electric Light Company brought electricity to Glastonbury homes. Street lights have never fanned out very far from the Center. Nobody seems to mind, for even in the 1970s Glastonbury people seemed to prefer their town to keep its rural character as long as possible.

Glastonbury approached the "horseless carriage," just coming into use in the early 1900s, with caution. P. K. Williams had the first automobile

Glastonbury Center, about 1904.
Town Records Building, left; Harriet Welles
Turner Burnham home, right, now site of
Welles-Turner Memorial Library.

in town, an Oldsmobile runabout, which he registered with the Secretary of the State in 1903, the first year the state required automobile registration. That same summer John S. Tyler of South Glastonbury acquired a Locomobile runabout which kept turning over and had to be righted by neighborhood boys. Both Herbert T. Clark and Aaron W. Kinne recalled this car and its balky behavior. They also remembered Roland Hollister's Cadillac 4-seater "tonneau," registered in 1904. Mrs. Addie Crosby owned East Glastonbury's first automobile, an Autocar runabout (with no windshield) in 1904. The next year three more local cars were registered: Dr. W. S. Kingsbury's Pope-Toledo runabout, S. P. Turner's Knox tonneau, and Charles F. Strunz' Cadillac tonneau. Mr. Strunz had previously owned a Royal motor bicycle, apparently Glastonbury's first motorcycle, which he registered with the State in 1903.

The remarkably few automobiles in town in the early years of automobiling may be a reflection of the Yankee "wait and see" tradition which seems to have characterized Glastonbury for so many years. The assessors' records do not show listings of any of the new-fangled motor cars until 1910, when the category "automobiles" was handwritten in below the printed heading "coaches, carriages and pleasure-wagons." The first separate assessment listing for automobiles was in 1914, when roads were somewhat improved, cars were better and cheaper and drivers for the first time were required to take examinations for licenses.

Glastonbury people had scarcely got used to seeing automobiles chugging along local roads when they were startled by the appearance of a flying machine swooping over the meadows. It was remarkable enough

Carl Hollister in a pusher propeller biplane
made by Frank Harriman in South Glastonbury.

to see such an object here, but more remarkable that the plane was Glastonbury-made.

Frank H. Harriman, who had moved his motor-manufacturing company from Hartford to Glastonbury in 1907, became fascinated with the Wright Brothers' experiments in aviation. By 1909 he had built and tested his own aircraft engine. Soon he began to design airplanes — a hydroplane, biplanes and a triplane. Herbert Clark remembered watching Harriman test his hydroplane on the river. Mr. Clark believed he may have been the first person to have seen a Connecticut-made plane actually take off and swoop through the air (it came back very soon to land on the water). The U.S. Government was interested in Harriman's aviation experiments and for a while had a "government inspector" living in a tent down near the Old Dock Road where Harriman was working, to keep an eye on developments, Mr. Clark recalled.

In 1913 Harriman constructed a concrete building, which is still used as a garage at 1123 Main Street, where he built and assembled some of the planes he had designed. The plane's fuselage was of wood, as were the propellers made at Taylor's nearby saw mill (formerly a cooperage where gunpowder kegs for a Maryland firm were made). The wings were covered with tautened linen, shellacked or varnished. At his own foundry, Harriman made iron, aluminum and bronze castings. When he realized the bearings were wearing too quickly, he tried making them of silver which he acquired by melting down some old silverware his wife had bought secondhand from a neighbor. (Twenty years later, Pratt and Whitney Aircraft was using silver to combat the same problem.)

But Frank Harriman lacked capital to make his venture a success. After a series of financial troubles, he went bankrupt in 1921 and left Connecticut for Long Island, where his inventions were eventually acquired and put into successful operation by a firm said to be still in business. Harriman is acknowledged today in aeronautical circles as a forerunner of modern aviation, and Glastonbury may claim the distinction of having been the proving ground for the first Connecticut-made airplane.

The advances in transportation (in spite of there being no steam railroad line) were beginning to spur the growth of Glastonbury's population. When trolley tracks began to be laid in the late 1880s, word went out that laborers were needed to cut and lay the ties. Response to this appeal brought the first Italian families to Glastonbury. Except for a few Irish immigrants who had arrived in this country to escape the devastating potato famine of the 1840s in their mother country and had come to Glastonbury, the Italian people were the first ethnic group to join the solidly Yankee, English-background makeup of the town.

Joseph Wright in his journals tells of hiring Irish boys as farmhands in the mid-1800s. Later, industries, particularly textile mills, brought a larger group of Irish families. Of Catholic faith, the Irish people had no place to worship in Glastonbury. They went to Portland, some walking, it is said, to attend Mass and bury their dead. But in 1878 St. Mary's parish of East Hartford established a Catholic mission, St. Augustine's, in South Glastonbury.

One of the first Italian families to arrive in Glastonbury to cut timber for the trolley roadbed, probably *the* first, were the Carinis. (At one time Bartholomew Carini was the largest landowner in town, being the possessor of 1500 Glastonbury acres.) The Prelis, Ferrandos and other families soon followed. When the sturdy chestnut trees had been felled, sawed into railroad ties and laid, the Italian men soon found other work, doubtless much more to their liking. They became orchardists, employed in the extensive Hale peach orchards.

Out on Belltown Hill, extending east from Matson Hill in South Glastonbury, was a large farm owned by James W. Pray. Mr. Pray became interested in the Italian newcomers and helped them to buy up the old farms on Matson Hill which had been, or rapidly were, being deserted by the old families whose descendants had gone west or left for the cities. On the land they acquired through Mr. Pray's long-term loans, the Italians began to build up peach and apple orchards of their own. These far outlasted the once-famous Hale orchards which dwindled after the death of J. H. Hale in 1917 and at last disappeared upon the appearance of the bulldozer in the 1930s. Today the blossoming slopes of Matson Hill in the spring and the later harvest of peaches, apples and blueberries testify to the skill and diligence of these Glastonbury fruit growers.

With the increase of Catholic parishioners, St. Augustine's on Hopewell Road separated from St. Mary's and became an independent parish in 1902. Meanwhile Catholics living in the north end, who at first attended

Brooks Quarry, across from Neipsic Cemetery, one of several 19th-century East Glastonbury granite quarries. Wadsworth Atheneum was built with Glastonbury stone.

Mass at St. Mary's, began holding services in a barn near the Williams Brothers silver factory in Naubuc. This group presently formed its own parish, St. Paul's, and built a church on Naubuc Avenue. By the 1950s the parish had outgrown the church building and a new large brick church of Colonial design was built on Main Street, dedicated in January 1958. St. Paul's parish continued to grow, along with the town, and a new Catholic parish was formed in East Glastonbury, where the town's residential development had increased the most. It began holding services, at first as a mission church and later as a separate parish, in the summer of 1970, at Gideon Welles Junior High School while the new church, of contemporary design, was being built on Manchester Road near the proposed Buckingham village center. Named St. Dunstan's after a 10th century abbot of Glastonbury, England, the church was dedicated on November 24, 1974.

Glastonbury industries brought a few German families to town, the first, the Korngiebels, coming in 1850. About 1880 the Kiedasch family advertised in the Connecticut Staats-Zeitung for a German Protestant minister to come to Glastonbury to preach. The ad resulted in the formation of St. Mark's Evangelical Lutheran Church, which first held services in the Music Hall on the Williams Brothers factory grounds. In 1902 the parish built a church on Grove Street. This was sold to St. John's Ukrainian Church in 1925, when the Lutherans built a new church on Griswold Street. St. Mark's, with its parish growing larger, built again next door on Griswold Street, the new modern sanctuary being dedicated on April 9, 1972, with the former church building becoming a parish hall. St. John's, after more than 70 years on Grove Street, was obliged to move when the street itself was absorbed into the redevelopment of Glastonbury Center. But the developer of that particular area, David McClain, came to the rescue with an offer of land for relocation, and in 1974 the church building came to rest on a new foundation.

A number of Polish families, like the Ukrainians, came to Glastonbury in the early part of the century to work in Clark's paper mill, Roser's, and the Williams Brothers silver factory. The Polish banded together, formed a Polish National Alliance and built their own community hall on Medford Street in 1914. A few Lithuanian families came here, too, for jobs in Howe's Spar Mill. Glastonbury industries have continued to attract employees whose residence here has broadened the once-tight Yankee makeup of the town's population.

Though the census of 1890 had shown a decrease in population of 123 persons during the preceding decade, never again did the census figures show a set-back. By 1900, more than 800 new people were residing here. It was a slow but auspicious start for the 20th century. The town had begun to grow at last, and the reasons were obvious. Technological advances — better roads, automobiles, the trolley line, improved communication, besides the strategic geographical location of the town just outside a major city — could hardly fail to stimulate the growth of Glastonbury. In the decades just ahead, two World Wars would sadden the town, but even these tragic events could not impede the building up of Glastonbury into a major suburban community.

South Glastonbury girls going berrying. (Photo by Carl Hollister.)

Chapter IX

Miscellaneous Disasters:
Wars, Depression, Floods, Hurricane,
and the Rise of Protective Agencies

On March 9, 1917, "under suspension of the rules and the House singing 'America'", an Act creating a Connecticut Home Guard was passed by the General Assembly. It was, apparently, the first official recognition that a state of war with Germany was imminent.

The Assembly's action and Congress' declaration of war on April 6, 1917, drew a response in Glastonbury — the appointment of a wartime committee and the formation of a Home Guard. No one had any idea how serious the threat of invasion by Germans on New England shores might be, and home-front mobilization became an all-out endeavor in Glastonbury, as elsewhere. Under the supervision of R. G. Pinney, W. E. Gates and Lewis W. Ripley, five volunteer companies of the Home Guard were organized here, more than in any other town in the state "of anywhere near the same size," Mr. Ripley later reported. The practice marches of these uniformed companies were familiar sights on Glastonbury streets during the two-and-a-half-year period of World War I.

By July 1917 men were being drafted. The town seemed to be uncertain for a while just how many of its young residents were being called up, for a notice appeared in the *East Hartford Gazette* on October 12 listing 48 known to be in service and asking that citizens let the Glastonbury Council of Defense "know at once of any others."

In September the Glastonbury Business Men's Association had appointed a special committee "to take charge of all activities in the present war." Mr. Ripley was chairman of this committee, which became known as the Glastonbury Council of Defense, and under his supervision a large number of sub-committees were formed to handle such activities as "Farewells, transportation of drafted men, equipment, correspondence, gifts, finances, service flags, Honor Roll, and soldiers and sailors' business affairs."

Glastonbury industries went into full production of goods for military use during World War I. As early as 1914 the Glazier Manufacturing Company made heavy overcoatings for the British, Belgian and Italian governments, and during 1917 and 1918 it produced "O.D." melton cloth for the U.S. Army. The Angus Park Manufacturing Company produced 200,000 yards of uniform cloth for both the U.S. and the French governments, and the Glastenbury Knitting Company in Addison turned out about 400,000 garments (underwear) for U.S. Army soldiers. The J. B. Williams Company manufactured a million tubes of "Sag paste" used to counteract the effects of poison gas. ("Sag" was "gas" spelled backward.) Meanwhile the Williams Brothers Manufacturing Company on Naubuc Avenue produced thousands of pairs of forceps for the U.S. Army Medical Department, and in addition made shackle bolts for anchors and airplane control parts. Roser's Tannery produced over a million square feet of pigskin for army purposes: saddles, leggings, wrist watch straps, Sam Brown belts and pistol holsters. Altogether Glastonbury was a major supplier to the war effort of that first "world" conflict.

Nineteen women's groups from churches, the Grange, lodges, Girl Scouts and clubs in October formed a Woman's Committee of the Council of Defense. The Woman's Committee was one of many such groups throughout the country which inaugurated in the name of defense a broad program of social work that continued after the war was over, becoming an accepted part of welfare service to communities. The women's activities included instruction in baby and child care, a welfare program for families whose husbands and sons were in the service, instruction in social hygiene for young girls, and instruction in good nutrition. Heading up this work were Mrs. S. H. Williams, Miss Amy Pratt and Miss Anne Williams. The work with children and the severe epidemic of influenza in the winter of 1917-18 spurred interest in securing the permanent services of a visiting nurse. Thus, from the organization of dedicated women working hard to help their town in an unfamiliar wartime situation, the Glastonbury Visiting Nurse Association was born. In February 1919 this association was formally organized with 66 charter members, Mrs. Williams being president.

Another concern of the Woman's Committee of the Council of Defense, and one directly connected with wartime circumstances, was food conservation instruction. Mrs. Stancliff Hale, as canning chairman, secured pledges of 41,058 quarts of canned fruits and vegetables. Mrs. Hale also conducted an inquiry into the hoarding of sugar. Besides sugar, coal was one of the scarcest items during World War I, and many Glastonbury homes and businesses were chilly during the winter.

The Glastonbury Branch of the American Red Cross was also active during the war years. Many women knitted socks, sweaters and helmets for the "boys," and in addition made hospital and refugee garments and supplies, surgical dressings and "comfort" bags.

By the time of the Armistice on November 11, 1918, 253 Glastonbury men were in, or had been in, the service. Most of them had served their time in Army camps in this country (chiefly Camp Devens). Sixty-two went overseas with the Army, but the town has no records of those who served abroad with the Navy or Marine Corps. Ten Glastonbury men were killed in World War I: Harry Q. Frost, Charles Leon Goodale, Cyrus Hilton, Alfred M. Hodge, Paul Lambert, Willard B. Mason, Thomas P. Moore, Thomas Paulina, Everett S. Treat and Jacob Ubert.

When it was over, over there, and the boys came home, the second decade of the 20th century was just ending and the town had added about a thousand more to its population than it had had in 1900. It was still a quiet town (in spite of "tin lizzies" and the telephone), and in the next decade it neither grew very much nor veered very noticeably from its largely rural character.

Shortly before the War, the heirs of James B. and David W. Williams had built in memory of their ancestors a red brick gymnasium, the Williams Memorial, next door to the high school, the old Free Academy. It was ready for the returning veterans as a recreation center, with a gymnasium and bowling alleys which were used by the townspeople for the next 40 years. The Williams Memorial was Glastonbury's first (almost its *only*) movie house. It was packed to the rafters every Saturday night by young and old, mostly young, who came to see such grand old performers as Charlie Chaplin, Douglas Fairbanks, Mary Pickford, Ben Turpin and Our Gang. A great puller was an exciting serial — a cliff-hanger full of hair-breadth escapes and last-minute desperate situations, all performed to the jangling ivories of a Tin Pan Alley piano.

The Williams family were long benefactors of Glastonbury. Once they had made a success of the thriving soap factory, they turned their at-

Advertisement for one of Glastonbury's most famous products, 1903.

tention to the civic needs of the town. It was a traditional pattern throughout the country, in the days before social legislation, for the reigning industralists to keep a benevolent eye on the needs of their home towns, and the Williams family lived up to this tradition. They lived graciously in large and well-appointed homes on Hubbard and Williams Streets on land which had been owned from the town's beginning by their ancestors, the Hubbards. Members of the Williams family in succeeding generations served in town offices, on boards and heading up civic associations. (A descendant, Richard G. Williams, served on the Town Council for the first ten years of its existence, most of the time as chairman, having previously spent 3 terms as Representative to the General Assembly.)

Samuel H. Williams served many years as chairman of the School Board and did much to upgrade Glastonbury schools. In 1915 Mr. Williams asked President Flavel S. Luther of Trinity College to survey the Glastonbury schools and report his findings to the School Board. President Luther accepted, and his report, while courteous, was rather devastating. He criticized the schools for lack of good equipment, unattractiveness, uncleanliness and underpayment of teachers. He also felt there were too many one-room schools and suggested a moderate consolidation. Consolidation was supposed to have been begun in 1909, but all that had been done was to bring the schools from district autonomy to supervision under one Town School Committee of six members, as a state law enacted that year had made mandatory. President Luther's only comment on the curriculum, a suggestion that the teaching of agriculture be included, presently was put into effect.

Glastonbury people took the report seriously, and built a new school quite soon in Buckingham. In the next few years, three more were built: on Hubbard Street, on High Street, and on Hopewell Road. All were small, the High Street School with four rooms being the biggest. It was 1939 before the last of the old one-room schools was closed.

As might be expected, the chief reason for the slow rate of new school building and lag in upgrading education had been financial. In 1915, the town's tax rate was set by town meeting. The selectmen would advise that a certain tax rate was necessary to meet expenses, but this would be disputed and a lower mill rate would invariably be voted. A compelling desire to keep taxes down was nothing new in Glastonbury history, or for that matter, in the history of civilization. But the consistent action of Glastonbury townspeople in trying to make do with an inadequate tax rate had at least two major repercussions. It retarded the building of schools sufficient to take care of the number of children in town, and it sent the town into debt, necessitating loans. In order to finance the construction of a new high school in 1922, the town was obliged to issue funding bonds for the first time.

When Francis S. Knox arrived in 1917 to begin his long tenure (36 years as Superintendent of Schools) he was faced almost at once with a problem resulting from the consolidation of schools: transportation for the pupils who formerly had walked to the little neighborhood one-room schoolhouses. The question of transporting elementary schoolchildren was controversial. Some people thought it ridiculous for the old district schools to be given up if it meant paying taxes to have their children bused. Others demanded better transportation than the farm wagons converted into carryalls which had been used, probably since 1902, to transport pupils to the high school. Even Mr. Knox seems to have been somewhat in favor of letting the children walk. "We need to make popular again the idea that walking is a delightful and health-giving exercise," he suggested in an annual report. But some parents thought the transportation issue important enough to take drastic action. "There was a strike of parents," reported Mr. Knox. "They refused to send their children to school. At the hearing conducted by a State Department (of Education) official, they said they wanted better transportation . . ."

And so, in 1917 school auto-buses began to cover the outlying areas of town. As Mr. Knox reported, the first motorized buses broke a good many axles on rough frozen roads and got mired in mud; but in the long run they proved their worth, for, as it turned out, transporting the children was the only way to keep the school system going, expensive or not. (Glastonbury, with its large area, in 1970 had almost the largest fleet of school buses in the state — 30.)

Mr. Knox's arrival as superintendent marked the start of a long gradual improvement in Glastonbury's school system. A major event in his administration was the building of a high school in 1922 on the same Main Street site as the old one, formerly the Glastonbury Free Academy, which was moved to a new spot south of the Williams Memorial. The

Glastonbury's first motorized school bus,
one of first in the nation — a 1917 Ford.

white-painted clapboard Academy, built in 1870, became in turn an elementary school, the Glastonbury Public Library, and briefly a school once more before its demise to make room for an expanding junior high complex in 1958.

During the first decade of Mr. Knox's administration such embellishments as physical education, music, art, foreign languages other than Latin, and vocational agriculture were added to the basic courses in the school program. Vo-ag had been recommended by Dr. Luther in his 1915 survey in view of the fact that Glastonbury was then largely a farming community. In 1916 a vo-ag course was given a try but it was abandoned two years later. It was 1923 before the agriculture curriculum, state-sponsored, was put into effect. It brought to town a man whose influence on the farmers and their work, chiefly fruit-raising, was to become great — J. Clair Dufford. Not only did Mr. Dufford work with the boys enrolled in his high school classes, but he met with Matson Hill fruit growers and visited their farms to inspect orchards for insects and disease, recommend pruning and spraying schedules, suggest fertilizers and to treat cows with "milk fever." The boys, too, as part of their vo-ag course, pruned and sprayed trees, tested milk and even dynamited stumps. Many years later Glastonbury was rewarded for its long and consistent work in vo-ag education by being chosen by the State as the site for a Regional Vocational Agriculture Center, constructed as an addition to the High School during 1963-64 with a state grant of $150,000.

The 1920s brought "modern times" to Glastonbury. This decade following World War I was a period of transition from an old-fashioned country town to a community with more modern government services. Volunteer fire companies were organized during this period, and the centuries-old constabulatory system reorganized into a rudimentary police department.

The hazards of fire were great long ago when the town was young. Wooden buildings heated by great open fireplaces and lit by candlelight or oil lamps were fair game for fire, and many must have burned down while the residents watched helplessly. At one time it was a law that every chimney must be inspected once a year as a safety measure, but this precaution could have had little effect. There were, of course, no fire companies in Glastonbury's earliest days. Neighbors, the first volunteer firemen, formed bucket brigades lined up from a burning house or barn to the nearest stream or farm pond. When the first textile mill came into being about 1814, an organized group of volunteer firemen, legend has it, were called into action when a fire broke out in the factory.

But many years elapsed before the official organization of volunteer firemen. It is a curious thing that Glastonbury could have let centuries slide by without a fire department of any sort. Yet apparently this was so. The lack of public water mains was undoubtedly one reason for the lag. It was not until about the turn of the century that the first water mains were laid part way down Main Street and along some side streets, with a few hydrants installed. About 1920 the Center Hose Company was organized in the north end, housing the hand-drawn gig it bought for the hose in a garage near the old Odd Fellows Building at the corner of Hebron Avenue and New London Turnpike. Once, on the way to a serious fire at the home of Lewis Kinne at Chestnut Hill Road and Main Street, the wheels fell off the gig as it was being towed by a car, and the hose was stuffed inside the car to get it to the fire. Later the Center Hose Company bought a Reo hose wagon and a 50-gallon chemical tank. Volunteers were called out by a fire alarm gong and a telephone system.

Naubuc Fire Company, photographed in 1931; now Fire Company 1.

In 1926 a bad fire burned down Dr. Harry Rising's barn and a shed back of St. Luke's Church in South Glastonbury. The South Glastonbury people had already been stirred over the disastrous fire which gutted Purtill's paper mill in Cotton Hollow in 1920, and now, in 1926, they took steps to organize their own fire company. Herbert T. Clark was named first chief, and a new Reo pumper was purchased. In the same year, the Naubuc Fire District was formed with Michael Muccio as fire chief. This volunteer company began operations with a 1922 Packard but soon bought a modern pumper, a 1929 American LaFrance. A PWA project helped remodel the old brick First District schoolhouse at the corner of Main and Pratt Streets into a firehouse in 1938, when William Connery (later first selectman) was fire chief.

When the Center Hose Company was organized in 1920, Glastonbury set up the first of several autonomous fire districts. Under state enabling legislation which authorized local establishment of fire districts operating as separate entities apart from the local government, neighborhood groups could organize and lay assessments for the financing of street lights and sidewalks, as well as hydrants and other means of fire protection. The Annual Town Report for 1921 lists two: Glastonbury Fire District and Naubuc Fire District (the latter preceding the organization of a Naubuc volunteer fire company by about six years.) Apparently the fire districts were established as much to acquire streetlights and some sidewalks in these areas as to finance fire protection, in the beginning. The Town Report for 1922 adds five more fire districts: Addison, Center, Hebron Avenue, South Glastonbury and Still Hill. Hydrants did not service all these areas. However, the East Hartford Water Company at that time maintained a reservoir at the rear of Keeney Street and laid a water line along Salmon Brook crosslots to furnish water to the Glastenbury Knitting Company at Addison and, farther down, to the Case Brothers paper mill, which made hydrants in that area possible. This reservoir, later taken over by the Metropolitan District Commission, was abandoned when the 1938 hurricane destroyed the dam. In South Glastonbury, Louis W. Howe operated a water company to supply piped water to that part of town. His reservoir was located in the Evergreen Lane area on Chestnut Hill.

The fire districts as self-financing bodies were not very successful. South Glastonbury managed to keep in the black, but collections in other areas lagged and in spite of sizable donations by industries such as the J. B. Williams Company and Roser's Tannery, the town eventually had to help out by paying the bills for fire engines and pumpers and other equipment as the volunteer fire companies were organized. During World War II, when thoughts of fire came uneasily to mind, the town voted to establish a town-wide Fire Commission. At the same time, 1943, an East Glastonbury volunteer fire company was organized and all the fire districts combined into three, each area being serviced by its own volunteer company. By the mid-60s, one more volunteer company had been organized and two new firehouses built, so that most areas of the town were within two miles of a fire station.

Back in the 1920s when the volunteer fire companies were being organized, Glastonbury's police protection was provided by constables, as it had been ever since the settlement of the town. Model Ts rattled blithely along Glastonbury's roads for years untroubled by traffic officers (except for an occasional zealous constable). In 1927 one of the six constables, Michael Muccio, was appointed Chief and provided with a police cruiser. Chief Muccio was on call 24 hours a day for the next (and final) 10 years of his life. He was killed in a car crash shortly before a legislative act creating a police department for Glastonbury went into effect in 1937.

Soon the new department bought a new cruiser and installed a two-way radio set-up. It was the start of a modern Police Department, heretofore not really needed but, as it happened, with a town-paralyzing hurricane, then wartime blackouts and finally an influx of new residents commuting back and forth on a new expressway, it was fortunate that the town had acted when it did to protect adequately the safety of its people.

The depression of the 1930s hit the town hard. A reflection of the severity of the depression here was the unusually large amount of un-collected taxes during this period. The depression had made tax-paying such a burden that it was decided to divide the annual tax payments, normally due in full on April 1, in two equal installments, the first being due April 1, the second on July 1. The two-payment system, voted by town meeting in March 1931, stayed in effect until the town made a changeover to the Uniform Fiscal Year in 1966.

It was the depression, creating an increased load of charity cases, that prompted the town to seek special legislation from the General Assembly to set up a Welfare Commission for Glastonbury. A Board of Public Welfare took office on January 1, 1940. For the first time, Glastonbury began to use the term, "welfare." For years the town had carried its welfare accounts under the heading "Poor of this Town," changing the category to "Charities" in 1911. Until well into the 20th century, the names of all those receiving public aid, including those supported in the Con-necticut State Hospital for the Insane, were published in the town reports. Probably these days such public notice would be considered an invasion of privacy.

Local welfare costs had been climbing all during the depressed '30s, but with President Roosevelt's federal relief program plus some state aid, the local total spent was far less than it otherwise would have been. It was the beginning, really, of a schedule of more and more financial assist-ance to various departments of local government from federal and state levels of government. And it gave, in effect, though few ever took notice of it, a measure of property tax relief for over-burdened local taxpayers.

Some financial help for the town and its depression unemployed came from the monumental alphabet programs put into effect by President Franklin D. Roosevelt. Grants for labor and truck hire for school and town projects came through from the PWA (Public Works Administration) and WPA (Works Progress Administration). Under one of these public works programs Glastonbury got a new brick post office built in 1936-37 on the corner of Main Street and Hebron Avenue. Over the years from 1806, when Glastonbury had its first post office across the street in Welles Tavern (the tavern-keeper, Joseph Welles, was postmaster), the flow of mail had demanded larger quarters (for the town's main post office) several times. The move to the new location was from the old Gaines Building on the west side of Main Street. The site chosen for the WPA-built post office necessitated the moving of the Gideon Welles birthplace, a handsome 18th century house which had been a Glastonbury landmark for many years. Incensed townspeople heatedly protested the federal government's choice of site but got nowhere.

In 1969, when the town's population had more than trebled its 1937 figure, the post office was declared too small to handle the enormous burden of daily mail and a new post office building was built on the old New London Turnpike, opening for business on May 25, 1970. Meanwhile, the town made plans to seek state aid to move the Gideon Welles house back to its original site, thus restoring the historic landmark.

In an almost uncanny stroke of foresight, the National Red Cross had sent out in 1934 an order to local branches to organize disaster relief committees. Mrs. James S. Williams, chairman of the Glastonbury branch, had responded promptly by appointing Richard S. Williams Disaster Relief Chairman. When the Connecticut River, which at flood stage rarely reached more than 27 or 28 feet, in March of '36 passed its previous recorded high and reached 30 feet, the Disaster Relief Committee was all set to go into action. Main Street was flooded to the north and south of Glastonbury, isolating the town except for the roads to the east. On March 19 the water rose rapidly, covering the Naubuc Avenue-Pratt Street area. By the time the flood crested at 37½ feet on March 21 it had forced the evacuation of 245 families. The three areas hardest hit were north Glastonbury in the Naubuc-Pratt Street area, Hubbard Street at Main south to Westview Lane, and South Glastonbury in the Nayaug area of Water Street and Tryon Street, Pease Lane and Ferry Road. The Academy and High Schools were among other scattered buildings flooded.

The town tackled its gigantic problem with remarkable efficiency. Led by the Disaster Relief Committee, hundreds of helpers pitched in, procuring boats to rescue the marooned, maintaining ferries, setting up cots in available halls and providing clothing and food with the help of the Red Cross. Under the direction of Dr. Whittles, then Health Officer, local doctors and nurses gave medical care and inoculated 1000 people against typhoid. (Several months later, 19 guests who had attended a wedding reception fell ill with paratyphoid-13, from eating potato salad contaminated by a "carrier" who had prepared it. All 19 were women. The men had escaped the disease because they had been inoculated against typhoid at the time of the flood.)

Like other Connecticut towns, Glastonbury had experienced floods before. The earliest recorded one occurred in March 1638 and began with "an exceeding great storm." It was recorded (39 years later) by Matthew Grant of Windsor, and noted also in Governor Winthrop's *Journal*. The next recorded unusual flood came in 1683 — or rather, there were two floods, one in July followed by another in August. They were mentioned in Mather's *Remarkable Providences*, published in Boston in 1684, as having completely destroyed the crops of Indian corn and "English grain." Others were recorded for the years 1692 (while Glastonbury was engaged in setting up its own Church Society and town government), 1801 (known as the Jefferson flood), 1841, 1843, 1854 and 1869. Although all of these were damaging, particularly those of 1854 and 1869, apparently none quite reached the height of the 1936 flood.

The Great Rain and flood of 1869 was probably the most destructive of any during the 19th century. Seventeen of the town's 18 bridges were destroyed by the roiling waters of the brooks, particularly Roaring Brook. In Eastbury the dams near the Crosby mill gave way, as did most other dams except the great one above Cotton Hollow. This huge stone structure withstood the strain, saving the two mills below and most of the Cotton Hollow factory village. But many of the little water-powered mills along the Glastonbury streams were damaged (up to thousands of dollars), and some had to suspend operations for several weeks. The Welles-Hollister grist mill and bake oven on Roaring Brook at Nayaug was completely destroyed. The mill was later rebuilt on the other (northwest) side of the bridge at the foot of High Street.

As it turned out, the great emergency effort in the flood of 1936 was in effect a dress rehearsal for another major disaster two years later — a hurricane. Ten days of heavy rain in September 1938 had soaked the ground, swollen the brooks and weakened the earthen shoulders of dams. On September 20, a cloudburst dumped tons of water on the forested hills of East Glastonbury, source of Salmon and Roaring Brooks. It was just too much for the ancient dams along the streams. Most of them gave way, and bridges were washed out along with adjacent roadbeds. The next day, September 21, the hurricane struck.

Like all towns in the path of this monster, Glastonbury was hard hit. Hundreds of the ancient beautiful elms and maples over-arching Main Street went down, blocking the road completely, and the uprooting and smashing were repeated all over town. Telephone and power lines were destroyed, gas mains damaged and many houses and barns damaged or demolished.

Former Conference House of First Church in 1936 flood.
This building, Main Street at Hubbard Brook, housed town's first
telephone exchange. (Courtesy of Mrs. Osgood P. Scribner.)

The next day the Connecticut River once again reached a very high flood stage, inundating the same areas which had suffered two years earlier. This time 96 houses were flooded and 900 people were evacuated, according to official report. This flood disaster posed a tougher job because of the tangled jungle of trees, wire poles and incredible debris. Lewis W. Stevenson, first selectman for many years (a plaza at the rear of the town Office Building has been planted and named in his memory) handled the emergency with speed and calm efficiency, directing the now experienced Disaster Committee.

Only the old-timers now remember the magnificent old trees, many of them planted centuries ago, along the town's principal thoroughfare, Main Street, once one of Connecticut's loveliest. These scars of the hurricane still remain, though a tree-planting project soon afterward got under way. In time these young trees may return to Glastonbury streets their former grace.

Although the hurricane of 1938 seems to have been the only recorded hurricane in the Glastonbury area, there was a violent tornado which swept through the town in August 1787. A report on this appeared in *The Connecticut Courant,* describing the phenomenon as a "tremendous hurricane" occurring at 3 p.m. on August 15 sweeping east through Stepney parish (Rocky Hill), crossing the river. In its course it flattened houses, barns, stone walls and trees, and killed a Rocky Hill woman, Mrs. Wait Robbins,

First Church, Congregational, Main Street, after 1938 hurricane.

and her 10-year-old son. Later a dress of Mrs. Robbins' was found caught on a barn belonging to her sister, Mrs. Joseph Moseley, across the river in Glastonbury. A sloop caught up in the river was hurled ashore on her beam ends. The cyclone passed through Eastbury and on eastward, petering out in Massachusetts.

A memorable event in the history of freakish storms was the blizzard of '88. These days the town is well-equipped to dig out the highways and keep traffic moving, but it was not always so. Once ox teams drawing sledges weighted down by men with shovels plowed the main roads, the manpower at hand for digging when necessary. So it was on March 11, 12 and 13, 1888. Ferry Lane was impassable for a week. "Selectman Moseley," said the *East Hartford Gazette*, "with a shovel brigade reached the East Hartford line on the 14th late in the day." There was no mail for three days. Yet the actual depth of the snow was only three and a half feet; it was the drifts, some 10 feet high, that caused the trouble.

Not long after Glastonbury had gathered its forces to meet the flood and hurricane disaster of 1938, it was faced with another mobilization effort. War clouds were gathering for the second time in a quarter-century. As in World War I, the mobilization of a World War II home front was the immediate local problem to be tackled. The first reference to defense preparations in Glastonbury's town records is in the annual report for 1940-41 on the Federal Educational and Recreation Program by its local

1938 hurricane damage to Buckingham Congregational Church.

supervisor, Emerson C. Reed. "During the past year," he reported, "the Adult Education and Recreation Program in Glastonbury has had a double job to do. The program has tried to give its normal services to the community and at the same time assist with the . . . demands brought on by the defense activities of our country." This program, which had included naturalization classes, English for the foreign-born, chair caning, nature study and other subjects, soon added to its curriculum the training of air raid wardens, auxiliary police, auxiliary firemen, first aid and home nursing training. These home defense training courses were set up at the request of a Defense Council organized late in 1941. First Selectman Donald H. Potter was chairman, but when he joined the Armed Forces, Martin Roser succeeded him to head up the Defense Council, later called the War Council.

On February 19, 1942, a special town meeting enacted an ordinance concerning black-outs and air raid protection. The ordinance, besides enabling the selectmen to order black-outs, provided for the appointment of special police from among the residents, giving them all the powers of the regular police and authorizing them to enter any premises within the town to extinguish lights. These special police were kept on as regular members of the Police Department after the war.

In 1917-18 there had been concern that the Huns might somehow invade the East Coast. But the uneasiness of World War I days became a conscious fear as World War II got under way. In place of the Home Guard units which had trained on local soil in uniform and with guns, in World War II air raid wardens patrolled the town and aircraft spotters were on duty around the clock.

Dr. Whittles organized and directed a comprehensive emergency medical service program, setting up casualty stations (fully equipped), nurses' registry, and procedures for health protection in the event of disaster. The need for such a program, and experience in dealing with major disruption, had been amply demonstrated in the two great floods and the hurricane of the '30s. J. Clair Dufford, as chief air raid warden, was another townsman who gave unstintingly of his time in organizing the town for a disaster which fortunately did not come.

By the end of the war nearly 1000 men and some 20 women had served in the armed services. Twenty-seven men gave their lives for their country: Harry E. Andrews, John N. Boeris, Theodore L. Chamberlin, Victor H. Comtois, Charles Froncak, John B. Kiesow, Matthew Kowynia, Frederick R. Lysik, Dudley W. Miller, Henry S. Paulman, Judson S. Ramaker, John Smyk, Frank J. Wachter, Steven J. Bemer, Goodrich Carl, William M. Connell, Charles Galli, Kenneth Kingsland, Francis J. Lewis, Edward Megson, Norman E. Miner, Donald R. Paquette, Herbert L. Pfau, Sterling L. Rocco, Mervin H. Sussman, Walter J. Zesut and Edward Polinick.

Mrs. Norma Sestero, who for many years was Glastonbury correspondent for the *Hartford Times,* edited a mimeographed newspaper, *The Home Town News,* which was sent during 1944 and 1945 to all the

G.I.s whose addresses she could acquire. (At that time Glastonbury had no local newspaper.) Besides chatty items about goings-on in town, the Home Town News carried excerpts from letters sent Mrs. Sestero by servicemen in all the major battle areas and outposts of that far-flung war, and from training camps around the U.S.A. Some letters came from boys who later were killed. Mimeographing and postage were financed by various civic organizations. Mrs. Sestero's service in getting such a paper to a large number of Glastonbury servicemen who were constantly on the go was certainly a major contribution to the morale of our local fighting forces.

Not until after World War II did any local newspaper manage to survive here. Though the town's expansion both in population and government services as the years went on created news in great quantity, it was brought to the people only through the columns of Hartford and East Hartford papers. *The Connecticut Courant* was brought to local subscribers by post rider very early, probably well before the Revolution. After 1817 the *Hartford Times* offered Glastonbury news, too. But it was many years before the town had a newspaper of its own. During the 1890s a weekly called *The Glastonbury Bulletin* was, published for several years. Meanwhile *The Weekly Gazette* (later the *East Hartford Gazette*) was covering East Hartford, South Windsor and Glastonbury, having begun publication in 1884. Though its Glastonbury coverage was later much reduced, the *Gazette* was the chief source of local news until 1948, when Mrs. W. Granville Taylor, Jr., published a short-lived weekly, called *The Glastonbury Bulletin* after its predecessor in the 1890s. In 1950, *The Glastonbury Citizen*, a weekly, was started by Louis Miller and acquired not long after by John Markham. Mr. and Mrs. Henry Hallas purchased this newspaper in 1953 and ever since have continued publishing *The Citizen*, which over the years has grown in size, news coverage, and circulation.

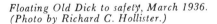
Floating Old Dick to safety, March 1936.
(Photo by Richard C. Hollister.)

Chapter X

Outgrowing Traditional Patterns:
From Town Meeting to Council-Manager

Glastonbury's growing pains, eased temporarily by World War II, soon became a constant condition, prompting ever-increasing efforts by the town government to keep the community fiscally healthy, and finally bringing realization that the form of the government itself must change if the town were to function efficiently.

When Pratt and Whitney Aircraft began operations in East Hartford in the late 1930s, it was the start of a new era, not only for East Hartford but for adjacent towns. Glastonbury, only a few miles south of the factory, was perhaps first in the surrounding area to feel the effects of a population push, as employees joining the fast-growing aircraft plant sought homes here.

Glastonbury's foresight in adopting zoning in 1930 had been remarkable, because at that time and for a good part of the decade very little new building was going on in town. Yet, realizing that a building boom might some day hit, the town created a Zoning Commission. It established three residential zones, a business zone in the Center and a small industrial zone. From 1930 to 1949, when there was an overhaul of the zoning regulations, there were numerous minor changes.

From the beginning the Zoning Commission had realized that flexibility in zoning would be necessary, and it was ready to deal with the subdivision problem when aircraft workers began to filter into the town in the late 1930s. Mrs. Laura Hale Gorton, daughter of J. H. Hale, the Peach King, one of the state's first women realtors, with the help of Charles and Felix Monzeglio, builders, started the subdivision ball rolling with a development tract in the old Hale orchard lands about 1937. But World War II slowed down any rapid building and it was not until after the war, when building supplies and labor again became readily available, that Glastonbury's population began to surge.

An early indication of what the future of Glastonbury's close proximity to the aircraft plant might mean was the construction in the north end of a federal public housing project for defense workers. Named "Welles Village" after the Welles family (early settlers) this project was accepted by town meeting in 1944. It has since been taken over by the town and operated as low-rental housing.

It was obvious after the war that the aircraft industry would not suffer from the cut-off of war contracts. Continuing defense orders, diversification and commercial contracts expanded the East Hartford plant into a large United Aircraft Corporation — and the demand for Glastonbury homes pressed on.

From the end of World War II to the present, population growth and all its problems have been the chief concern of the town. The influx of people from all parts of the country had far-reaching effects. New houses lining new streets gave Glastonbury a new look and a new character — suburban.

The change-over from rural to suburban did not come suddenly. There was no flash flood of jerry-built housing developments submerging the town in a sea of problems. The chief factor in the restraint of such a situation was the action of the Town Plan and Zoning Commission ("Planning" had been added in 1947) in revising the zoning ordinances in 1949. Already under way was the construction of the new Glastonbury Expressway which would lessen considerably the running time between Glastonbury and Hartford. Forearmed with the knowledge that this would open up the town still further for population expansion, the Commission engaged a planning consultant, Professor Flavel Shurtleff of Wesleyan University. Professor Shurtleff prepared land-use maps which guided the changing of zones, showing the need for vast new areas of single-family house lots with larger square-footage and wider minimum frontage requirements and more business- and industry-zoned areas. Since then there have been innumerable zoning changes as the town has grown in size and service needs. Many of these changes have been necessitated by the very makeup of the town's topography and sub-soil: ledgy hills, swampy areas and other factors bearing on drainage conditions. Perhaps because Glastonbury never became a member of the Metropolitan District Commission, municipal water and sewage systems have serviced very little of the town's far-flung area, though new sewers in the early '60s were installed to service Glastonbury Center, and sewer extensions began to crawl slowly through the southern and eastern sections in the '70s.

With many new families arriving in town in the 40s, already existing town services which had been adequate for a pre-war population of less than 7000 needed to be expanded and upgraded. More classroom space in the schools was the most urgent problem. In 1946 an addition to the High Street School was built; in 1947, an addition to the Naubuc School; in

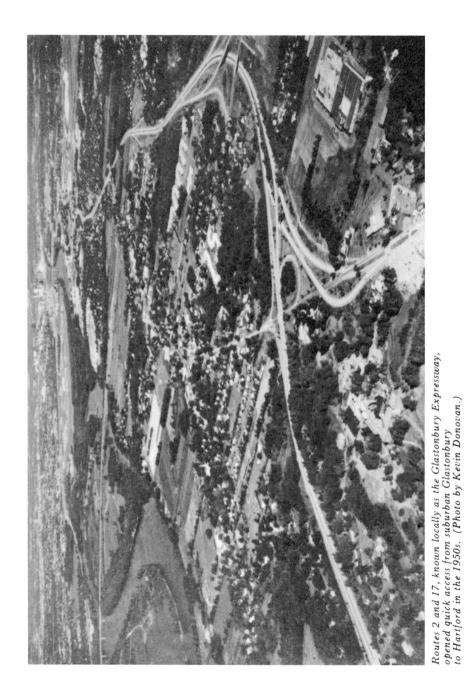

Routes 2 and 17, known locally as the Glastonbury Expressway, opened quick access from suburban Glastonbury to Hartford in the 1950s. (Photo by Kevin Donovan.)

116

1948, Eastbury School was built; and in 1952 a junior-senior high school went up on Hubbard Street. The decision to build this junior-senior high school, which was to involve the largest single expense in the town's history up to then ($2,002,900), came only after a long period of wrangling by the citizenry. One factor in the decision to build a new school rather than add on to the old one was that it would provide a suitable location for the World War II Memorial Gymnasium which a Committee of 21 had been endeavoring to find a place for since 1946.

In a 10-year period (1944-1954) the school population increased by more than 800. The overall population had zoomed by nearly 3000, almost a 50 per cent increase. It was obvious that still another school was needed, and in 1954 land was purchased on a service road named Buttonball Lane, put in while the Expressway was under construction. The Buttonball Lane School opened in 1955. That same year an $800,000 addition to the still-new junior-senior high school was begun and land purchased for yet another elementary school on Hebron Avenue.

The suburbanization of Glastonbury brought in its wake certain enduring benefits, perhaps the chief of which was the upgrading of the quality of public education. Newcomers took a keen interest in the sort of education their children were getting. And when teachers began to clamor for better pay in 1947, they got it. Superintendent Knox authorized a survey of curriculum needs, conducted by the teachers themselves in 1951. The "curriculum laboratory," so-called, was subsidized half by the town and half by the teachers, who met after school with two professors from the University of Connecticut working on theories, practices and materials necessary to put into being a unified curriculum for all Glastonbury schools. It was the start of a continuing process of curriculum development by the Glastonbury teachers.

Mr. Knox's tenure of 36 years was the longest of any superintendent of schools in the town's history. He was succeeded by R. Daniel Chubbock in 1953, when there were still schools at Addison and Buckingham staffed by only two teachers apiece. Yet the school system had become big business, with a budget of half a million dollars and over 100 employees serving more than 2000 school children. In 1956 Laurence G. Paquin succeeded Dr. Chubbock as superintendent. He was faced at once with problems of teacher shortage, demands for increased teachers' salaries, increasing demands from parents and a shortage of funds. The problem of teachers' salaries was to become a chronic one. Dr. Paquin's mention of "demands of parents" referred largely, probably, to an insistent plea for kindergartens, which the town had never had, though they had been advocated by Mr. Knox. Kindergartens were established at last in 1959 after several years of private cooperative kindergartens staffed by mothers.

During Dr. Paquin's brief tenure (he left in 1962) the school system embarked on a project which brought nationwide recognition to the town of Glastonbury: a $1,400,000 federally-sponsored program to develop audio-lingual materials for the teaching of modern languages. The Glastonbury school system entered into a two-year contract with the federal government in 1959 for a pilot program which convinced the office of the NDEA (National Defense Education Act) to proceed with the larger program. This involved the production of tapes, records and texts for the teaching of French, Spanish, German, Russian and Italian. It was the first time that the federal government had ever contracted with a local community for a special project in education.

Glastonbury was the central agency for the program, the local teachers working on the project forming the nucleus of a group which included researchers all over the country. It was found expedient to set up a "Glastonbury" office in New York, which was a convenient place for the professional experts to make their recordings and tapes. The government arranged with Harcourt and Brace, publishers, to publish the textbooks and teachers' manuals, all of which — and the tapes and discs as well — carried labels noting that these were the "Glastonbury" materials. For Glastonbury's service the town received approximately $140,000. With the money, foreign language laboratories (specially-equipped taping and listening booths with monitors for teachers) were installed in both the high school and the Academy Junior High.

The federal grant for the audio-lingual language materials project was a boon to Glastonbury, but it could not match the impact on the townspeople created by the bequest of $150,000 made to the town by Mrs. Harriet Welles Turner Burnham. Mrs. Burnham left this sum in her will for the specific purpose of building a town library as a memorial to the Welles and Turner families, with an additional sum of $200,000 for maintenance of the library. The money was released by the executors of Mrs. Burnham's estate in 1941, but there were so many delays for one reason or another that it was 10 years before construction got started on the location Mrs. Burnham had chosen, the site of her home on Main Street, Glastonbury Center. But perhaps it was worth the wait, for the Welles-Turner Memorial Library, opened in October 1952, was indeed a building fulfilling Mrs. Burnham's wishes, "not only proper and adequate for the housing of a library but an ornament to the town and a handsome memorial structure." In 1964 a 4400 square foot addition, financed by the Harriet Turner Burnham Fund, was constructed at the rear of the library, a functional box not visible from the street. In addition to the Welles-Turner Library, Glastonbury has two neighborhood libraries staffed by volunteers: the South Glastonbury Public Library, established in 1926, and the East Glastonbury Public Library, formed in 1960. Glastonbury's first public library was established by town meeting in 1895, with an initial appropriation of $200.

All phases of the town government showed the strain of the population explosion which began in earnest in the early '50s. But perhaps the greatest immediate concern was expressed by the Board of Police Commissioners. In 1952 the chairman, Joseph A. Goodhue, reported that Glastonbury's police budget was 35 to 40 per cent lower than that of the average town, and that furthermore two full-time officers and one cruiser were inadequate to protect the growing population, then about 9000. With a forthcoming special appropriation the commission added three more full-time officers and one more cruiser. Under Chief Terence McKaig's direction, up-to-date methods were put into effect, such as a teletype system, more systematic record-keeping, and outside training courses for policemen. A much-needed service was the Police Auxiliary Ambulance Association, established in 1954 with funds from a public drive carried on by the Police Department. Over the years the Ambulance Association has developed into a trained unit of 24 volunteers. Public subscriptions with a small assist from the town keep it going and have provided a garage and headquarters building behind the Town Office Building.

The impact on property taxes of the spread of residential development was noted early by all taxpayers. In the 10-year period from 1944 to 1954 taxes went up more than 50 per cent. Budget and tax rate continued marching along with the zooming population. The local government was becoming big business, though not until 1960 was a full-time accountant engaged to handle the ever-increasing number of town governmental transactions.

The death of Lewis W. Stevenson on August 10, 1953, was a severe blow to the town. "Lew" Stevenson had been a selectman since 1920, a record of 33 years in office, 27 of them as First Selectman. Over the nearly three-centuries' span of Glastonbury's Selectman-Town meeting government there had been a number of elected town officers with many years of service, but the 20th century apparently produced most of the long-term records. Both Republican and Democratic parties often endorsed the same candidates for certain offices. Robert O. Rider, town treasurer since 1921, resigned in 1956, completing a tenure of more than 35 years. Herbert T. Clark, first elected assessor in 1909, then registrar of voters in 1919 and at every town election from then until 1964, had a record of 55 years of service to the town. And this does not include his annual duties as an election official at the polls, starting in 1898, the year he was made a voter! Town clerks with long records include Thomas Welles, mid 1700s; Thaddeus Welles, mid 1800s; Frederick R. Curtis, 1896-1930; and John A. Miller, first elected town clerk in 1937, who served in that office until his death in 1970, a tenure of 33 years broken only by two years' duty with the Armed Forces in World War II.

The loss of its biggest and oldest industrial firm, the J. B. Williams Company, sold in 1957 to Pharmaceuticals, Inc., of Cranford, N. J. was sad news to Glastonbury. The soap factory on Williams Street, known familiarly as "J. B.'s", employed 230 local people. All except 70 were laid off when Pharmaceuticals moved almost all operations of the plant to New Jersey in 1960. "J. B.'s" had greatly expanded its production during the 20th century, having established a large plant in Montreal, Canada, about 1922, and later set up operations in England and Argentina. Over the years it had acquired such well-known products as Conti Shampoo,

Kreml hair tonic, Skol suntan lotion and Lectric Shave, and produced and marketed these as well as its own famous Aqua Velva after-shave lotion.

After the J. B. Williams Company was closed down here, a group of 10 former employees organized Glastonbury Toiletries and set up a manufacturing operation at the old plant. In addition to its own soaps and other products, Glastonbury Toiletries as the 1970s began was manufacturing on contract for the new Williams owners (Pharmaceuticals had bought the J. B. Williams name along with the business) all Williams shaving soaps and creams, the base for Conti shampoo and concentrated professional products for the beauty parlor trade.

The Consolidated Cigar Corporation, which had come into Glastonbury about 1920, leasing land for the growing of broadleaf tobacco, had become the town's biggest taxpayer by 1957. In 1924 Consolidated Cigar built a warehouse for storing and packing tobacco on Hubbard Street. Twenty-five years later the corporation built a warehouse and office building on Oak Street, which it greatly expanded in 1957. The many acres of gauze-tented shade-grown Connecticut wrapper tobacco were a picturesque sight in the Neipsic, Hebron Avenue, Keeney Street and Old Maid's Lane flat-land areas.

A considerable loss to Glastonbury's tax list was the closing of Roser's Tannery. Over the course of its 90-year existence, the tannery had maintained a wide reputation for producing quality pigskin. But technology was threatening its markets; plastics were superseding leather to a growing extent. Furthermore, Roser's, like the J. B. Williams Company, was a family-run business, and by the 1960s, the day of family-contained industries was on the wane everywhere. Large business corporations, constantly adding new enterprises to their holdings, controlled much of the nation's industry. When the Allied Kid Company of Boston made a purchase offer for the tannery in 1965, the Rosers sold. The tannery continued in business here until 1969, when the Glastonbury plant closed its doors.

Roser's Tannery buildings were bought in the fall of 1969 by Flanagan Brothers, Inc., manufacturers of engine parts for the aircraft industry. Flanagan Brothers, owned by James F. Flanagan and Thomas J. Flanagan, came to Glastonbury in 1957 and located their shop, then known as the Blue Hills Machine Company, on Nutmeg Lane. After the company bought the Rosers' buildings it made extensive alterations on the inside, moving in during the summer of 1970. Then the Flanagans remodeled the outside, cleaned up the adjacent millpond and stocked the pond with fish, giving fishing privileges to Glastonbury school and town employees, senior citizens, and boys and girls, as well as the firm's own employees.

One substantial taxpayer which kept its home base here was Arbor Acres Farm on John Tom Hill in the southeast part of town. The success story of Arbor Acres Farm, a poultry-breeding enterprise known worldwide, surpassed even that of the Hale Orchards of earlier times. It was, actually, the success story of the Hales' foreman, Frank Saglio, and his family. Frank Saglio arrived in America from his native northern Italy about the turn of the century and moved to Glastonbury six years later to take a job with the Hale Orchards. In time he became foreman, and by 1917 had saved enough money to go into farming on his own. He bought a hundred acres on John Tom Hill and began the operation of a family farm.

One of his five children, Henry, by the time he was 12 was spending most of his time raising chickens, which he housed in a discarded piano crate. With the help of Michael Aglio, who had come to live with the family, Henry had increased his laying flock to several thousand birds by the mid-'30s, and then decided to concentrate on poultry-breeding. Word of the new meaty broiler strain (the now famous Arbor Acres White Rock) which Henry Saglio produced by combining three distinct blood lines, spread rapidly. But by 1940 Saglio, realizing, as he later said, that "backyard hunches" could scarcely be relied upon, hired a geneticist, Richard Allen, When, in 1948 the farm was awarded the highest rating of all the nation's purebred entries at A & P's national "Chicken of Tomorrow"

Ebenezer Plummer House being moved down Main Street from Douglas Road to present site, 2094 Main Street, in 1947.

contest, Arbor Acres fame was assured. Diversified farming was now discontinued and brothers Charles and John Saglio joined Henry in expanding the poultry business.

During the 1950s the company set up coast-to-coast branches, including research centers. Arbor Acres acquired its first foreign plant, appropriately in Italy, in 1958, and gradually established other units throughout the world. The Glastonbury-based company had become an important international "agribusiness" and it attracted the attention of the Rockefeller-founded International Basic Economy Corporation, which was concentrating on expanding food production around the world. In 1964 IBEC acquired a controlling interest in Arbor Acres, and Henry Saglio became a member of IBEC's Board of Directors. Glastonbury's famous Arbor Acres poultry was produced and marketed by 18 plants in the U.S.A. and 23 plants overseas. For greater efficiency, many of these were consolidated later, some plants being enlarged and some closed down. By 1975 eight plants were being operated domestically, and 17 facilities abroad were producing and distributing Arbor Acres breeding stock to many countries, including the Philippines, Pakistan, Thailand and the Republic of China. The poultry stock goes into eastern European countries such as Czechoslovakia and Jugoslavia, and some has been sold on an experimental basis to Soviet Russia.

But Glastonbury's income from the taxes on all its business and industry — large and small — was not enough to counterbalance the expense of providing services for a booming population, as the decade of the 1950s got under way. Rising taxes spurred efforts to acquire a Town Plan which would guide development of the town in a more orderly fashion. There was a legal reason, as well, for instituting such a plan. State enabling legislation for zoning (1949 revision) specified that zoning regulations should be made in accordance with a comprehensive plan. By 1953 Glastonbury still had none. Professor Shurtleff's land use maps had been a first step. A more detailed design was needed, and in 1953 the Town Plan and Zoning Commission engaged a technical planning firm to prepare a new plan.

New maps, surveys and studies of various factors bearing on the town's geographical, economic and social makeup and potential growth were carried out by the professional planning concern, and new zoning regulations were drawn up. When all this material was completed the Plan was put before townspeople at public hearings. The package did not go down very well with the taxpayers who crowded the High School auditorium for the final hearing. Farmers, particularly, were incensed because a large amount of their acreage had been re-zoned, some for a minimum of 2-acre lots, some for a 5-acre minimum. Most of the farmers had no intention of selling their land at the moment, but all knew that in time their farms would have a residential value and they did not want this potential lessened. The large lot sizes had been specified for two reasons: to slow down development in outlying areas which would be costly to service; and to avoid underground water pollution in ledgy areas where septic fields would not function adequately.

The town bowed to citizen feeling. The 2- and 5-acre lot size requirements were deleted, and the 1-acre minimum specified for rural residential zones was extended to the rural (outlying) zone. A decade later a new zone, "country," put back a 2-acre minimum. But by then everyone was aware of the septic pollution problem. The new Plan, which had admittedly been geared to reduce the pressure of rising taxes insofar as seemed possible, increased the areas zoned for industrial use. As time went on, more and more land was zoned industrial. But industry was slow to take advantage of the sites made available by zoning.

Way back in the 1930s, the Town Zoning Commission had pointed out in a soft aside that the time was coming when a new, more businesslike form of town government would be needed. But almost a quarter of a century went by before any action was taken on this tentative suggestion. It was the League of Women Voters, organized locally in 1950, which spearheaded the movement for a new form of town government for Glastonbury. At a town meeting in October 1952, the League introduced a resolution calling for the appointment of a committee to look into the matter of changing to a more efficient local government system. The motion was "unanimously carried without discussion," noted the annual Town Report for the fiscal year ending August 31, 1953.

The committee was duly appointed. But progress toward such an object — complete turnover of a nearly 300-year-old government — was slow. When the committee finally reported back to town meeting 15 months later, it made no recommendations. The reason given was that the committee had not been directed to make "specific" studies. The committee was dismissed and another immediately appointed, empowered to make "specific suggestions" for "a more suitable form of government." In November this committee gave its report and its endorsement of a change from the old Town Meeting-Selectmen form to the Council-Manager system. The report was "accepted and placed on file." Five more years were to pass before the town, after due consideration, much publicity and free-for-all hearings, was able to bring itself to the point of scrapping the old — the time-honored grass-roots New England small-town democratic system where everyone, if he wanted to, could have a voice in town meeting — and instigating the new — the modern, efficient, businesslike Council-Manager government.

Chapter XI

The 1960s to the 1980s:
New Responses to New Challenges

The setting up of a modern town government at the turn of the 1960s came none too soon. Serious problems loomed as the century advanced. Glastonbury faced the dilemma of responding to the needs of modern times while trying to preserve the quality and character of its historic, rural environment. In the decade ahead the town would be confronted with multiple problems, mostly stemming from the population growth of the entire area: problems of land use, of pollution, the restiveness of youth, and persistent pressures from the "core city," Hartford.

Changing the form of government took time. Under the provisions of the new Home Rule Act, voted by the Legislature in 1957, Glastonbury adopted a charter, something the town had survived without for nearly three centuries. This charter, drawn up by a nine-member committee and approved by town referendum in 1959, provided for a Council-Manager form of government. The new government, headed by a nine-member Town Council, was elected in October 1959. Sayre B. Rose was elected first chairman; regrettably, ill heath caused him to resign soon after. Richard G. Williams was named in his place and served for 10 years.

In the midst of preparations for the change in town government, the question of a larger, more suitable town hall had to be faced. Since 1930 the town offices had been located in the brick Second District School at Main and School Streets, which had been vacated when the elementary Academy School was built. By 1955 the old school, pride of an earlier generation, was almost at the bulging point with the pressure of ever-increasing town functions. Town officials, board members and Town Court used the rooms in relays. With the prospect of one of the most important construction projects the town had ever undertaken — a new Town Hall — a public building committee was established in October 1955. The committee spent a year studying possible locations for the office building, finally selecting a site on Main Street diagonally opposite the Academy School. At town meeting on October 8, 1956, the site was approved by a close vote (202 in favor, 197 against). The office building was dedicated in March 1960, in time for the welcoming of the new town manager.

Fifteen sessions of interviewing applicants for the position had been held by the Town Council before it made its choice for town manager: Donald C. Peach, who was at that time assistant town manager of Bloomfield.

The year 1960 was one of difficult transition. But the changeover from the old Selectmen-Town meeting system was accomplished with creditable smoothness by the able young town manager. Mr. Peach understood well the nature of the problems that lay ahead, and in his first annual report to the townspeople he warned of "constant pressures for more schools, public works projects, and other capital items as well as higher costs for municipal operations . . ."

His admonitions accurately forecast the sixties. At the start of the decade the population had reached 14,497, an increase over the 1950 figure of 64 per cent. During the next ten years the number of people who called Glastonbury "home" would continue to grow, though not quite as fast.

Annual town expenditures tripled during the '60s (from 2.5 million in 1960 to 7.6 million budgeted for 1970). As might be expected, the main cause of the increased cost was the greatly enlarged school population, which grew from 3479 in 1960 to 5590 in 1970. When Mr. Peach arrived, the Academy elementary was being converted to a junior high at a cost of $900,000, a wing on the Hebron Avenue School was being completed, Buttonball was getting an addition and the next year would see the start of a new school, Hopewell. The need for new schools and additions to existing ones would continue through the decade.

The policy-making body of the new town government, the Town Council, met regularly to pass on a wide range of projects and proposals. The Council that first year adopted personnel rules including fringe benefits for town employees; organized a central accounting and purchasing operation for town departments; codified town ordinances (with the help of the League of Women Voters); and authorized the seating of Circuit Court #12, which supplanted the old Town Court, in the Town Office Building. In the course of its long history, the Town Court had handled chiefly minor local cases until the increasing popularity of the automobile began to crowd the docket with traffic cases mainly involving out-of-towners. It had thus ceased to be a strictly local court.

A major proposal of the Council in its early years was to change the town's fiscal year which for as long as anyone could remember had begun on September 1, to a year beginning on July 1. The new arrangement, known as the Uniform Fiscal Year because it conforms to the fiscal year of the State, was adopted by town referendum in 1966.

When the town had decided to abandon its centuries-old Town Meeting form of government, many townspeople wondered if citizen participation in town matters would be a thing of the past. The opposite turned out to be true. For many years past, a principal motivation of public interest in town affairs seems to have been a desire to keep taxes down. About the only exception was the matter of education. During the last century there had been spokesmen advocating better and more schools, better and better-paid teachers, school buses, kindergartens and so on. Still, plenty of tight-fisted Yankees opposed all increased expenditures, on general principles!

But as the 1960s got under way, public interest in other areas of community well-being began to be evidenced — in protection of the environment and in planning for the town's future growth. A subject of relatively new concern was the need for conservation of open space and protection of water resources. In the fall of 1961 the Town Council established a Conservation Commission "to review and suggest definite conservation programs." This significant step was largely the result of prompting by the Glastonbury Sub-Chapter of the Nature Conservancy, a national organization formerly known as the Ecological Society of America. The Glastonbury conservancy group received its charter on the same day as the Connecticut Chapter of Nature Conservancy, April 30, 1960, with the specification that it be known as a sub-chapter because Glastonbury was the only community in the country to form a local Nature Conservancy chapter, all others (there were then 14) being state chapters. In its concern for the ecological environment, Glastonbury was 10 years ahead of the times.

The Conservation Commission's first project, a major one, was to propose the town's purchase of a large tract of land bordering Neipsic Road, 188 acres, including a reservoir, owned by the J. B. Williams Company, which had been bought by a New Jersey firm and was moving out of town. The commission wanted the land for a town park and recreation area, with 20 acres to be used as the site of a future junior high school and 39 acres for "future general town purposes." Although the purchase price was $230,000, the net cost to the town, after grants from the Hartford Foundation for Public Giving, the state and the federal governments and a modest sum for a power easement, was $121,860. This project, which involved a considerable expenditure of taxpayers' money — for once only partially for a new school — was approved at a voter referendum, the land bought and the park established. The Gideon Welles Junior High School was built at the east end of the property in 1967.

An important gift to the town was the public swimming pool located on the east bank of Roaring Brook at Hopewell Road, presented by the Glastonbury Grange in 1960. (The Grange adds color to Glastonbury life with its annual October Grange Fair held on the grounds of the old Community Club in South Glastonbury, preceded by an elaborate, high-spirited and colorful parade. Great crowds line the parade route for this Saturday spectacular and attend the fair with its old-time cattle-drawing and greased-pole shinnying.)

In 1964, a group of 15 private citizens presented 51 acres of scenic property in the Cotton Hollow area of Roaring Brook to the town for a nature preserve. Other public-spirited citizens gave abutting land. Now the scene of Sunday walks, the area was once South Glastonbury's industrial section: Pratt's Forge, the powder mill of Revolutionary days, the 19th century stone mill with its 50-foot dam, a saw mill, grist mill and ancient iron works.

The Conservation Commission, continuing its policy to preserve open land along Roaring Brook to prevent pollution, acquired Smut Pond in Hopewell, a gem in a setting of natural beauty, deeded to the town by the J. T. Slocumb Company in 1967. Smut Pond, also known as Brainard Pond, was the site of the old Wassuc Company twine and cotton mills a century ago. Other major acquisitions were the Shoddy Mill — Coon Hollow nature preserve, a 77-acre wetlands area in East Glastonbury near the source of Roaring Brook, and the Lambert lowlands bordering Smith Brook at Main and Hillcrest, purchased by the town with the aid of federal and state grants.

While the Conservation Commission was quietly seeking the gift or purchase of "open space" lands, the newly-appointed town sanitarian was conducting a study of the purity of local brooks, streams and drainage ditches. It should have been no surprise that he found considerable pollution in all parts of town, with raw sewage and industrial wastes emptying into streams and thence into the Connecticut River.

Some years ago, a series of small sewer lines had been piped through the back yards of houses near the Center, and a small sewer had been installed down Main Street to the vicinity of the Moseley farm; all these lines emptied into the nearest streams and flowed directly into the river. In the 1930s the State Water Commission had called for a stop to such pollution practices, and to the town's increasing industrial pollution. But little was done until in 1960-62 a primary sewage treatment plant was constructed behind the Academy School and a new sewage line installed through the Center. By 1965-67 there were major sewer extensions in the Salmon Brook and Hubbard Brook drainage areas. Then, in 1968 the State Water Resources Commission ordered the town to construct a secondary treatment plant. The town voted approval of the needed bonds in 1970 and the new water pollution treatment plant was built at a cost of $6,500,000, the federal government contributing 55 per cent of the cost and the state, 30 per cent. The plant went into operation in March 1973, and in June the State Department of Environmental Control's protection tests indicated that the new facility "was delivering an effluent of excellent quality." Meanwhile plans were laid for a six-and-a-half million dollar sewer project in the Roaring Brook drainage area of South Glastonbury and Hopewell, presently under way.

Long needed, but hard to face up to because of the cost, public sewer projects will continue through the final quarter of the 20th century, reaching even into the far corners of the town. So said Alvin L. Bean, the town's Public Works Director, who has predicted that by the year 2000, 90 per cent of the town's area will be serviced by sewers.

Improvement of the environment was a major concern of civic committees appointed by the Town Council during the '60s. A Heritage

Committee was named to maintain the colonial character of the town; a Historic District Commission to regulate a short-lived Historic District on Main Street; a Water Resources Commission; a Refuse Disposal Commission; a Community Beautification Committee, and others. Toward the end of the decade the Town Council adopted a 5-year Community Development Action Plan (CDAP) under provisions of the State Department of Community Affairs, and appointed a Citizens Advisory Committee to review the town's needs in housing, economic development, public utilities, culture, and other aspects of Glastonbury life.

The "position papers" prepared by this group in April 1970 brought to light some jolting statistics on Glastonbury's changing status. A survey of Police Department activities during 1961-68, for instance, revealed that criminal arrests in the town had increased 99 per cent in that 7-year period; motor vehicle arrests, 331 per cent; automobile accidents, up 69 per cent; and complaints (in general) had increased 61 per cent, while the population of the town had grown by only about 33 per cent. Among other suggestions, the committee recommended that the police force numbering 31, including one policewoman, be increased.

Obviously, Glastonbury was no longer a "small town." The CDAP group found need for an addition to the 10-year old Town Office Building, including more space for the Police Department. Other space expansions for town purposes recommended by the committee included enlargement of the landfill dump area, on the old New London Turnpike. The landscaped landfill dump (considered a model of its type) established in 1966, had been designed, with the best professional advice, to last 25 years. But by the mid-'70s its capacity was nearly exhausted because the amount of waste an affluent society could accumulate in a short period of time had been greatly underestimated. The proximity of the dump to Roaring Brook also limited the possibilities for extension. A dreary search for other sites began. One was found on Old Maid's Lane, South Glastonbury, suitable for tree stumps and branches, and this area went into use in 1973. In August 1974 a large tract on Tryon Street bordering the Portland line was optioned for future landfill dump use whenever the New London Turnpike site had to be closed off.

A major environmental problem tackled by the town government in the latter half of the '60s was that of planning and zoning for land use. A Town Plan which had gone into effect in the mid-'50s was judged to be pretty much outdated ten years later. Actually, much of the land the Plan had earmarked for certain uses still remained underdeveloped. It seemed sensible to review the Plan and update it. A firm of planning consultants was engaged in 1965 to undertake this work, financed largely by funds from the federal government. At about the same time the town engaged its first professional planner to act as executive for the Town Plan and Zoning Commission in handling applications for subdivisions and other developments and in generally providing liaison between various town agencies (engineering, sanitation, etc.) One of the first suggestions to come from this new office was a proposal to redevelop the Glastonbury Center area, which was fast becoming traffic-choked, while nearby acreage remained inaccessible and unused. In 1966 a Redevelopment Agency was appointed to work on the project and to apply for federal funds for it.

Both projects, the revised Town Plan and the Center Redevelopment proposal, in the works simultaneously, took time to prepare. Both had setbacks. A preliminary Town Plan, put before the TPZ in 1969, was sent back to the consultant firm for revision; and a proposed Center Redevelopment plan was voted down at a town referendum in June 1969.

A new town Comprehensive Plan of Development was completed in January 1970. Intended to guide Glastonbury's growth until 1986, the Plan was presented in the form of a map (compiled from data in a 230-page report) showing recommended locations for future highways, schools, and zones for residential, industrial, recreational, institutional uses and so on. According to its spokesman, the Plan outlined "the logical continuation and projection of the town's current direction of development." It provided for a principal commercial district in the Center, with "mini-cluster" neighborhood commercial areas at South Glastonbury, Buck's Corners, East Glastonbury, Mill Street-Hebron Avenue, and Manchester Road-Hebron Avenue. Some of these were once the centers of rural Glastonbury hamlets which grew up around 19th century factory sites. The accepted Plan also endorsed the town's efforts to preserve open space, greenbelt areas bordering brooks, and the Glastonbury riverside meadows.

In an April 1970 referendum, Glastonbury people, reversing their earlier vote, approved the Center Redevelopment project by voting to appropriate $495,000, the town's share of the projected $6.5 million cost of the plan. The Center renewal, which town officials estimated would take at least five years to complete, was the most ambitious plan for the development of Glastonbury ever to be undertaken in the nearly three centuries of the town's existence.

The latter half of the decade of the '60s was in some ways a period of social strain for Glastonbury residents. The great surge of unrest which swept the country — opposition to the undeclared war in Vietnam and revolt of the youth; "core city" problems of race and over-population; lack of low-income housing and protests of minority groups — all these had their effect on Glastonbury, as on many other urban and surburban areas of the country. Not surprisingly, the schools were first to reflect the unrest. Dr. Hugh McG. Watson, arriving in 1966 as the new Superintendent of Schools, was faced almost at once with the problem of involvement with Hartford's black ghetto school situation — in short, with "busing."

A two-year plan to bus elementary Black pupils from Hartford's North End was submitted by the State Board of Education to several suburban towns, including Glastonbury. Some towns accepted the proposal. It was a heated issue in Glastonbury, many residents being wholeheartedly in favor of the plan, others just as vehemently against. But it was up to the Board of Education to make the decision, and when the final votes were cast, it was a tie vote. The proposal was lost, The next year, '67-'68, the subject of busing came up again, this time under the title of "Project Concern," administered by the Hartford Board of Education. Meanwhile the Glastonbury Board of Education had studied the results of the previous year's experiment. The Board again voted and this time the measure was passed. Forty-six youngsters from Hartford's North End were bused into Glastonbury in the fall of 1968 to join with pupils (almost all white) in the Hopewell and Eastbury schools, costs being borne by the Hartford Board of Education.

Project Concern pupils from Hartford continued in the local schools, which by the year 1973-74 had a minority enrollment (excluding the "Project" children) of only three per cent. In that particular year an additional 50 pupils were sent to Glastonbury under a federal grant which supplied extra teachers for the affected grades, K (kindergarten) through 5, making a total of 85 outside enrollees. The next year the federal grant was not made (no reason was given by the federal office), but funds granted to Hartford for busing purposes still allowed extra children to enroll in Glastonbury schools. A racial breakdown of the local school population for '73-'74 showed that, of a total elementary school population of 1776, there were 39 Black students, 50 "Spanish-surnamed" Americans, and 15 Asian-American children.

In the 18th century, Glastonbury had had considerably more Black residents than in the 20th, as noted in an earlier chapter. The number dwindled rapidly all through the 19th and 20th centuries (one of the last descendants of Glastonbury slaves being Bill Russell who, older residents may remember, lived at the Town Farm. His ancestors were slaves belonging to Noah Tryon and Alexander Hollister). In the early 1960s, the number of Black families living here could probably be counted on the fingers of one hand. But Negro families slowly began to move back into Glastonbury, some buying houses in middle-to-upper-middle income neighborhoods. They were professional people, mainly, a few teaching in the Glastonbury school system. (Superintendent Watson recruited actively for teachers at Hampton Institute in Virginia). A study of the school population makeup in the fall of '68 revealed that there was a total of 20 Black pupils whose homes were in Glastonbury, four in high school, three in junior high and 13 in the elementary schools, out of a total school population of 5198. There were also 10 pupils of Spanish-American extraction, a totally new ethnic group to make its appearance in the old Yankee town.

The opening of a large addition to the Naubuc School coincided with the start of the new decade in January 1970. The addition was the first school building in the state constructed on the "open space" classroom plan. Most of the classroom area is arranged in triple or quadruple units without permanent partitions (dividers being movable); second-floor units are grouped around a sky-lighted library center. For acoustical privacy, floors are carpeted, ceilings acoustical-tiled, and most walls covered with tackboard. The auditorium doubles as a cafeteria, and the stage, classroom size, is used also as a music room. The gym has a separate entrance and may be sealed off from the rest of the school for use as a community recreation center during evenings, weekends and vacations. In compliance with a recent state law, the two-story addition has an elevator, chiefly for the use of physically handicapped pupils.

The year 1970 also marked the start of a major school construction program — that of a new high school addition which, together with the existing high school, would accommodate 1800 pupils with "core facilities" for expansion to a 2400 pupil capacity. For the past five years school enrollment predictions had indicated the need for high school expansion after 1970. Though Glastonbury's birth rate, like that of many other Connecticut towns, was leveling off, migration into town was continuing at a good clip. The past decade's 40 per cent increase in population was bound to keep the schools filled for some time to come. In line with the kind of citizen participation in town affairs noted in an earlier chapter, representatives of the community had met together in 1968 as a "school facilities study committee" appointed by the Board of Education to look into school building requirements for the next decade. The report recommended, among other projected school needs, the building of the high school addition, estimated to cost $7,265,000. This large addition, completed in October 1973, was the town's chief building construction project of the early '70s. Foremost in the designing of the addition was a new emphasis on creating recreational facilities for the community as a whole, as well as the students. The new structure was primarily an athletics and auditorium complex. The auditorium, large enough to seat 1200, was named in memory of Francis S. Knox, who had served the town as superintendent of schools for 36 years, starting in 1917. The mammoth gymnasium, dedicated as a Veterans' Memorial, included a large indoor swimming pool. For some time previously, residents of the north end of town had clamored for a swimming pool in their own neighborhood; others, like East Glastonbury and Hopewell, already enjoyed such privilege. A north end pool had been decided against, however, as being an expense the town could not take on. But now with an indoor pool proposed for the high school addition (a proposal which had been turned down years earlier as being too pampering) a solution to the problem seemed ready-made. The high school pool could very well serve as a community pool for general use after school hours. The idea went over nicely. The pool and athletic facilities, as well as the auditorium, are given consistent use by Glastonbury residents.

The fact that Glastonbury was about as close to an all-white suburb as any town could be in the closing years of the 1960s pointed up its still insular character. Scarcely 10 or 15 minutes away from Hartford, the community seemed far-removed from the troubles of the city. Up until the advent of "Project Concern" Glastonbury had remained pretty quietly on the sidelines, going about its own business and proceeding with local government much as it always had. A gesture the town had made in recognition of the gathering problems of the urban and suburban area had been to join the Capital Region Planning Agency in 1960, sending two representatives to help in "coordinating local planning among towns in the Hartford Area and . . . formulating plans for the development of the Area as a whole." During the school year 1967-68, the Board of Education voted to affiliate with the Capitol Region Education Council and its subsidiary, Metropolitan Effort Toward Regional Opportunity (Metro), set up to act as a center for the sharing of certain educational services among the 28 member towns of the Regional Council.

The hesitant reaching-out toward other communities to give and receive help — a regional approach towards solving local problems — coupled at the same time with a strong urge to remain apart, to retain independent status as an ancient self-governing Connecticut town, created an "identity crisis" for Glastonbury as it began the decade of the 1970s. The very word "regionalism" spelled danger to some town officials. Yet without that label, both Glastonbury's police and fire departments had for years been acting in a regional capacity by cooperating with neighboring towns in apprehending lawbreakers who crossed town lines and in fighting fires of major proportions. An area in which the town had actively, though unsuccessfully, sought a regional solution was that of trash disposal.

But as the '70s approached, the whole regional concept seemed a matter of concern to local town leaders. Both Richard G. Williams, chairman of the Town Council, and Donald C. Peach, the town manager, in annual reports of the waning 1960s warned that Glastonbury's autonomy might be in danger, with the State taking over more and more of the responsibilities which were traditionally those of the towns. In his annual "Letter to Fellow Citizens" in the '67-'68 town report, Mr. Williams cautioned specifically against "regionalism, which can well lead to the elimination of town governments," and he asked that local citizens be on guard to oppose any bills presented to the General Assembly which would be "detrimental to Glastonbury and our sister suburban towns." In 1970, the 10th anniversary of the Council-Manager government, Mr. Williams retired as chairman of the Council. Mr. Williams' farewell letter to citizens qualified his earlier admonitions against "regionalism" by suggesting that neighboring towns work together to solve mutual problems. "I am completely convinced," he said, "that if we are to retain any semblance of local autonomy, we must cooperate to the greatest possible extent . . . with other towns. If we do not do this, I feel certain that it will not be many years before the State government takes over more and more duties of government until it finally assumes full responsibility and local, close-to-the-people governments cease to exist."

No one denied that environmental problems of the entire urban area were becoming increasingly pressing or that some of these, such as water and air pollution, could not be contained within town borders. Possibly, however, the issue which most worried town officials concerned the future of local zoning authority. By 1970 population pressures were great within the everspreading urban Hartford area. Glastonbury still had many acres of unused land (about 60 per cent of its total 34,321 acres), and professional urban trouble-shooters and regional study committees began to eye the cautious zoning practices of Glastonbury and other self-contained suburban towns.

The '70s continued many of the main concerns and developments of the 1960s. Preservation of the total environment, both man-made and natural, was a major ongoing aim. In spite of Glastonbury's geographical inclusion in an urban capitol region, most residents felt that the town had its own pleasant character and that as the town continued to grow an effort should be made to resist undue pressure from without and from within to turn it into Anyplace, U.S.A. Residents felt a continuing tug of war between the demands of growth and their desire to preserve the character of the town.

There could be no doubt of the pressures resulting from growth. The 1970 U.S. Census reported Glastonbury's population at 20,651, more than 42 per cent above the figure 10 years earlier. Furthermore, this population was highly mobile. Less than half of the people in town lived in the same house they had inhabited only five years earlier. The youthful segment (the under-18s) had kept pace with the general population growth, increasing from 5393 in 1960 to 7728 in 1970, or 43 per cent, placing new strains on the school system. During the same period those over 65 had also increased in number: from 1158 to 1455, over 25 per cent.

The sizable youth population, many of whose concerns mirrored those of young people throughout the nation in the concluding years of the 1960s, came to the attention of the local government. In various ways the town had set out to help those in trouble, or looking for jobs or companionship. Presently there was a Youth Services Commission, a Youth Services Bureau, a drop-in center and a special youth police officer. Among the duties of the latter was the conducting of a "Police Explorer Post," a pre-police training program for the 14- to 18-year-olds. Yet, though the high school age group was large, trends in the town's youth population were perplexing for the School Superintendent and the Board of Education as they made plans for the amount of classroom space needed in the future. The under-18 group was growing, but the birth rate was declining, and inflation had put at least a temporary damper on the building of new homes for young families with children. School Superintendent Watson reported in 1974 that forecasts beyond a five-year period could not be considered reliable. He cautiously projected a decline of about 650 pupils in the Glastonbury public schools by 1983 but warned that school enrollment predictions would have to be updated every year. He foresaw the need for no new elementary school construction during the next 10 years. But at the same time, pressure on upper elementary school classroom space was great enough to warrant the expansion of the 600-pupil

Academy Junior High to an 800-pupil upper elementary school.

Though increasing at a slower rate than that of the young, the numbers of elderly people living in Glastonbury were also continuing to grow. The needs of older persons had been formally recognized back in the '60s with the appointment of a town Committee for the Aging. Among other suggestions, the committee proposed the construction of housing for those over 65 with low or moderate incomes, and 55 specially designed residences were built with the help of state funds on a town-owned site off Hubbard Street in 1971. Forty more units were added here in 1982. Meanwhile in 1975 fifty residences for senior citizens, called Center Village, were built in the redevelopment area. After many years' delay, the Interfaith Housing project, Wells Street, got under way in 1982. A great boon to older people was the "Dial-a-Ride" bus donated by Flanagan Brothers, who had bought the Roser's Tannery buildings, and the George H. C. Ensworth Memorial Fund, a charitable trust set up by the will of Antoinette L. Ensworth for the benefit of public or charitable organizations in Glastonbury. (This Fund had also helped to establish the Youth Services Bureau.)

At the same time that Glastonbury was moving to meet the increasing needs of its population, young and old, it was taking steps to preserve the character of the town in which this growing population lived. Pressures from without were not easy to resist. More and more state and federal money was coming our way, often with strings attached, and though it was welcomed for the easing of the property tax burden as well as for its enormous help in construction projects such as the redevelopment of Glastonbury Center, it demanded in return a degree of local conformity to standards and goals set in the State Capitol and in Washington. The social and economic pressures which characterized the era also placed new burdens on Glastonbury: increased crime, for instance; the energy crisis; out-of-town investors proposing real estate developments which could radically change the appearance and character of the town; but most of all the unprecedented rate of inflation and a threatened depression. All these pressures impinging on the quality of life in Glastonbury and on the character of the town occupied increasingly the attention of the citizens.

Redevelopment of Glastonbury Center was a project which had been voted down in a referendum of 1969 in part because many townspeople were in doubt about the change it might force upon the character of the town. But something had to be done about the traffic snarls in the Center, and about the need of local businesses to expand. In a second referendum held in April 1970 the redevelopment proposal passed. An appropriation of $495,000 in local money was approved, representing one-eighth of the estimated total cost, the remainder to be borne by the federal government and the State. In October 1971 with the signing of a federal-town contract, this major face-lifting operation got under way. A Redevelopment Agency went into action, beginning negotiations with property owners which eventually enabled the town to purchase for re-sale to developers parcels of land in the 89-acre redevelopment area. By first acquiring title to the land, Glastonbury was able to control to some extent the manner in which development took place.

Rejecting proposals from some quarters to make the area uniformly "colonial" in design, the Redevelopment Agency permitted a variety of design styles, including contemporary condominiums, stores and offices, restored historical buildings, colonial-styled shops, a market mall with parking areas, and so on. At one end of the Center was an imaginative commercial-residential section called Glen Lochen, wherein even the land was re-contoured and full-grown trees were planted.

The Market Place, Glen Lochen, in the redevelopment area, gives old Glastonbury a new look. (Photo by Dick Matthews.)

Returned closer to its original site in the redevelopment area was the Gideon Welles birthplace, brought back in the summer of 1974 from its backyard exile in 1936, when the WPA-built post office had usurped its corner position as a Glastonbury landmark. Largely through the efforts of Richard E. Ballard, chairman of the Heritage Committee, funds were found to make possible the preservation of this historic building and to help in its renovation, for use mainly by senior citizens. Meanwhile the Glastonbury Bank and Trust gave the historic Welles-Chapman Tavern to the Historical Society, which moved the building across the street next to the Gideon Welles house. Local merchants provided materials at cost or made donations to help in the renovation of both buildings. In the former tavern, space is leased to tenants, thus providing an income for the property's upkeep and mortgage payments. With the relocation of a section of the old New London Turnpike, once known as Colchester Avenue, at its junction with Main Street and Hebron Avenue, the final phase of a program to change completely the rotary at Glastonbury Center began. The traffic bottleneck at the three-cornered rotary had exasperated drivers for a long time, and there was a general feeling of relief that the situation was to be remedied.

In one way or another as the town was refurbished, its heritage kept surfacing. A hundred years and more ago, the village of South Glastonbury had been a thriving part of the town, both economically and agriculturally. But during the early years of the 20th century, business had shifted to the north. As the final quarter of the century approached, there was interest in the renovation of what was once good and characteristic of the town. While the "up-north" Center redevelopment was getting started, the south end began to stir once again. A local builder, Edward Kamis, bought up a number of the existing old buildings in South Glastonbury's center and, joined by local merchants including the gas station proprietors, restored or remodeled the buildings. A group of businessmen organized a South Glastonbury Village Association, partly to foster community spirit (lighting street lanterns at Christmastime, for instance). New businesses set up shop in the restored buildings, a few new structures were put up, and in general South Glastonbury emerged with an attractive new-old image.

Community spirit was strong in South Glastonbury, partly because of the good-humored and much publicized doings of some of the residents of Nayaug, the old river-bordered area first settled three centuries ago by

Gideon Welles' birthplace, built 1782, as it appeared before its removal to make room for post office at corner of Hebron Avenue and Main Street. In 1974 it was moved back near its original position.

John Hollister and Richard Treat. A roadside sign erected in the 1960s at the Water Street approach to the Roaring Brook bridge announced "ENTERING NAYAUG . . . By-passed By Progress and Blessed By The Lord . . . Population — More Horses & Cows Than People . . ." From time to time the improbable goings-on in the little community were reported straight-faced in the columns of the Hartford newspapers. On one occasion Nayaug got mentioned in *Time* magazine, which noted the placing of a "Rattlesnake Crossing" sign to keep out developers. Publicity was also accorded Nayaug's efforts to prevent the town from paving Dug Road, "the last dirt road in town." Among the leaders of the fun was Nayaug's so-called mayor, James T. (Jim) Kinne, a direct descendant of Nayaug's founder, John Hollister. As time went on more and more residents far from the actual boundaries of the old Roaring Brook area took part in the Nayaugian festivities.

Nayaug's fun and games were clearly related to a deeply felt need for a sense of community throughout the town as urban pressures continued to change Glastonbury's former small-town character. When, early in the '70s, residents of the Buckingham area became concerned over town approval of what they considered an environmentally unfeasible development (without sewers or water) they formed the Buckingham Civic Association and brought suit against the Town Plan and Zoning Commission. In the end, the suit was settled out of court. The Buckingham Civic Association announced two basic purposes: to keep pace with needs of the residents, as they occurred; and to preserve "the present rural character of Buckingham." In deference to this expressed neighborhood feeling, the TPZ in October 1973 authorized the formation of a special East Glastonbury committee to make recommendations for a plan for a business center at the intersection of Hebron Avenue and Manchester Road which had been designated on the 1970 Town Plan. This committee, assisted by a professional planner from the State Department of Community Affairs, made suggestions also for all of East Glastonbury, particularly for its recreational facilities.

An earlier East Glastonbury neighborhood organization was the Diamond Lake Association, formed when the area was first developed in the 1940s. But the first such group in town was probably the South Glastonbury Community Club, begun in the 1920s. Both of these were founded essentially as social rather than civic organizations.

Following the lead of Buckingham, a neighborhood group in 1974 formed the Addison Bog Civic Association. The Addison area, which was beginning to grow for the first time since the Glastenbury Knitting Company had closed its doors, was giving signs of a speedy and rather dense development. It was here, near the East Hartford town line, that the town had recently purchased 3.8 acres as a site for an elementary school (though there were no immediate plans for building). Addison residents planned to keep an eye on the development and the association set up a policy to maintain the community's woods and provide picnic places, hiking trails and bicycle paths.

A neighborhood village center which could radically change Glastonbury's 300-year-old face was approved in 1973 for Buck's Corners. Here, on a 33-acre site, once the farm of Benoni Buck, a Revolutionary supplier, might rise a cluster of varied-purpose buildings, residential and commercial. Land for a new Congregational church at this location had been bought some time ago.

In the face of citizens' efforts to keep a sense of small-town neighborliness in the growing town, the fact could not be blinked that familiar urban ills were continuing to creep in. Police Chief Francis J. Hoffman reported in 1975 that crimes had increased greatly over the past year — mostly, as the Chief said, crimes against property rather than person. Not very long ago townspeople had thought nothing of going off for the day without locking a door or a window, and many never bothered to lock up at night. But times had changed. To meet the growing problem of crime, the town took steps in the 1970s to strengthen its law enforcement. It had financial help from the federal government through the Justice Department's Law Enforcement Assistance Association, which made possible the setting-up of a crime prevention unit with a specially-appointed crime prevention officer. This prevention work turned out to be so successful that, paradoxically, it resulted in the reporting of more crimes! Merchants who formerly suffered shoplifting without complaining to the police, at the behest of the crime-prevention worker began to report incidents of stealing. And so with other areas of unreported criminal or mischievous activity.

A "911" emergency reporting system, recommended by the Citizens Advisory Committee, was instituted in 1972, making Glastonbury a forerunner in the use of this centralized emergency dispatching program designed for eventual use the country over. In this system, the phone number 911 is the call-for-help number of police, fire and general disaster, and enables police to trace immediately the address of the distress call. The Fire Department, as one response to a growing complexity of emergency situations, organized volunteer rescue squads, the members receiving training in first aid and various rescue techniques. Some were scuba divers, some were police officers, and the units were available for use by the Police Department as well as the Fire Department. Glastonbury had had drownings from time to time throughout its history. Samuel Welles, a captain in the early colonial militia, drowned one day in 1675 while crossing the river. A descendant of his who drowned two centuries later was Oliver Welles, brother of Gideon. The setting up of rescue squads was a practical measure for a river town.

Fire Company No. 1 had occupied headquarters in the remodeled District No. 1 brick schoolhouse at the corner of Main and Pratt Streets since 1938, but in 1970-71 the old schoolhouse-fire station was torn down and in its place an up-to-date firehouse was built. Costing $405,000, the sleek modern structure houses not only fire fighting equipment but provides headquarters office and classroom space, a hose drying tower, communication equipment, and an emergency generator.

When a major ice storm with high winds struck the town in the pre-Christmas week of 1973, the Fire Department with its emergency generator was of enormous help. Firemen in all four companies and ambulance crews were on 24-hour duty, as were other town officials including Civil Defense Director Alvin Bean and Town Manager Peach. The town was very hard hit. So many trees were down from one end of town to the other that it looked as if the hurricane of 1938 had made a return visit. Complicating the business of getting back to normal was the mess the fallen trees and branches had made of electric wires and transformers, and the near-zero temperatures in the wake of the storm. The Connecticut Light and Power Company imported crews from out-of-state to help restore power, removing live wires and freeing the lines from fallen branches, but even so some areas were without electricity for seven days — and that meant for many no lights, no heat, no refrigeration, and, because so many people got their water from wells, worst of all, no water. Neighbor helped neighbor, and volunteers in great numbers offered service to the town. Glastonbury took a long time to recover from the savage effects of the storm. Yards were littered with downed trees and heavy branches for weeks, and roadsides in some parts of town were lined with piled-up branches for months awaiting the town pickup, which was gradually accomplished. For the first time in years, the Civil Defense Center was called into action to cope with a disaster. The storm, dubbed "Felix," cost the town more than $100,000.

Although Glastonbury had to protect itself against the unleashed forces of nature during the ice storm, the townspeople did not lose sight of the fact that the more usual circumstance was that nature needed protection from suburban man. Back in 1961 Glastonbury had got a lead on most local communities in the country by establishing a Conservation Commission to stand guard over the ecology of the town and to initiate open space preservation measures. By the mid-'70s this commission had accomplished a great deal, and enthusiasm for its work had spread. Additional open space acquisitions included the purchase of a 15-acre tract of wetlands on Coldbrook Road and a neighborhood playfield and part of the Addison Bog, as well as 30 ledgy acres west of Manchester Road near Hurlburt Street, deeded to the town through the open space provisions of the subdivision regulations. The commission also accepted conservation easements on a parcel of land bordering Roaring Brook near Ash Swamp Road, and another parcel along Salmon Brook. Through its conservation chairman, Mrs. Bertrand H. Brown, Glastonbury joined Wethersfield and Rocky Hill in setting up a Great Meadows Conservation Trust which was gradually acquiring river meadow land.

The Water Resources Commission, which had been appointed some years ago to study water supplies and make recommendations for keeping water free of pollution, in the early '70s was combined with the Conservation Commission. A principal aim of the enlarged commission was to analyze the environmental impact of all proposed local development. Joining the conservation fight was a high school Eco-action Group. One of its projects was the compilation of a list of open space areas worthy of preservation. Meanwhile the revised zoning regulations tightened up environmental controls and designated many of the town's brookside valleys and swamps for open space preservation.

Geologists had given the name "Glastonbury gneiss" to a type of granite rock formation which runs in a wide band across the town, and on northeast through the state. This granite underlying the topsoil was partly responsible for directing the residential growth of the town toward what the Citizens Advisory Committee feared might become a "homogeneous middle-to-high-income bedroom suburb." Erosion and seepage of waste water, particularly in these ledgy areas, continually plagued residents and administrators. It was expensive to guard against such problems, and home owners ultimately had to pay the costs. Low-cost housing was not practical; builders mainly produced high-priced homes, especially as inflation hit hard at mid-decade. This circumstance helped to bring into Glastonbury ever higher-income families whose spending habits influenced to a certain extent commercial enterprise, encouraging such businesses as specialty and gourmet shops, and tending to give the town a more sophisticated air than it had had in all its growing-up years.

The Community Development Action Plan (CDAP) which had been prepared by the Citizens Advisory Committee in 1970 in compliance with a state requirement for the granting of funds, reflected the desire of almost every town board to keep Glastonbury a village with its own distinctive character. In part the Plan was a summary of town board proposals, though it included some independent suggestions from the CAC itself. It covered many aspects of economic, social and administrative functions, and its suggestions made clear the struggle between growth and the preservation of environment and community character upon which growth was constantly encroaching. The increased services for young people and the elderly, expanded "protective" services, and measures for ecological conservation discussed earlier in this chapter were mainly implementations of proposals made by interested citizens participating through CDAP.

Citizen participation in every area of government is a tradition that goes back to the 1600s, even before Glastonbury became an independent town. Although many aspects of running the multi-million dollar town government are now handled by paid administrators, participation by citizen committees in recent years has increased. Concern for the quality of life is everywhere evident. For example, in March 1973 a special citizens committee on educational policy produced a report which included recommendations that the schools stress "awareness of differing values and a sense of our humanity" and "the role of aesthetics in the environment" as well as "the need for responsible use of natural resources." Con-

*Ancient houses still beautify Main Street.
Timothy Hale House, left, and Hale-Rankin
House. (Photo by Duffy.)*

sideration for the less fortunate continues high on the list of community responsibilities, as it had been 325 years ago when the town was first settled. At the mid-point of the '70s, the private Human Rights Council (organized some years ago through the efforts of a local doctor, a clergyman and other interested citizens) relinquished its duties to a town Human Rights Commission. Instances of discrimination against minorities reported to this Council had been very few, but its members felt a commission under the town aegis could operate more effectively. Among the new commission's duties would be the preparation of a plan for minority hiring and representation on town boards.

As the 200th anniversary of the American Revolution approached and history-minded groups everywhere began to make plans for a celebration in 1976, the Historical Society of Glastonbury called together representatives of about 60 local organizations to form a Bicentennial Committee. In February 1973 the Town Council accepted this group as an official town committee. Because of the program the committee had drawn up, following the themes of "heritage, festival, horizons" (signifying past, present and future) and presented for approval by the American Revolution Bicentennial Administration, Glastonbury was one of the earliest towns to be given a "certificate of recognition" as a "bicentennial community" and one of only about 1500 towns in the country then so designated.

Glastonbury had had another bicentennial celebration in 1853, this

141

one to commemorate the date of May 18, 1653, when the General Court of Connecticut Colony had first given permission to communities on the east side of the Connecticut River to have their own military training bands, which of course included our own community, then a part of Wethersfield. It was the first recognition the General Court had given of any corporate power in the colony except its own, and it is from that time that the town dates its first beginnings as a separate entity.

"Glastonbury's" celebration, held on May 18, 1853, began with the firing of a "national" salute of 31 guns and the pealing of all church bells. A crowd estimated at between 6000 and 7000 persons gathered to watch a parade, and come remained to hear a speech on the history of Glastonbury by the Rev. Dr. Alonzo B. Chapin and several talks by homecoming natives, including Gideon Welles, in a tent loaned by Yale College, set up on the Green. According to the style of the period, the talks were sentimental. Nevertheless, some of the sentiments expressed could well hold true today. Over the years Glastonbury has gone through great physical changes. But large areas of the town have not been marred, as many of Connecticut's old towns have, by great swaths of multi-laned super highways, neon-lighted strips, or by railroads. Its residents can still feel pleasure from the same things recalled by Reuben Hale in a letter which was read aloud at the bicentennial celebration on the Green in 1853: "There is to me a . . . pleasure in recalling my impressions of the dear old town: its green meadows and sandy hills, its sunny brooks and arching elms. Its pleasant walks and hospitable firesides remain now as they were then, for railroads and canals have spared them . . ."

The country aura which in 1853 had inspired such sentiments at Glastonbury's bicentennial celebration was still exerting its spell at the time of the nation's bicentennial in 1976. Strawberry fields beckoned pickers, luscious raspberries appeared on roadside stands and blueberries crowned Matson Hill, already blessed with peaches and apples. The ancient cider mill on Main Street pressed hundreds of gallons of cider in the fall, and piles of Glastonbury pumpkins made bright splotches of color to vie with the maples turning red and gold. And in the winter, cross-country skiiers could glide through open fields for miles, far from the noise of auto traffic. A 38-acre wooded bluff above the Connecticut River west of the Old Church Cemetery was acquired by the town in 1978 as part of its program of open space preservation. Here were bridle paths and pleasant walks. Nearby on Main Street the Connecticut Audubon Society in co-operation with a group of Glastonbury people interested in the environment set up, in 1981, the Holland Brook Connecticut Audubon Center in the old District Four schoolhouse which for many years, enlarged, had been used as the American Legion Hall.

It was partly the attraction of this nostalgic rural atmosphere that led the town into practical and philosophical conflicts with various units of federal, state and local government in the latter part of the 1970s. The very geological makeup of the town, with its ledgy sub-soil and flood plains unsuitable for highly concentrated building, contributed too to the impasse between the people and big government over the issue of low-cost housing. Continuing pressures from the economically distressed Hartford upon the surrounding towns for help in relieving the city's plight caused consternation in uncrowded Glastonbury.

In May 1979 Donald Peach resigned as town manager, an office in which he had served for nearly 20 years, ever since the town had changed its government from the Town Meeting to the Council-Manager form. His successor, Richard Borden, former town manager of Cheshire, arrived here to assume his duties as Glastonbury's town manager in October 1979. He came at a time when a decision had to be made as to whether the town should accept federal funds to help provide low-cost housing. In previous years the so-called Community Development Block Grant funds had been used for redevelopment of the Center. But with the Fair Housing Act's requirement that federal money must be used to help build low-cost housing, the townspeople raised objections to accepting the money and the Council voted to get out of the block grant program.

Meanwhile the neighboring town of Manchester was being sued by Hartford and the Federal Department of Justice for housing bias, and there were hints that Glastonbury, which had turned down two proposals for low-cost housing tracts, would soon have to contend with a similar suit. This threat materialized in December 1980, when Glastonbury was charged in a civil suit with violating the Fair Housing Act.

Largely because of the persistent lack of public sewers and water, the 1970s' plan for residential-commercial "village centers" was revised as the decade of the '80s got under way. There was as well opposition to the centers from neighbors in both Buck's Corners and Buckingham-Manchester Road locations. The plan was changed in 1980 to permit "convenience commercial centers", without low-cost housing in those two neighborhoods.

The South Glastonbury village center plan was left on the books, drawing opposition from the local people. South Glastonbury, long established and by now well supplied with water and sewers, had not changed much in outward appearance since early days, and its residents clung together to resist any potential encroachment on its placid community life.

By the 1980s Glastonbury's industrial development was beginning to forge ahead. The courting of industry to help out with the tax load had been going on for some years, and now these efforts began to bring results. The mills of heavy industries were nowadays not welcome, as they had been in the 19th century when smokestacks signalled prosperity. Still, in the 1970s it was generally agreed that a section set apart from residential areas for light industries or office buildings would be very desirable, and an Industrial Park, some 230 acres off Hebron Avenue, was established, attracting several enterprises of the sort the town wanted.

All these projects, designed to bring vigor to the old town, had given it a new look, but the re-design of the tri-cornered Station 35 intersection, one of the final steps in the Center Redevelopment, was the most striking change. A central Green, traditional for old New England towns, was something Glastonbury had never had, probably because it had originally been part of

Wethersfield, and its settlement grew up along a main street. The triangular traffic intersection that had plagued motorists, and maybe even horse teams, for years was re-designed with the closing of access to the old New London Turnpike. Down came century-old buildings, a fate, deserved or not, which had befallen a score or so of old structures over the five-year period of redevelopment. In their place appeared a wide expanse of Green liberally planted with shade trees, criss-crossed by sidewalks and embellished by a fountain. The central Green seemed a fitting ornament to the town, even though it had not originally been planned around a Common.

The 1980 census gave Glastonbury's population as 24,970. In the decade of the 1960s the town had grown by about 42 percent. The decade of the '70s came nowhere near matching the growth rate of the 1960s, but there was still a significant 17 percent increase in population.

The new families tended to be small, reflecting a nationwide trend. And expectations of a decreasing number of school-age children prompted the closing of a school for the first time in many years. The High Street School closed its doors to pupils in 1978. Since 1973, when the town's peak school enrollment had been 6000, the number of pupils had declined (in 1974 to 5848; in 1980, 5073.) The Board of Education's projection for 1985 was down to 4604, a big drop.

In the meantime, demands on town services grew heavier than ever. The Town Office Building, adequate when built in 1960, had already been outgrown when in 1978 a proposal for a large addition came up for approval in a referendum. It was turned down, apparently because the voters were opposed to increased taxes, prompting a cry of "negativism" from both Council and Manager. Various town departments began to seek space elsewhere. The Public Works Department took over half of the then-vacant High Street School, while the Board of Education, which had been burned out of its headquarters in the old J.B. Williams office building, occupied the other half until it returned to the rebuilt Williams building in 1981. Declining school enrollment made possible the use of one of the buildings of the Academy School for town offices. In July 1981 the Town Council voted to remodel the Academy "A" building (the original 1922 High School) to serve as Glastonbury's town hall and to turn over the Town Office Building to the Police Department. The Police, housed since 1960 in the basement of the Town Office Building, for some years had been pleading for more space. As the town had grown, so had the crime rate. In a voter referendum in November 1981 funds were approved to satisfy the space needs of both town and police administrations.

A year later preparations were made for the great move, and soon the administration would conduct the town's business in more spacious quarters. Here in the old Academy "A" building would meet the many town boards, commissions and committees manned by volunteers, appointed or elected. Time, as it headed toward a new century, had increased the pressures and the urgencies and the duties which these civic groups must undertake.

Glastonbury has had a strong tradition of public service for nearly 300 years. Its citizens, all along, have faced issues confidently, and many of these issues have been critical. Through all the years of Glastonbury's existence it has successfully managed to gain independence from its mother town, to live in peace with its native Indians, to participate in the American Revolution, to build industries, some known world-wide, to become a pace-setter in public education, to withstand disasters, natural and economic, to change the form of its government to suit the times, and withal, to grow old gracefully. If the course of the town's future is anything like its past, Glastonbury will continue to adapt to change while preserving those qualities which make it, for thousands of people, a favorite town in which to work and live.

Chapter XII

Toward a Fourth Century:
Change and Continuity

The '80s were just getting under way with a remarkably healthy economic outlook for the town, when on the planning agenda of the Economic Development Commission there appeared an innovative, ambitious and handsomely designed upscale-retail and office building complex first known as the Pointe Meadows Project. Why the final "e" on point never seemed to be explained. But it didn't matter. The name was soon changed to Somerset Square.

Somerset Square, which had been designed by the architectural firm of Robert A.M. Stern, well-known for his PBS series on "Pride of Place," became in effect a symbol for Glastonbury. A symbol of the new, young, upwardly mobile population beginning to augment the old-time Yankee makeup which had characterized Glastonbury for over 300 years.

The name Somerset had been chosen because of the town's original namesake, Glastonbury, Somerset County, England. The entire project was planned for an 80-acre site west of Main Street (opposite Griswold Street) on former tobacco land. That it covered floodland once off-limits for developers did not seem to hinder the project for long. Construction engineers drafted extensive and elaborate drainage systems and the PAD (Planned Area Development) plan proceeded.

Attractive retail shops were centered by a large square restaurant incorporating a series of small cafe-type eateries each featuring regional decor, with an upstairs disco, the whole dubbed The Great American Cafe. It was an ingenious concept and became very popular, particularly at lunchtime.

To follow the progress of Somerset Square from its inception on the drawing boards, its acceptance by the town and its impact on Glastonbury townspeople is, in a way, to trace the story of the economic enthusiasm and following disillusionment of the 1980s-into-the-'90s decade. For, as a recession loomed, the original ownership of "The Shops at Somerset Square" faltered, was reorganized and new ownership took over, trying to bring in more of Glastonbury's young and financially able.

It may have been Somerset Square's upmarket concept of what Glastonbury was or might be becoming, together with the burgeoning of great-house development in the town's eastern hills and other scenic areas, that inspired the Town Council's appointment of a Strategic Planning Committee in September 1985. Only a year before, an updated Town Plan of Development had been prepared and accepted by the Town Plan and Zoning Commission. But this, a state-mandated task, had to do with land use only.

Strategic planning, a corporate/organizational practice sometimes known as long-range planning, encompassed a long view of Glastonbury's future growth and needs. Explained the Preface to a final report made in July 1990: "It is our response to the charge from the Town Council to make the general public interest groups and town management more aware of where the town is now and where it wants to go ..."

Where it wanted to go, judging from details of the report, was just about where it had always wanted to go: to continue to be a semi-rural community, with protected open space along with managed growth; good schools; care for unfortunates; village service centers; reasonable taxes and a certain amount of industry (light) to help out the tax base. Some particular desirables were suggested including a light rail service and a theater for both movies and plays.

There were, of course, other suggestions — actually more than suggestions – recommendations and encouragements. For instance, "beefing up" the land acquisition fund, adapting zoning to encourage "affordable" housing, and generating "broad-based community support for our educational system."

The Strategic Planning Committee over the course of its five-year study compiled a great deal of information about the town, held public meetings, conducted surveys and enlisted the help of "hundreds" of residents. Three task forces to analyze issues, totaling 48 members, readily recognized the town's evolving demographics (an older population, more women working outside the home, single-parent households, and newcomers of various ethnic backgrounds) and in general took note of the new challenges in store for changing times. "The need to do more in less time ... has implications for our government, our leaders and our organizations and volunteers," one group summarized.

Undaunted by all these challenges, the Strategic Planning Committee envisioned an "ideal picture" of the town in 2020, which, in the Committee's own words "incorporates the values we seem to hold paramount and — despite some tinges of "motherhood and apple pie" — shows a concerned community open to the new, while preserving the best of its history."

The fiscal year 1984-85, when the Committee began its work, despite a bad flood in June '84 and hurricane Gloria in September '85, had been a banner year for Glastonbury. Richard S. Borden, Jr., town manager, reported that the town had ended the fiscal year in "an outstanding financial position." Financial good news continued for yet another year with a General

Fund surplus of over a million dollars and property values of almost $400,000,000, reflecting the extraordinary growth of population (over 18 percent in the last 10 years) and corporate/commercial development.

The times were euphoric. An Historic District was approved for a section of Main Street. There were enhancements such as concerts and the longstanding art and antiques shows on the Green. There was continued vigilance in preserving the environment (including a request for a rattlesnake caveat to protect that endangered species — 300 years after a town vote to pay bounties to anyone who brought in a rattlesnake tail with rattles still attached.) In all, measures were drafted by the local government to assure continuation of the good life in the town. There appeared to be full employment, a flourishing real estate market, and generous banks.

But by the time the Strategic Planning Committee had presented its report in July 1990 after five years of deliberations, Glastonbury was struggling with a new problem: a slowdown of the economy all over New England. The 9-member Planning Committee, augmented by the task forces looking ahead 30 years, had foreseen a rosy future. While it was generally agreed by the approving Town Council and others that this point of view was admirable, tough challenges had developed that needed to be handled.

No one could have guessed that a Hartford-based limited partnership, Colonial Realty, would cause economic trouble for a large area of New England. The ripple effect caused by the financial problems of this and other firms quickly reached Glastonbury. Presently the area's principal employers — United Technologies, Hartford insurance companies, and others — began a new trend labeled by the media "downsizing," meaning reducing the work force, some of whom were Glastonbury homeowners. The economy slumped, and with it the real estate market, the job market, and retail sales.

Glastonbury had been growing for years, as our suburban area had become more opened up through new highway construction and the Wethersfield-Glastonbury Putnam Bridge. Increased population meant increased problems: more traffic in and out of town and within the town, overcrowded schools, lack of space at Welles-Turner Memorial Library, the first appearance here of two recently identified diseases, Lyme Disease and "AIDS", and, of all unexpected and rare events, a murder, reportedly planned by two students of Glastonbury High School. The murder was committed in August, 1987. Dennis Coleman was convicted of the crime. He is said to have been assisted by others in carrying out details of the strangulation and removal of the body of Joyce Aparo, the mother of one of the group.

Seemingly in few other decades than that of the '80s into the '90s, except for periods of war and postwar times, has our town passed through greater change: the exuberance of good times followed by economic anxiety, and the perception of a nationwide lowering of traditional cultural values. Emerging on the horizon was a pervasive call for increased social sensitivity and attention to the problems of those not so fortunate as suburbanites. All this characterized the waning decade of the 20th century in Glastonbury.

Even before the start of the 1990s, Glastonbury, like other Connecticut towns, was faced with financial strictures, largely the result of a cutoff of state funds. Yankee stubbornness, thrift and independence, which had been fairly quiescent for a good long time, suddenly emerged. Joined to the old-timers were the newcomers; families from other states and other countries who had come to this quiet, suburban rivertown in recent years. Now they found themselves allied in a joint effort to preserve a way of life they had found good without emptying their pockets in the process.

What the alliance of old and new meant for Glastonbury, as voting day at the polls had made plain in 1986, was a message to the town government to stand pat, or in the words of that old New England saying, to use it up, wear it out, make it do or do without. On that November day in '86 voters turned down a referendum request for $4 million for an expansion of the Welles-Turner Library. And a second try for a revised expansion and renovation of the library was again turned down at a voters' referendum in June, 1990 though by only 116 votes. This was a surprise and a disappointment to the Library Board. Two years earlier a town referendum had approved issuing bonds up to $6.9 million for renovation of the high school. At the June 1990 referendum additional money for the high school renovations had been approved, though the library expansion plan had failed.

One of the proposals calling for "renovation" was to bring fire code requirements up to date. "As there were no fire codes when any of Glastonbury's schools were built, there are some problems to be faced," reported the Board of Education. It was a surprising fact to have emerged so close to the end of the 20th century, and it resulted in the formation of an architectural study to determine code violations in all the schools. This in turn appears to have been partly responsible for a November 1990 referendum (unsuccessful, as it turned out) appealing to townspeople for approval of $11 1/2 million for renovations, code compliance, and more school classroom space. Another try in 1991 for more funds for expansion and modernization of the schools was again turned down, though narrowly. But persistence finally won out and in June '93 the town electorate passed a $12.2 million referendum for expansion and renovation of the five K-5 elementary schools.

With town expenses increasing, it should have been obvious that a town budget of $44 million for '88-'89 would mean increased taxes. So it should have been no surprise that a taxpayers' protest group organized, calling itself STOP (Stop Taxpayers Overpaying.) When it first began its campaign to bring down town expenditures and taxes this group met with some opposition from critics who derided STOP's lobbying efforts. As time went on the group gained more support and in 1992 placed on the voting list a successful Independent candidate, Ted Niehay, for Town Council.

The nine-member Town Council is the main political arena of the local government. Like many old Yankee towns, Glastonbury has tended to elect Republican majorities to its Town Council (always there are at least three minority members.) Henry A. Kinne, who altogether had devoted 20 years of service to town boards, 14 of them on the Town Council as member or as chairman, decided in 1985 not to seek reelection. His Republican successor and the first Town Council chairwoman was Sonya (Sonny) Googins, who served for 16 years on the Town Council, including four terms as chairman, continuing into the 1990s. Democratic chairmen during that period were William Constantine and Charles Monaco.

Richard S. Borden, Jr., who had arrived in 1979 to become Glastonbury's second Town Manager, guided the town through times of affluence and periods of financial stress, working with the Town Council to keep Glastonbury on a steady course. During his tenure the town flourished, despite the continuing pressures of growth, and continued to maintain its excellent "Double A Prime" credit rating.

... a lingering recession," Town Manager Borden called the unhappy economic times that characterized the close of the '80s and start of the '90s. But, thanks to a still-increasing town population bringing benefits as well as some problems, Glastonbury by 1990 was still doing all right. (The official 1990 U.S. census population figure for Glastonbury was 27,901, an increase of 14.7 per cent over 1980.)

Citizen participation has from the beginning been a mainstay in New England villages and is so in Glastonbury, where community spirit remains strong. Volunteers compose the membership of the various town boards and committees, and volunteers throughout the town participate in such programs as protection of the environment, youth and family services and an array of other services. Parents volunteer at schools, and volunteers help in many other community ways including church outreach programs.

More than 150 volunteers man the town's four fire companies, who will be under the supervision of a full-time paid fire chief authorized by the Town Council in 1995. The Fire Department celebrated its 60th anniversary in 1986.

Providing transportation to doctors' appointments or to hospital clinics continues to be a particularly helpful service for those who can't drive. In 1992 a health needs assessment conducted by Connecticut Research Associates found Glastonbury "healthier than the state overall." The town's achieving this accolade owes not a little to such quiet volunteers as FISH (Friends in Service Here, providing transportation for some patients to doctors, clinics and hospitals), the Glastonbury Volunteer Ambulance Association, and other helpful groups who augment the care of the Visiting Nurse Association and the town's Health Department.

At intervals during the 20th century the United States has called upon citizen participation on a larger stage, to defend human rights and democracy in global conflicts from Europe to Asia. Glastonbury provided soldiers for all these military actions: World War I (U.S. participating in 1917-1919); World War II (1941-45); Korea (1950-53); Vietnam (1966-72); and the brief Persian Gulf War (1991.)

In August, 1990, Iraq invaded Kuwait, and in January the U.S. and its allies counter attacked Iraq. On February 23, the Iraqis were overpowered and defeated in a brief war. Twenty-seven Glastonbury men and two women, Karin Johnson and native Deborah Behrens (apparently the first local women members of the armed services to be sent to a European war theater) served in this war. The town held an Honor Day "to support our troops" on February 10, and it annually honors its veterans in Memorial Day observances.

Richard Borden in 1992 announced that he would resign as Town Manager at the end of the year to take a similar post in Merrimack, N.H. Assistant Town Manager Richard J. Johnson was named to take his place after six months' interim duty as Acting Town Manager while the town conducted a national search for candidates for the job. Johnson, who had been second in command since 1985, was well-acquainted with top administrative functions. One of his first acts after taking over the town management was to put into effect a Town Council "early retirement incentive" program for long-term employees, a downsizing designed as an economy measure. In this respect Glastonbury was following a restructuring process common at the time. Nevertheless, by midyear of 1994 Johnson found it necessary to do some rehiring for key jobs.

A significant change effected by Johnson was the restructuring of the Public Works Department, which for years had handled many of the vital public services, such as care of the roads. In the less complicated, rural days of the town, maintenance of roads, highways and bridges had been a principal concern of local government and had been handled by the Selectmen. Of course this highway duty, with the ever-increasing responsibilities of an expanding township, is still a top priority, but now the department formerly known as Public Works operates under the aegis of a Public Services Department headed by a Town Engineer/Manager.

In the winter of '93/94 the Public Services Department's snowplows had a hefty workout. One snowfall after another blanketed the town from Christmastime till spring; meteorologists declared the year to be the snowiest since Connecticut officials had begun keeping records. The winter's snowfall of 83.1 inches was a 99-year record, and by winter's end the town had plowed a grand total of 54,208 miles of local roadways (including multiple returns to the same areas.)

Heavy snowstorms were not the only severe weather problems the town has had to cope with over the past 10 years. Hurricane Gloria struck in September 1985 with such force that trees and branches were downed all over town making roads impassable and causing a power outage that affected some areas for six days. It did not match the 1938 hurricane which smashed the First Church Congregational but it was bad enough.

The turn of the decade of the '90s seemed to be characterized by a slew of new terms and catch words: "political correctness," "multi-culturalism", cultural awareness, the information highway, and many more.

A signal that the Electronic Age was really here came in the 1984-85 school year when a program on how to use computers was begun in the 4th Grade. The next year (the first for Dr. R. Stephen Tegarten as Superintendent of Schools) computers for instruction in computer use and for word processing were installed at Gideon Welles Junior High and Glastonbury High School. In 1994 the schools had 300 computers and were needing, and asking for, more. The town had installed a new computer system by 1988 for data processing, and the Police Department, too, upgraded its computer system. From then on schools, businesses and town residents were well connected to the computer age, here as everywhere. Anyone who used the Welles-Turner Library became familiar with computer use. In 1993 the library installed a new computer system for its index catalog which linked Glastonbury with a network of 34 other Hartford area libraries and was later expanded. Word processors soon began to replace or augment typewriters in many Glastonbury homes, and fax, modem and E-mail became familiar terms.

It was by way of the schools that Glastonbury townspeople became most aware of the new directions that society was taking. Even before the start of the '90s it had become obvious that public school education had veered

A computer class at work, Glastonbury High School, 1995.

152

from a centuries-old course strictly bent on basic book-learning to a wider objective: primarily to prepare the young for participation in a global economy. The schools were encouraged as well to broaden student interest beyond the classroom to the community itself. "We use our schools as social agencies, really, to prepare our students for life" (rather than just teaching the basics) reported a public school teacher (not from Glastonbury) in a TV "sound bite" sponsored by the Connecticut Education Association.

Glastonbury schools along with the rest of the state had begun to provide greater emphasis on social issues and community involvement. The Board of Education was scarcely unaware of the increased responsibilities that the times (and perhaps the nudging of the State Board of Education) were placing on local public schools. In 1992, under the chairmanship of Inez Hemlock, the Glastonbury board formally adopted "a belief statement" which spelled out several fundamental concerns. These stressed the conviction that as "all children can learn," partnership with parents and community was a responsibility of the educational system, and (coming full circle with the original colonial law establishing public schools) that schools have a responsibility to teach children to read and write, and (widening out the circle to bring it into compliance with modern times) not only to read and write but to compute, listen, speak and think clearly.

In spite of the irony implied by the wide-ranging term "political correctness," great strides were being made through legislation as well as through the increasing public awareness of the need for sensitivity toward certain population groups: ethnic and racial minorities, the disadvantaged, women, and homosexuals. "Awareness" in hiring policies at the Town Hall and in the school system was an early first step in implementing political correctness.

Since 1973, the peak year of school population (listed at 6000) the number of school-agers had dwindled year by year, apparently reflecting a low birth rate, a phenomenon throughout the country. Twenty years later, in spite of an increased population in the town, the school enumeration listed 4836 students, some eleven hundred fewer than the 1973 peak. But more space was needed due to an expanded curriculum calling for special rooms for new and diverse uses reflecting the technological changes of the times, more emphasis on art and music and other special courses, some required by state mandate.

The diminishing number of school age children in the South Glastonbury area had prompted the closing of the High Street School in 1978. After its abandonment the High Street School became a problem building until in 1991 the town voted to lease it for 99 years to the Congregational Church in South Glastonbury. The Church planned to use the building not only for Sunday School classes and the Nursery School it had sponsored for many years, but as a meeting place for community groups and other community functions. After many months of work on renovation and restructuring, done at no expense to the town, the 90-year-old High Street School opened in the fall of 1994 for a South Glastonbury area center.

As the decade of the '90s got under way the Board of Education found itself planning for a reversal of the decline in school population. Estimates showed that by 1995 Glastonbury would have well over 5000 school-agers, increasing the school population by at least 500 over the '90-'91 figure. Noises were being made for a necessary new elementary school. But for the present, without town referendum approval, alternative solutions would have to be considered, the Board regretfully concluded. Charged not only with overseeing the care and needs of the aging school buildings but with setting policies for increasing numbers of children and teenagers in an atmosphere of changing cultural values, the Board was finding its duties more and more complex.

Recognizing the disturbing fact that even a relatively tranquil suburban community like Glastonbury was not immune from social ills, the Board of Education early in the decade adopted policies which showed that such problems were here already. These policies included one on suicide prevention and one dealing with alcohol and drugs. The latter policy was already in place when the school administration was called on in the spring of 1994 to deal with the arrest by Glastonbury police of both drug dealers and drug users, students at the High School.

There was parental consternation when the schools took steps to implement a state mandate to provide "planned, ongoing and systematic instruction on "AIDS." In this connection the State Board of Education found it necessary to help teachers with their "levels of comfort" through workshops. In Glastonbury the emphasis was on being careful and taking health precautions. The sessions were part of the school's general health program.

Again there was concern when in June, 1993 the Legislature enacted a law requiring local and regional districts to devise plans for "educational quality and diversity" in Connecticut's schools, popularly known as the state's "new racial desegregation law." Glastonbury residents worried that their children might be forced to attend Hartford's troubled schools, a situation which could lead to loss of local control. But as required a committee was set up in January 1994 to work out a voluntary "diversity" plan for presentation to the legislature. The committee of 62 members included representatives of the Board of Education, the school system, town officials and churches as well as townspeople and students. They were handed a problem which was indeed a puzzle: how to go about rearranging a school body which reflected the make-up of the town's population, not seen as outstandingly diverse.

In tackling the thorny subject the diversity committee soon found that the school system already had in place programs to involve students from other communities. "Project Concern" children from Hartford had been enrolled in Glastonbury schools since 1966; there was the East Hartford/Glastonbury Magnet School (an ethnically and culturally diverse "special interest" school for young children) and other Magnet schools were planned. There were also "Sister School" programs including exchange visits with schools in other towns, combined field trips, shared curricula, arts performances, and other programs. The committee recognized the need for continued attention to Glastonbury newcomers with limited English and suggested, among other possible services, that the teaching staff be "diversified linguistically." Still, the committee's final report of the diversity study took note of community families' "expressed concern about forced change which might impact on school quality, and their strong desire to have local control and parental choice."

There may be more diversity in Glastonbury schools today than there has ever been before. Glastonbury schools have taken under their wing young people who have come here with their parents from many countries worldwide. By 1994 10 per cent of the school population was made up of minorities. Of these, 110 had classes in English as a Second Language, and some got tutorial support. But, says Jacqueline Jacoby, Superintendent of Schools, they soon get "weaned away" and join regular classes. However, this ethnic and social mix does mean the schools have had to learn how to deal with a variety of cultures.

In 1994 the Board of Education addressed the matter of the schools' observance of religious holidays. There had been a flurry of reactions throughout the community when, at Christmastime in 1993, a school administrator, anxious to observe the rule of separation of church and state, sent a staff member home to change her sweater which bore a Christmas tree design. The Board proposed a policy of consideration of "each others' religious beliefs or non-beliefs," and recommended guidelines for treating a broad spectrum of religious holidays, including Christmas, Thanksgiving, Three Kings Day, Hanukkah, St. Patrick's Day, Ramadan, Divali, Hinamatsuri, Passover, and Easter.

Although the cultural mix may have been most noticeable in the schools, the many countries represented among the newcomers also had a significant place at the polls on voting day. In 1993 the Registrars of Voters listed as voters persons from 34 different countries not including our neighbor, Canada: Belgium, Chile, China, Costa Rica, Dominican Republic, El Salvador, Egypt, England, France, Germany, Guatemala, India, Indonesia, Italy, Ireland, Japan, Korea, Mexico, Philippines, Poland, Puerto Rico, Romania, South Africa, Spain, Thailand, Greece, Israel, Portugal, Nicaragua, Nigeria, Mozambique, Mongolia, Peru and Turkey. American citizens, all. Glastonbury also has immigrants from other countries including Afghanistan and Azerbaijan.

Changes in family structure over the past decade have had a particular effect on the schools. The need for two incomes for family support, and the growing increase in the numbers of career women, have introduced a "parenting" aspect of public education. This includes serving breakfast and reduced-cost lunches to some, heretofore considered a service available in urban areas, not suburban towns with an upscale image. The schools now provide emotional counseling for children suffering from depression or needing help in dealing with all sorts of problems, including peer pressures (academically and socially) and "copy-cat" indulgence in alcohol, tobacco and drugs.

Counseling and other non-academic duties have had an impact on the amount of time devoted strictly to academic subjects yet are considered so important that, coupled with the increasing demands of learning, they may soon make necessary extended school hours or even days. So predicts Superintendent Jacoby. A similar assessment was made for the national schools in a spring 1994 report of the National Education Commission on Time and Learning: "The six-hour, 180-day school year should be relegated to museums, an exhibit from our education past."

To Jacqueline Jacoby belongs the distinction of being Glastonbury's first woman Superintendent of Schools. Mrs. Jacoby was appointed in May 1993 to take the place of R. Stephen Tegarten, who had resigned to accept a job in his native Indiana. Jackie Jacoby, who had formerly been Deputy Superintendent of Schools, faced a formidable administrative challenge. The Glastonbury school population whose direction would be in her hands was nearing the projected 5000, and thus was larger than the entire population of each of 48 Connecticut towns.

The enormous proliferation of information being generated in this "New-Age" has an important effect on the schools. Not only the availability of information, but the need for it, is greater than ever, said Mrs. Jacoby when asked about the changes in public school education as she has observed them during the 14-year period of her connection with Glastonbury schools.

"We require more of kids," she noted. "Literacy has a more expanded definition than it used to have. For instance, reading is at a much higher level." The main difference in the schools today, she observed, are that we are dealing with more and more technological instruction and handling a more diverse student population.

Coping with the problems of youth and with rapidly evolving social conditions is not the sole province of schools. Police have a part to play, too. The Police Department in recent years has stepped up its agenda of community youth service. Various programs are carried on, such as DARE (Drug Abuse Resistance Education) for 6th graders, and the "Officer Friendly" program for pre- and elementary schools, providing cautionary advice on such things as distrust of strangers, bike safety, the bad effects of drinking alcohol and smoking. Programs for teenagers are carried on as well.

As the population increased over a 10 year period, so did the number of police officers. In spite of the loss of seven officers (mostly through retirement) whose long terms of service totalled 137 years, the roster of sworn officers increased more than 20 per cent. By 1994 there were 53 police officers, including three policewomen, and in addition there were 20 trained community service officers for supplemental duty.

Glastonbury's Police Department was the first in the state to receive national accreditation from the Commission on Accreditation for Law Enforcement Agencies. It is no wonder that the department won this honor, for it achieved a "state of the art" standing as it kept up with the technological changes of the times. The department maintains a main computer databank as well as a computer-teletype providing contact with police departments nationwide, laptop computers for on-site use, portable radios in every cruiser, night vision scopes and a whole range of up-to-date police equipment.

Though violent crimes seldom occur in Glastonbury, vigilance is constant. "The town is a relatively affluent stable community," points out Police Commander Thomas J. McKee. "The river is a buffer," he believes, "and so were the tollbooths." Nevertheless, we do have burglaries — sporadically — as well as other law violations. Drug investigations are difficult, says Commander McKee. There are no urban street-corner gang meetings, for instance, and it is not easy to track down drug users and dealers. Commander McKee is not without sympathy for young offenders, however. He feels that in the past few years they have had to "grow up quicker" because of the intensified pressure of demands from parents, peers and society.

Tracking down one notorious drug dealer who had picked Glastonbury as the ideal spot for his international dealings from a "safe house" a few years ago, was probably the most dramatic criminal action ever handled by the Glastonbury Police Department. Acting on a tip from neighbors who had observed suspicious activity at a house on the street, police, after a 10-month investigation, captured the suspect and broke up a major drug-dealing ring. All the department's advanced special equipment, including a "crime van" and electronic communication devices, were used in the capture. Specially trained Glastonbury police officers, the Emergency Response Team, worked with Hartford's "Swat Team," and some officers were sworn in as U.S. marshalls in order to listen in legally on wire-taps, as they awaited the arrival of a tractor-trailer loaded with drugs en route from Mexico by way of Texas to Glastonbury for distribution to other points.

It was obvious that the recession was still lingering in the early 1990s. The year 1992 was a somber one for family businesses and others competing with chains. Kamins store, an expanded independent version of the traditional five-and-dime, a landmark at Glastonbury Center, went out of business to the regret of its many customers. And before the end of the year Franklin's Pharmacy, a standby for Glastonbury residents for the past 70 years, followed. These two occupants of Main Street at the junction of Hebron Avenue — the old trolley Station 35 — left a noticeable void in the attractiveness of the Center for months before the spaces were filled.

Another long-time pharmacy, Pagano's, which had been in business in Glastonbury since the 1930s, closed its doors in May 1994. And that April

South Glastonbury suffered a blow when Glastonbury Drug, a family-run pharmacy that had been a Nayaug fixture for 30 years, went out of business. The only independently run pharmacy then left in Glastonbury was Towne Pharmacy, which had occupied its spot in the One-Stop-Shop mall on New London Turnpike since about 1960. All these closings were an indication, perhaps, that the old ways of doing business were vanishing as the new century approached.

A supermarket tussle among several nationally-known grocery firms seeking to locate in Glastonbury took up many hours of public hearings in 1992. This urgency to get into Glastonbury was an implication of market confidence in a growing upscale consumer population. Eventually the winner emerged: Finast/Edwards, whose plan to build a "superstore" on Glastonbury Boulevard not far from Somerset Square was first approved, then challenged in a court case which was dismissed. During the course of the "supermarket war" Glastonbury's central supermarket, the independent Frank's, affiliated with the Shop Rite chain. Then, coincidentally with the ground-breaking for the new Edwards store, Frank's was sold to the Stop and Shop chain. Meanwhile a Manchester concern, Highand Park Market, came into town, locating at the Buckingham Shopping Center. Gardiner's Market of South Glastonbury, a family-run grocery store for 45 years, was a standout and by the mid-'90s still retained its independence.

In the palmy days of the mid-'80s the office park areas off Hebron Avenue, zoned for such use some years ago, began to flourish. Handsomely designed corporate office buildings in a manicured green rolling landscape gave visible proof that Glastonbury had found a successful way not only to replace the old manufacturing plants but to enhance the grand list on which taxes are based. The Economic Development Commission, appointed to advise the Town Council, made strides in attracting quality commercial and light industrial corporations, with benefits to employment and taxes. Noticeable during this period of growth was the spread of bank branches to various parts of the town.

Some of the branch offices in the Corporate Park area bear familiar names: Metropolitan Life, Liberty Mutual, and Travelers, as well as MCI Telecommunications, Nabisco and A-Copy. When the early years of the 1990s slowed the increase of corporate building, and the economic recession made its mark on the Gateway Corporate Park, some firms were delinquent in paying taxes, and the town took over buildings and land. However, according to Community Development Director Kenith Leslie, the vacancy rate has been negligible.

Connecticut towns ever since their settlement had obeyed the Biblical injunction to "Remember the Sabbath day, to keep it holy. Six days shalt thou labor and do all thy work; But the seventh day is the sabbath of the Lord thy God ..." But modern times, as the 21st century drew closer, induced the Connecticut legislature to re-think the hallowed Commandment.

Interestingly, it was a labor law that first permitted retail shop openings on Sundays. In 1976 drug stores were permitted to dispense drugs and medical supplies on Sundays, as well as various other things like baby supplies and newspapers. Food stores with no more than five employees were allowed Sunday openings. By the mid-'90s shops in general, food markets to great retail outlets and malls were being well-patronized on Sunday afternoons. With husband and wife both working, shopping on Sundays became almost a necessity. And locally this was no exception.

Despite Sunday shopping, church membership in Glastonbury appears to have remained nearly constant over a long period, church secretaries report. But membership is cyclical: as members move away from town, new families arrive. In areas where residential building has increased, church membership grows. For instance, in South Glastonbury, the Congregational Church admitted 76 new members in 1992-93. St. Dunstan's Catholic Church in Buckingham, too, has experienced an increase in church membership. This "church in the woods" observed its 20th anniversary in November 1994.

Congregation Kol Havarim, founded in 1984, dedicated its new synagogue on Hebron Avenue in 1987. The ceremony marked the acquisition of a Torah and furniture to house the sacred texts owned by the congregation. In the same year St. Luke's Episcopal Church of South Glastonbury celebrated the 150th anniversary of its building, and in 1986 the Glastonbury United Methodist Church marked the 100th anniversary of the building of its meeting house. Another Glastonbury church, the Lutheran Church of St. Mark, celebrated its centennial in 1985. St. Paul's Parish observed its 40th anniversary in 1994.

Churches have continued to develop and expand their services to the community. Most participate in the Glastonbury Clergy Food Fund, administered by St. James Episcopal Church, which buys food for the hungry with money raised through sponsors of a 6-mile "Crop Walk" held once a year as part of a Church World Service project. Some $2,000-$3,000 raised in Glastonbury goes to buy food locally, says the Rev. George W. Jenkins, rector of St. James Church. The Glastonbury Clergy Food Fund helps support the town Social Services Department's Food Bank.

Along with programs that participate in helping those in need of food and fuel, several churches help build awareness of society's need to protect the environment and preserve what remains of the natural features that drew the earliest settlers from Wethersfield to this side of the river.

... "be sensitive to environmental factors ..." warned the Strategic Planning Committee in its report to the Town Council in July 1990. Protection of the environment had come to State legislative attention as long ago as 1886, when the first waterways protection law was passed to forbid the dumping of industrial waste and sewage into the Quinnipiac River, near Meriden. This first recognition of the water pollution problem in the state appears to have had little impact over the years on pollution control of the Connecticut

River. For by 1994 some untreated Hartford sewage was still flowing past Glastonbury's river front.

Years ago Glastonbury had taken steps to control the flow of its own pollution into the Connecticut by constructing two multi-million dollar sewage treatment plants. Efforts to protect our ecological environment is and has been a continuing aim of our Conservation Commission. Acting since 1972 as the local arm of Connecticut's Inland Wetlands and Water Courses Agency, the Commission remains on the alert to protect Glastonbury's vast outlying areas, much of them traversed by streams. Developers, reaching farther and farther from the central settlement, have had to mind their land acquisition manners, and protective zoning regulations are strict.

For some time the Town has had its eye on residential developers, and other users of the land for industry, and zoning measures have required that a certain amount of acreage (according to zone classification) be set aside for preservation. By 1994 Glastonbury's "open space" amounted to about 25 per cent of the town's 55.5 square miles. This was an increase of five per cent in the acquisition of preservation land over the past decade, in spite of the continuing spread of residential building in all parts of town. The open space land has been acquired for preservation over many years by various means including gifts, easements, purchase (the town was granted funds for preservation land purchase through referendum approval in 1988) or agreement with land owners. A significant acquisition in 1990 was an 80-acre parcel on the Hebron town line along the Blackledge River containing the 80-foot Blackledge Falls.

The rescue of one of Glastonbury's most precious ecological assets, the Great Pond area at the south end of town, is a story of dedication, persistence, and finally success. Great Pond is a remnant of a huge body of water named Lake Hitchcock by geologists, which 4000 years ago covered a site that stretched roughly from New Britain to Vermont. It is the habitat of rare plants and water wildlife.

For 30 years adjacent acres had been mined for gravel by the Balf Company of Newington. As Balf edged closer to the pond area, concerned conservationists headed by H. William Reed formed the Friends of Great Pond. After months of hearings and meetings, this group, with the cooperation of the town's Conservation Commission and the Nature Conservancy, in 1991 successfully negotiated an agreement with the Balf Company. The result was Balf's donation of 52 acres which, together with 75 already owned by the town for recreational purposes, meant a total of 127 acres of preserved land. Balf also pledged funds toward a maintenance endowment trust to be under the stewardship of Nature Conservancy. The resultant Great Pond Preserve for the protection of a unique ecological area and for active recreation is a boon to Glastonbury in general and especially to the town's south end.

The eastern part of South Glastonbury is graced with beautiful orchard-covered hills, where apples and peaches grow in abundance, along with pears and plums. Rose's berry farm, widely known for its pick-your-own strawberries, raspberries and blueberries, is here, near neighboring slopes of grape vines. Some other fruit growers open their orchards in season to customers willing to do their own picking. Known as the Matson Hill area (it also includes Belltown Hill and Clark Hill) the orchard land for more than a hundred years has been owned and cultivated by generations of Italian-American families. The hilltops offer long spectacular views.

For years the Matson Hill section of Glastonbury has been in some respects a land unto itself, devoted to the production and marketing of fruit. In 1992 the state passed legislation granting tax relief to orchards and dairy farms maintained as businesses, legislation aimed at preserving agricultural land. It was not only Matson Hill that benefited from tax relief. So also did the John Tom Hill dairy farm and orchard sections located on the eastern stretches of Hebron Avenue.

But the downturning economy of the late '80s began to affect the farmers. Earlier, both tobacco growers and dairy farmers had suffered. Now, in spite of a widening market for Glastonbury fruit and seasonal roadside stands, some orchardists began to sell off parcels of the land they had inherited from forebears.

When in 1994 the Town Planning and Zoning Commission began preliminary hearings on its mandated 10-year update of the Town Plan of Development, an alarm bell sounded in the farm country. For, among its various prospective revisions, the committee had inserted a proposal to protect by way of conservation easements "ridges, steep slopes, hills, woodlands and wildlife areas." Owners of the land so characterized spoke up indignantly in objection to being singled out for discriminatory restrictions on their property. Two longstanding issues clashed in the preliminary hearing: individual property rights versus the public interest; and ecology versus the economy. Both were brought out in the questioning of committee members by land owners, who maintained that the market value of their land would be lowered if restrictions were placed on their acreage. This was not the first time the issue of property rights had been raised as the local government sought to guide the growth of the town in an orderly way. Objections were made when the first Town Plan was drawn in the 1950s and the subject of limiting development on steep grades was introduced. Objections were again raised in the 1970s by property owners who felt their rights were threatened by the establishment of an Historic District. The District was defeated the first time around but approved on a second try in 1984 after much work spearheaded by what Town Council Chairman Sonny Googins called "a tenacious Historic District Committee."

One of the most confounding issues of the decade, and one which brought into conflict matters of public concern, was that of "affordable housing." The State Legislature enacted a law in 1988 requiring the towns to increase their supply of what was then considered low income housing, known thereafter as "affordable." Although the Town Council in 1989 created a Housing Partnership advocacy group to help carry out this mandate, there were problems. The first affordable housing project, Cove Point Landing, sailed through zoning and Council hearings in spite of its location not far from the river and flood-land. But subsequent projects did not fare as well. In 1992 a developer sought a zone change to build 134 units of housing, including affordable housing, in the Neipsic Road area. Neighbors opposed the project on grounds of increased traffic and drainage problems. The proposal was eventually turned down.

In the summer of 1994 another housing proposal that caused the town much concern brought up issues which were perplexing for many who were advocates of both affordable housing and protection of the environment. The Hartford-based Christian Activities Council, to which many Glastonbury churches belong, sought to build affordable housing on land it planned to buy from the Metropolitan District Commission at the corner of Hebron Avenue and Keeney Street. Opponents lined up against the Christian Activities Council to fight the project, mainly on environmental grounds. The Metropolitan District land in question was part of a large acreage which had once been watershed land with two reservoirs.

In August the Town Council rejected the housing plan. The Christian Activities Council then appealed the decision to Hartford Superior Court, where the Neipsic Road area housing project was already scheduled to be heard. In November these cases were joined by another appeal of a Town Council denial of affordable housing, this one proposed for a floodland site on Welles Street. Meanwhile a cooperative affordable housing project to build 32 dwelling units on Griswold Street was under way to add to the town's goal of 220 affordable units by 1999.

In the swirl of debates over land use, housing, minority rights, school curricula, and all the rest, Glastonbury celebrated the 300th anniversary of its founding. In 1693 by vote of the General Court Glastonbury had become a town independent from Wethersfield, having been the eastern part of Wethersfield's colonial settlement since 1634. Official year-long Tercentenary observations included special events of many sorts: fireworks, a family day particularly for children, town tours, including some in a simulated trolley car on Main Street, reenactment of the town's separation from Wethersfield, an historical pageant, and much more. The celebration culminated in a long parade with floats and marching bands on a chilly November day. Co-chairs of the Tercentennial observance were Tink Henderson and Betsy Katz, who headed a large town-wide committee, assisted by many volunteers.

Throughout the year many organizations, including churches, schools and service groups, contributed to the town's celebration in their own way. The establishment of Glastonbury having been contingent upon the founding of a church and settling of a minister, that church, now known as the First

A spectacular "birthday cake" celebrating the town's Tercentenary was a highlight of Family Day. (Tercentenary Committee Photo)

Church of Christ, Congregational, celebrated its 300th anniversary concurrently with the town.

The Historical Society sponsored lectures and a concert series, undertook exterior renovation to its headquarters, the Old Town Hall, and its Welles-Shipman-Ward House. The Society in 1993 published a book, *The Letter Kills but the Spirit Gives Life*, by Kathleen L. Housley, a biographical study of Glastonbury's noted Smith Sisters, early advocates of women's rights.

Word was received in the Tercentenary year that Curtisville, a 19th century mill village in the Naubuc area, had been named to the National Register of Historic Places as the result of an architectural survey authorized by the Historical Society. The town's Tercentenary Committee sponsored a permanent computerized genealogy file of descendants of the town's founders and early residents, compiled from information sent from many states across the nation, and established in place at the Historical Society. A Tercentenary shop offering souvenirs, books and artifacts connected with Glastonbury was maintained in donated store-space in Somerset Square, and later was carried on by the Historical Society as a Welcome Center at the Welles-Chapman Tavern.

The visit of 96 residents of our namesake town, Glastonbury, Somerset County, England, on a hot July week was a highlight of the Tercentennial year. Local families hosted all the visitors, who included the mayor of the English Glastonbury and members of that town's brass band. It was a festive week, one of the most notable events being a Sunday evening concert on the Green, given jointly by the English band and our own Glastonbury band.

The week climaxed with a grand finale in the High School gym, featuring a concert by the English band and an exchange of gifts. The Glastonbury visitors presented to our town a replica of an ancient ceremonial chair from their Town Hall, which has been placed on display in the Welles-Turner Memorial Library.

To plan, supervise and raise funds for historical events every month of the year was an enormous organizational feat for a Tercentennial which brightened a year otherwise marked by a nagging economical slump.

Three hundred years have wrought changes which could not have been envisioned by the handful of families who settled Glastonbury in the 17th century. Yet, as a new century and a new millennium nears, the town they formed remains steadfast in following the advice of the Colony's General Court to the petitioners for the new town: that they "be cautious how they improve it."

Through good times and bad, Glastonbury has endeavored to improve life in the town for a greatly expanded and increasingly diverse population. It has kept its sights on its cherished environment, has fostered up-to-date educational programs, has taken steps for the continued safety of its people and property, and all in all, has attempted faithfully to carry out the original mandate of its founders.

Appendix

Original Land-holders, 1640

The identification of the men who were the earliest Glastonbury land-holders is difficult. The Rev. Alonzo B. Chapin in his 1853 history says that there were 34 lots laid out in the survey of 1639-40, and lists the original lot owners. But Sherman W. Adams, writing in Stiles' history of Wethersfield published in 1904, says there were 38 lots (or farms). His list of owners is different from that of Dr. Chapin's. In some cases Chapin has given names which Adams lists as second or third owners. Since Adams spent many years of his life studying the early history of Wethersfield and examined Chapin's list with some care, Adams' list is probably more accurate.

Chapin's List Published 1853		Adams' List Published In Stiles' *History*, 1904	
Lot No.	Owner in 1640	Lot No.	Owner in 1640
1.	George Wyllys	1.	John Strickland and perhaps others
2.	John Deming	2.	Francis Norton and perhaps others
3.	Robert Bates	3.	John Deming
4.	Richard Gildersleeve	4.	Thomas Morehouse and Thomas Sherwood
5.	Joseph Sherman	5.	Richard Gildersleeve
6.	Thurston Rayner	6.	Thomas Tapping and John Fletcher
7.	Thomas Welles	7.	Rev. John Sherman
8.	First owner not known	8.	Thurston Rayner
9.	First owner not known	9.	William Swayne
10.	Rev. Henry Smith	10.	John Reynolds
11.	Samuel Sherman, Richard Gildersleeve	11.	Andrew Ward
12.	Samuel Smith	12.	Rev. Henry Smith
13.	Thomas Uffoot	13.	Richard Law
14.	George Hubbard	14.	Edward Sherman
15.	George Wyllys	15.	Samuel Smith
16.	Robert Rose	16.	Thomas Ufford
17.	John Gibbs	17.	George Hubbard

Chapin's List Published 1853		Adams' List Published In Stiles' *History*, 1904	
Lot No.	Owner in 1640	Lot No.	Owner in 1640
18.	Nathaniel Foote	18.	Edward Wood
19.	Mr. Parke	19.	Robert Rose
20.	Abraham Finch	20.	John Gibbs
21.	John Plum	21.	Nathaniel Foote
22.	John Thomson	22.	Nathaniel Dickinson?
23.	John Edwards	23.	Abraham Finch, 3rd
24.	Frances Kilborn	24.	John Plumb
25.	Thomas Coleman	25.	First owner not known.
26.	Jeffrey Ferris	26.	John Thomson
27.	John Whitmore	27.	John Edwards
28.	John Robbins	28.	Widow of Thomas Kilbourne
29.	Thomas Wright	29.	Thomas Coleman
30.	Robert Cooe	30.	Jeffry Ferris
31.	James Boosie	31.	John Whitmore
32.	Leonard Chester	32.	John Robbins
33.	Clement Chaplin	33.	Thomas Wright
34.	Matthew Mitchell	34.	Robert Coe
		35.	James Boosey
		36.	Leonard Chester
		37.	Clement Chaplin
		38.	Matthew Mitchell

Petitioners for Separation

A petition was submitted to the General Court of the Connecticut Colony in 1690 asking that Wethersfield people living on the east side of the Connecticut River be allowed to separate and "be a township of themselves." In the same year an Agreement was signed concerning the building of the Meeting House, evidently required by the General Court before the town could be established. In the first book of Glastonbury town records this Agreement appears in the hand of Samuel Smith, as follows:

"February: 13: 1690. Att a metting of the inhabitanus one the east sid of the grat Revuer blonging to weathersfild it was agred that the matting hous shold stand upon john hubbords land one samuell smith his plaine the a boue said samuel smith and john hubbord doe ingage to giue land conuenentt for metting house as witnis ours hand . . ."

A list of 24 names is appended, as follows:

epherine goodridg (Goodrich)
Joseph Smith
John Harinton
Thomas bruer (Brewer)
ebenezer hall (Hale)
John Strickland
John hall (Hale)
william hous
Samuell hall (Hale)
patrack stearne
Richard Treatt, siner
Thomas Treatt
Richard Smith
John holister
Jonathan Smith
Samuel hall Jr. (Hale)
Samuel Smith
John hubbord
Joseph hils
John Kilbornn
Samuel welles
Thomas hall (Hale)
Richard Treat, Jr.
william wickham

It is likely that both Alonzo Chapin and Sherman Adams had seen the petition for separation, which at the present writing cannot be located in the State Archives. Both historians add 18 names to the above 24 householders signing the petition. The additional names are: Jonathan and Benjamin Hale, Deac. Thomas Hollister, Joseph Hollister, Sen'r and Jr., Benjamin Smith, Thomas Loveland, Joseph Bidwell, Richard Fox, Nathaniel Talcott, Deac. Benjamin Talcott, Thomas Kimberly, Daniel Wright, David Hollister, Edward Benton, William Miller, Samuel Gaines, and Ephraim Hollister.

Notes

In the following notes the Historical Society of Glastonbury is referred to as HSG.

Chapter I: Invitation from Wahquinnacut

p. 1.   For general information on the Wongunk Indians see John W. DeForest, *History of the Indians of Connecticut*, 1853. The most recent study of Connecticut Indians at the time of the white settlement is a University of Connecticut master's thesis: Mary Guillette Soulsby, *Connecticut Indian Ethnohistory: A Look at Five Tribes*, 1981.

5-6.   On the settlement of Wethersfield, see Sherman W. Adams and Henry R. Stiles, *The History of Ancient Wethersfield*, 1904.

Chapter II: Crossing the River

For information on early Glastonbury, see the Rev. Alonzo B. Chapin. *Glastenbury for Two Hundred Years*, 1853.

p. 11.   Legends throughout this book are usually those recounted by Florence Hollister Curtis. The HSG has a collection of Mrs. Curtis's writings, published and unpublished. Mrs. Curtis (1850-1951) had been interested in history and writing about it probably half her life.

13-14.   Herbert T. Clark, "Early Roads of Glastonbury," undated manuscript on file at HSG provides information about Glastonbury's first thoroughfares.

16.   The story of Richard Treat teaching Wongunks is from J.W. De Forest, *History of the Indians of Connecticut*, which has further information about the Treats' missionary work with the Indians.

Chapter III: Cutting The Apron Strings

p. 19.   *Glastonbury Town Records*, Vol. 1, gives actual votes concerning town negotiations with the Rev. Timothy Stevens. For biographical information on the Rev. Timothy see Virginia Knox, "Timothy Stevens Settles," *Publick Post*, spring 1968.

21-22.   Research conducted by the author in Glastonbury, England, and other Somerset County towns indicated the name may have been suggested by the then governor, Robert Treat, whose family had come from the Somerset area, as had several founding families of Glastonbury, Connecticut.

23. "Samuell Loveman," who beat the drum to call the people to worship in 1701 was doubtless Samuel Loveland, born 1677.

23. Records of the First Ecclesiastical Society contain descriptions of both second and third meeting houses. An agreement with Josiah B. Holmes, 7 March 1837, states that he is to "erect and finish" a meeting house for $4800, its dimensions to be 44' × 56' with a portico 8' × 44'. A committee, having toured other Connecticut churches, gave the following architectural instructions: the portico was to be supported by four fluted columns "in the true Grecian Doric order;" there were to be 8 windows of 60 lights; window blinds made "after the manner of those at the East Hartford Meeting House;" doors "equal to those in the meeting house at Collinsville;" stairs and galleries finished like those at the South Baptist Church in Hartford; and "altar or pulpit which together with a communion table" should be similar to those in the Farmington Meeting House. This third Glastonbury meeting house burned down in 1866.

27. That two kitchen windows were a characteristic of early Glastonbury houses was the observation of Dr. Whittles.

30. Recent research indicates that the house at 1597 Hebron Avenue, known as the Treat Tavern, may have been built by Daniel Wright, Jr., before 1730 and that it was here that Eastbury Society was organized in 1731.

31. Glastonbury's Tercentenary Map, 1935, gives the date of 1776 for Welles-Chapman Tavern.

32. Joseph Wright's diaries, 1837-1863, mention meetings of town boards held at both "Chapman's" and "Bates."

Chapter IV: The Struggle For National Independence

p. 40. For the Revolutionary period in Glastonbury I have drawn on both Mrs. Curtis' and Dr. Whittles' accounts, as well as on Stiles' *History of Ancient Wethersfield* and records of Glastonbury town meetings.

41-43. The dispersal of Yale students to Glastonbury, Wethersfield and Farmington is recounted in several publications including Franklin B. Dexter, *Biographical Sketches of the Graduates of Yale College with Annals of the College History, 1885-1912*, and Brooks M. Kelley, *Yale: A History*, 1974. Ezra Stiles (who became president of Yale July 8, 1778) in his *Literary Diary*, ed. F.B. Dexter, 1901, mentioned that he visited the Yale classes in "Glassenbury" November 14, 1777, and noted that the freshman class had joined the juniors here, while the sophomores had been sent to Farmington. Tutor Baldwin had replaced Tutor Buckminster. Stiles says: "I saw the Junior Class being at Recitation with Mr. Baldwin and made a Speech to them. Mr. Wells tells me College wants Regulation for they have left the more solid parts of

Learng & run into Plays & dramatic Exhibitions chiefly of the comic kind & turn'd College says he into Drury Lane."

Chapter V: Wheels of Progress

p. 48. For information on Glastonbury ships and shipping see Barbara Cox, "Sailing Ships of Glastonbury," *Publick Post*, winter 1968. The HSG has miscellaneous documents concerning local shipping, including three logbooks.

52-3. On charcoal burning, see Bernice Swan, "Charcoal Industry in Glastonbury," *Publick Post*, July 1956. Mrs. Curtis' manuscript on old Wassuc also provides reminiscences of the smoking charcoal pits.

The Hartford Manufacturing Company petitioned the Legislature for incorporation in 1814, stating that "they have built a factory at Roaring Brook in Glastenbury for the manufacture of cotton and woolen fabrics."

54. For information on early industries see Herbert Clark, "Early Industries Along Roaring Brook," *Retrospect*, May 1940; manuscript notes for a talk given by Dr. Whittles, HSG, March 1962; William S. Goslee, Glastonbury chapter in J.H. Trumbull, *The Memorial History of Hartford County*, 1886: and *East Hartford Gazette*. Glastonbury edition, Nov. 29, 1901.

The "subsequent enterprises" following the closing of the Glazier woolen mill, continuing textile manufacture, included Brookside Woolen Company, Hopewell Mill, and Matson Mills, Inc.

59. Town records indicate tanners were part of Glastonbury's business community from the beginning. Leather "sealers" (inspectors) were first elected by an order of the General Court of Connecticut Colony in 1656. Presumably pigskin was tanned as well as hides of other animals.

Chapter VI: Spirit and Mind

p. 60. A small Baptist Church located on what today is Woodland Street between Clark Hill Road and Belltown Hill Road is shown on Warren and Gillett's map of 1811. Mrs. Curtis describes it in a manuscript (HSG) and tells of its being moved (by then abandoned) around the corner to Matson Hill Road to become the first Matson Hill schoolhouse.

In 1979 the Asbury Church joined with the East Glastonbury Methodist Church, forming the Glastonbury United Methodist Church ("United" being a denominational term denoting the merging of the Methodist Church sect with the Evangelical United Brethren.)

The Asbury Church sold its church building on Buttonball Lane to Wethersfield Community Church, an Evangelical Free Church. Glastonbury members of this church, who had formerly commuted across the river to the Wethersfield church, then formed their own parish, to be known as the Glastonbury Community Church.

60-2. The archives of most churches supply information about their own history, as well as papers on church history written over the years by church members or ministers.

Crowding at the 9:30 a.m. Sunday service of the First Church Congregational by 1982 prompted the expansion of both north and south sides of the church to provide an additional 144 seats. An administrative wing was added at the rear of the church.

66. Chapin's 1853 history has material on Glastonbury's early schools, culled from town records. See also Louis W. Howe, manuscript, "Common Schools," 1939, HSG. School visitors' reports contain interesting data. Earl H. Hodge writes of "The Grammar School in South Glastonbury," *Retrospect*, September 1948. Henry T. Welles in *Autobiography and Reminiscences* (1899) recalls his schooldays at this school.

67. The football death of Charles Raze Gager was reported in the *East Hartford Gazette*, October 3, 1902.

Chapter VII: Simple Pleasures and Complex Issues

p. 71. An inventory of paupers' clothing is given in the article, "Over the Hill," *Retrospect*, March 1952. In 1980 the town sought to close the Still Hill Boarding Home, which then housed five men, but community opposition prevailed and presently the Home is in operation.

72. An article on "The Old Town Hall on the Green," *Publick Post*, fall 1958, names Parley Bidwell as builder of both the Old Town Hall (Historical Society Museum) and the South Glastonbury Methodist Church (S.G. Public Library).

74. Manuscript reminiscences of Oliver Hale, born 1775, tell about Josiah Strickland and his grog shop.

75-8. HSG has a good collection of material, published and unpublished, about the Smith Sisters.

Adams, a champion of abolition, presented many such anti-slavery petitions. But no evidence that Glastonbury's was the first has come to light.

The 1790 census enumerated 75 Blacks in Glastonbury, of whom 33 were listed as slaves. Two, Syphax Moseley and Prince Simbo, were listed as heads of households.

81. Eliza Bunce, a school teacher, accompanied her husband, Dr. Henry Bunce, to the Civil War battlefield to serve as a nurse. A local chapter of the Daughters of Veterans of the Civil War, founded in 1926, was named Eliza Bunce Tent in her honor. Mrs. Dana B. Waring, in a talk at the HSG, 1962, "Vignettes of Glastonbury During the Civil War

Period" (printed in the *Publick Post*, spring 1963) told about Eliza Bunce's Civil War nursing.

Chapter VIII: From Steam to Electricity

p. 86. For maps of Connecticut River channel changes see Stiles, *Ancient Wethersfield*.

88. For Roser Tannery history see *Roser: A Tradition in Tanning*, private printing, 1954.

89. Granite quarries were being operated in Glastonbury as early as 1825, according to Charles W. Burpee, *History of Hartford County*, Vol. II. By century's end there were four, all in East Glastonbury except for Town Woods Quarry near today's Apple Hill. Glastonbury quarries supplied stone for the Hartford Seminary Foundation and other well-known buildings as well as for Hartford's street curb-stones.

90. For Hale orchards background see J.H. Hale, "The Story of the Hale Nurseries," Hale catalog, 1896.

93. An earlier telephone exchange may have been located in the ell of the Ebenezer Plummer House at its original site, the intersection of Main Street and Douglas Road, some long-time residents believe.

95-6. For additional information on Italian families in Glastonbury see Joseph Pero, *Joey: My Mother's Favorite Son*, private printing, 1980.

Chapter IX: Miscellaneous Disasters

p. 102. The Hopewell School built in 1925 burned in 1943 and was not rebuilt.

105. For volunteer fire company history see Glastonbury Annual Town Report, 1961-2.

108. Dr. Whittles in a report on the work of the local Disaster Relief Committee, 1936, told about the potato salad poisoning.

Chapter X: Outgrowing Traditional Patterns

p. 115. United Aircraft Corporation changed its name to United Technologies in 1975, consistent with the company's emergence as a world-scale technological corporation.

117. Information on the Glastonbury foreign language materials project is from a report by the project director, Mary Thompson.

120. Glastonbury Toiletries went out of business in 1977 after 17 years, finding competition difficult.

The Consolidated Cigar Corporation, which had owned 1900 acres of tobacco land in Glastonbury in 1976, by 1982 had sold all but 200 acres. Gulf Western Industries had acquired Consolidated Cigar and converted its shade-grown cigar-wrapper leaf process to a more economical sheet-wrapper product for cigars.

Chapter XI: The 1960s to the 1980s

p. 127. By 1982 Glastonbury had 7300 acres of "open space" restricted from development: state forest and parks, town-owned parks, greens, playfields, hiking trails, natural areas, pools, steambelts and inland wetlands, conservation easements both public and private, private camps, reservoirs, and golf courses, all this more than 20 percent of Glastonbury's total 35,321 acres.

128. For the second time an Historic District Committee was appointed and in 1982 proposed the establishment of an historic district on part of Main Street.

129. There appears to be no all-inclusive local record of the number of Glastonbury men and women who served in either the Korean or the Vietnam wars. Peter Monaco was the only Glastonbury man killed in Korea. Lieut. Col. Russell P. Hunter, Jr., missing in action in Laos, 1966, was officially declared dead in 1974. Maj. William W. Roush, an Army "Green Beret," was killed in Vietnam in 1968.

139-9. The South Glastonbury firehouse in 1982 was pronounced too small to accommodate a new fire engine and equipment. The neighboring Community Club, a 1760 house, was taken down to extend the site for a new firehouse, which was begun that October.

143. The federal lawsuit for housing bias brought against Glastonbury in 1980 was settled in November 1982 by a "consent decree" in which the town agreed to institute several measures designed to encourage low- and moderate-income housing. This lawsuit was by no means the first time the town had been brought into court. In 1695 the County Court ordered judgment for Luke Hill to recover 48 shillings from the selectmen of Glastonbury, his bounty for having killed 8 wolves.

Chapter XII: Toward a Fourth Century: Change and Continuity

p. 148. The trial of Karin Aparo on a charge of conspiracy to murder her mother had not been scheduled by fall, 1995, and the case was still pending in Superior Court. This Glastonbury murder was the subject of a book and made-for-TV movie shown in 1993.

150. Projections place Glastonbury's population at 30,600 by the year 2000, to increase to 31,425 by 2005, according to the town's Community Development office.

150. Sonya (Sonny) Googins was elected to the State House of Representatives in November 1994.

150. Bernard Dennler retired as Fire Chief in 1995 after 46 years as a volunteer fireman.

151. A search for documentation of Glastonbury women members of the U.S. Armed Forces who served overseas in Korea or Vietnam has been unavailing. However, it is known that Theresa Preli Devine served in the Philippines as an Army nurse during World War II. Florence Megson served with the Red Cross in Guam in World War II.

152. The Welles-Turner Memorial Library in 1995 celebrated the 100th anniversary of the establishment of a free public library in Glastonbury.

154. Glastonbury's first case of AIDS was reported to the local Health Officer in 1984. By November 1994 there had been, in all, over those 10 years 17 cases reported in town, but none since February 1993. Lyme Disease was first reported in 1988/89, with four cases cited. The number had reached 18 by 1990 but dwindled to eight in 1994. These few cases of communicable disease were a great contrast to those reported in 1949: 126 cases of measles, 78 of chicken pox, 34 of mumps and 13 of scarlet fever.

154. The state-ordered School Desegregation Plan grouped towns by regions for study, placing Glastonbury in Region 9 with the following towns: Avon, Bloomfield, Bolton, Canton, East Granby, East Hartford, East Windsor, Ellington, Enfield, Granby, Hartford, Manchester, Rocky Hill, Simsbury, South Windsor, Suffield, West Hartford, Wethersfield, Windsor and Windsor Locks.

157. The Police Department received national accreditation in 1986 under Police Chief Francis J. Hoffman. Chief Hoffman retired in '87 after 17 years' service and Chief James M. Thomas was sworn in to take his place.

157. A telecommunications van was set up in the 1980s by the Civil Preparedness office under the director, Robert F. DiBella, for use in emergencies.

159. Inez Hemlock, in giving a brief history of St. Dunstan's Church in *The Glastonbury Citizen*, called this 20-year old Catholic Church "The Church in the Woods."

160. Over the years as more dwellings have been built, disposal of waste has been a perennial concern. By 1983 the landfill dump at 2340 New London Turnpike had reached capacity. A transfer station for trash disposal was set up, and through an arrangement with Hartford, solid waste was sent first to that city's landfill and then to the Connecticut Resource Recovery Facility. The town's recycling program annually collects hundreds of tons of newsprint, glass, etc.

160. During the decade 1984/94, 91 new streets were added, according to the Public Services Department, an indication of how fast the town has grown and spread.

161. Glastonbury's first "affordable housing" (designed as such) was Welles Village, built in 1942 by the federal government to house defense workers. The town purchased the units in the 1950s. Welles Village, with Federal subsidy, is under the management of the Glastonbury Housing Authority. The community has its own Welles Village Association.

163. As a Tercentenary project the Historical Society had the old school bell from the former Glastonbury Free Academy mounted on a granite boulder on the circular turnaround green behind the Town Hall.

163. A cooperative project carried out at Glastonbury Center by both the Town of Glastonbury and community volunteers was the Tercentenary Park, a long flower garden backed by a post-and-rail fence, with benches and a commemorative brick walkway. The garden was named in memory of Paul Love, a volunteer who had grown and tended flowers at the Welles-Chapman Tavern and the Gideon Welles Birthplace.

Appendix

165. The additional list of 18 names, supposedly petitioners for separation from Wethersfield, must be in error. It includes names of three persons not yet born in 1690, Jonathan and Benjamin Hale and Joseph Hollister, Jr; as well as Ephraim Hollister, aged 6; David Hollister, 9; Thomas Kimberly, 9; Nathaniel Talcott, 12; Benjamin Talcott, Daniel Wright, and Joseph Hollister, Sr., 16; and Thomas Hollister, 18.

Sources

In addition to the sources of information listed below are town officials and others credited in the text, whose help and courtesy are much appreciated.

BIDWELL, RAY W., "Flood Waters Disclose Relics of Indian Past," *Retrospect*, a publication of the Historical Society of Glastonbury, November 1938.

CHAPIN, ALONZO B., *Glastonbury For Two Hundred Years: A Centennial Discourse*, Hartford, Case, Tiffany and Co., 1853.

CLARK, HERBERT T., "Early Industries Along Roaring Brook," *Retrospect*, May 1940.

CLARK, PHYLLIS H., "The Development of the Glastonbury Junior-Senior High School, Including a History of the Glastonbury High School, 1902-1952," *The Glastonbury Citizen*, June-September 1952.

CONNECTICUT, *Colonial Records*, transcribed by Charles J. Hoadley, Hartford, Case, Lockwood and Brainard, 1868.

CONNECTICUT, *State Archives*, Connecticut State Library, Hartford.

COX, BARBARA B., "Sailing Ships of Glastonbury," *The Publick Post*, a publication of the Historical Society of Glastonbury, Winter 1968.

CURTIS, FLORENCE HOLLISTER, *Glastonbury*, Woman's Club of Glastonbury, 1928. "Prudence Eaton" series, *East Hartford Gazette*, 1928; 1929; 1931.

DE FOREST, JOHN W., *History of the Indians of Connecticut*, Hartford, W. J. Hamersley, 1851.

EBSTEIN, BARBARA, "The Harriman Motor Works, Inc.," *The Publick Post*, Fall 1969.

EAST HARTFORD GAZETTE, article on blizzard of '88, March 23, 1888. Section on Glastonbury industries, November 29, 1901.

FOX, FRANCES WELLS, et al, *Wethersfield and Her Daughters*, Hartford, Case, Lockwood and Brainard, 1934 (Section on Glastonbury by Lewis W. Ripley.)

GLASTONBURY CITIZEN, THE

GLASTONBURY, *Town Records*. These record events from 1690 onward. Annual Town Reports, 1870 to date.

GOSLEE, HENRY S., "Glastonbury Sketches," *The Connecticut Quarterly,* Vol. II, October, November, December 1896.

HARTFORD COURANT, THE

HODGE, EARLE H., "The Grammar School in South Glastonbury," *Retrospect,* September 1948.
(See also "The Glastonbury Seminary," *Retrospect,* October 1939.)

KNOX, VIRGINIA A., "Glastonbury Ferries," *The Publick Post,* July 1956.
"History of Glastonbury Churches," talk, Eunice Cobb Stocking Chapter, DAR, 1968.
"Timothy Stevens Settles," *The Publick Post,* Spring 1968.

PARSHLEY, MARY H., "Glastonbury – A Mining Town?" *The Publick Post,* Winter 1967.
"Academy Hall," *The Publick Post,* Spring 1969.

PRATT, ALFRED H., "The Anchor Industry in Early Glastonbury" *Retrospect,* Winter 1939.

RHINES, OLIVE S., "Earlier Days in Glastonbury," *The Connecticut Antiquarian,* Bulletin of the Antiquarian and Landmarks Society of Connecticut, December 1960.

STILES, EZRA, *Literary Diary,* Vol. II, ed. by Franklin Bowditch Dexter, New York, Charles Scribner's Sons, 1901.

STILES, HENRY R., *Ancient Wethersfield Connecticut,* New York, Grafton Press, 1904. (Sections on Glastonbury by Sherman W. Adams.)

SWAN, BERNICE, "Charcoal Industry in Glastonbury," *The Publick Post,* July 1956.

TRUMBULL, J. HAMMOND, *The Memorial History of Hartford County,* 1633-1884, Boston, Edward L. Osgood, 1886. (Section on Glastonbury by William S. Goslee.)

VAN DUSEN, ALBERT E., *Connecticut,* New York, Random House, 1961.

WELLES, HENRY T., *Autobiography and Reminiscences,* Minneapolis, Marshall, Robinson, 1899.

WHITTLES, LEE JAY, "The Role of Glastonbury During the Revolution," *DAR Magazine,* April 1962.

WILLIAMS, SAMUEL H., *Schools of Glastonbury, 1840-1940,* privately published, 1945.
Shaving Soap Manufacturing in the 1870s, privately published, (1945-46?)

WRIGHT, JOSEPH, *Journals,* 1837-1863. Typed transcripts in the collections of the Historical Society of Glastonbury.

Index

Turramuggus (Tarramuggus), 7, 9, 13
Twain, Mark, 87
Tyler, John S., 94
"Tyro's Casket," 64

Uncas, 15
Uniform Fiscal Year, 107, 125
United Aircraft Corp., 115, 153
University of Connecticut, 91

Van Dusen, Albert E., 6
Vietnam War, 154
Vocational Agriculture, 104

Wahquinnacutt, 4
Ward, Dr. and Mrs. James, 26-27
Waring, Mrs. Dana B., 152
Wars, 151
Warwick Patent, 6
Wassuc Manufacturing Co., 54, 87, 127
Water Resources Commission, 139-140
Watson, Dr. Hugh McG., vi, 129, 130, 133
Webster, Noah, 42, 64, 65
Welfare Commission, 107
Welles, Ann Hale, 83
Welles, Ashbel, 48, 49, 50
Welles-Chapman Tavern, 31-32, 71, 107, 135, 150, 163
Welles, George, 41-43, 48, 49, 50
Welles, Gideon, 50, 72, 82-83, 138, 142
Welles, Gideon, House, 107-108, 135, 136
Welles, Henry T., 64, 152
Welles, Isaac, 31
Welles, John, 43, 48, 49
Welles, John, Jr., 48
Welles, Jonathan, 33-34
Welles, Joseph, 31, 32, 50, 107
Welles, Oliver, 138
Welles, Oswin, 57
Welles, Capt., Robert G., 81-82
Welles, Capt., Samuel, 7, 28
Welles, Samuel, Jr., 38
Welles, Samuel (squire), 50, 62, 83, 138
Welles-Shipman-Ward House, 26-27, 43, 49, 64
Welles, Thaddeus, 73, 80, 82, 119
Welles, Thomas, 33, 48, 119
Welles, Thomas, Gov., 50
Welles, William, Jr., 41-42
Welles-Hollister grist mill, 109
Welles Village, 175
Wethersfield, 1, 6; proprietors, 7-10; church, 11; petition for separation from, 18-19, 23; boundary dispute, 86
Whigs, 72-74, 79

Whittles, Dr. Lee J., 10, 25, 44, 108, 112, 169
Wickham, John, 38
Wickham, William, house, 24-25
"Wide-Awakes," 79
Williams, Anne, 100
Williams Brothers Manufacturing Co., 58, 97, 98, 100; music hall, 98
Williams, David W., 101
Williams, James B., 58-59, 92, 101
Williams, Mrs. James S., 108
Williams, J. B. Co., 55, 59, 92, 93, 100, 106, 119, 120, 126
Williams Memorial, 101, 103
Williams Park, 88
Williams, P. K., 93
Williams, Richard G., 102, 124, 132
Williams, Richard S., 108
Williams, Samuel H., 92, 102
Williams, Mrs. Samuel H., 100
Williams, William, 58-59
Wilson, Kenneth M., 54
Winthrop, Gov. John, 5, 8
Wollcott, Henry, 7
Woman's Club of Glastonbury, v
Woman's Committee of the Council of Defence, 100
Woman's Congress, 76
Women's rights, Smith Sisters petition to Legislature, 77, 78
Wongunks, see Indians
Woodbridge, Rev. Ashbel, 21
Woodbridge, Howell, 38, 40, 49, 53
World War I, 99; names of 10 killed, 101
World War II, 111-113
Wright, Daniel, Jr., 169
Wright, Eleazar, 41
Wright, James, 30, 86
Wright, Joseph, 68-69, 72-73, 78, 79, 96
Wright's Island, 68, 86
Wyllys, Samuel, 7

Yale, 21, 65; in Glastonbury, 41-43, 169
Youth Services Commission, 133

Zoning, earliest regulation, 59, 128, 133, 143

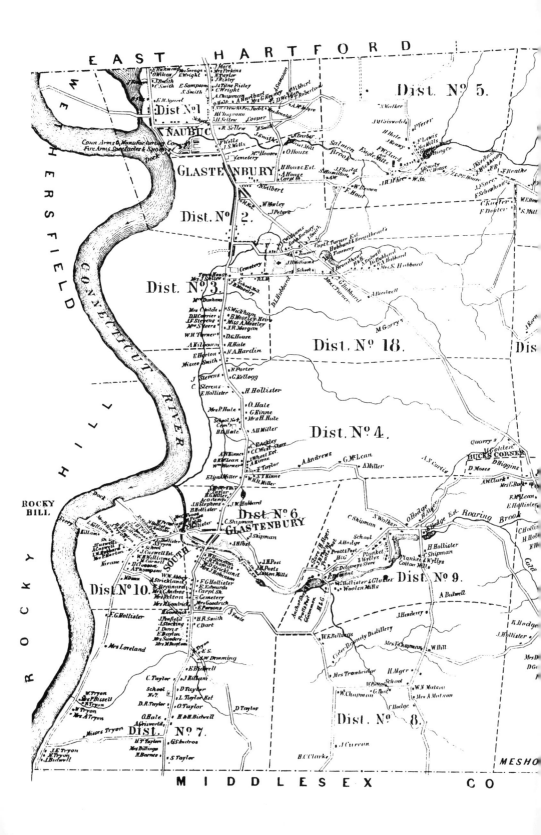

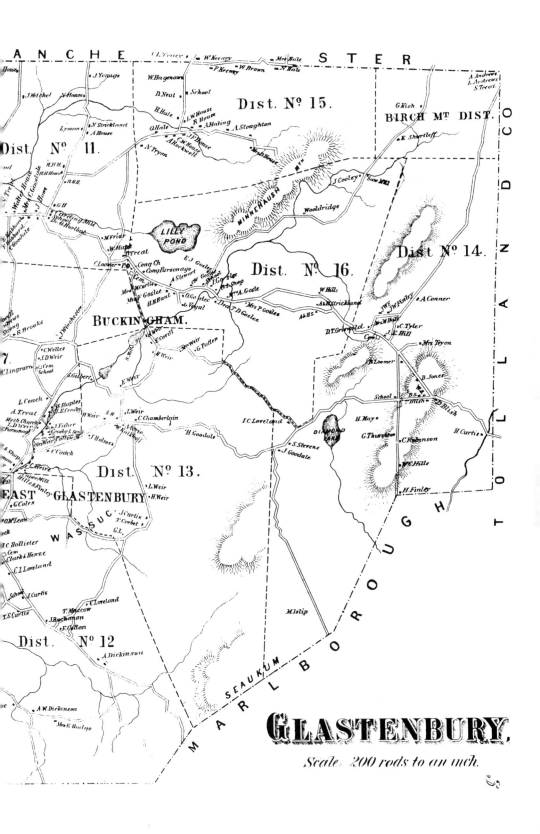

MAN CHE STER

Dist. Nº 15.

BIRCH Mt. DIST.

Dist. Nº 11.

Dist. Nº 14.

LILLY POND

MINNEHAUSH Mtn

Wooldridge

Dist. Nº 16.

BUCKINGHAM.

Dist. Nº 13.

EAST GLASTENBURY

DIAMOND POND

Dist. Nº 12.

GLASTENBURY.

Scale 200 rods to an inch.

MARLBOROUGH TOLLAND CO

SEAUKUM

SOUTH GLASTENBURY

Scale 30 rods to an inch.

Dist No 6

Roaring Brook

J. W. Kinne
O. R. McLeon
Wm Warner
Elijah Miller
J. Wheet Est
J. Kinne
S. T. Kinne
F. Taylor
Wm H. Miller
S. T. Kinne
J. Shipman

Powder Keg Mfg
P. Taylor
H. G. Miller
Academy
J. H. Stevens
J. W. Hubbard
B. Hollister

B. Hollister & Son

C. Shipman
Cong Parsonage
C. Shetfield
Store
Cong Ch.
School No 6
G. Merrick
C. Manley
R. E. Merritt
W. Bates
Chas Bates
Hotel
M. E. Church

J. H. Post
Epis Ch.
R. West
A. A. Redwood
Store
G. Hawley
F. Strickland
Emily Dayton
Mrs. Jones
Mrs. Treat
Dress Shop
Store
W. Goodrich
Mrs. J. White

M. Westley
S. Shipman
Masonic Hall
G. Pratt
Henry Coles
J. Strickland
Shippman
F. Glazier
Coble Sh.
S. Strickland
Epis Parsonage
Fr West Tav
Fr. W. West

Jay S.
William
P. O.

A. H. Williams
Mrs. L. Collins
Chas House
W. Pease
M. & J. Hollister
Grist Mill
W. Pease
Mrs. S. Pease
W. H. Pease

W. Dean
Old Grist Mill
M. Hollister
C. Hollister

J. Couch

CEMETERY

L. V. H. Risley
R. Risley
Epis Ch.
Mrs. Risley
G. L. Ford
G. Sanson
Asa Welles
G. Welles

Shop
T. Welles
Shoe Shop
J. Welles
Masonic Hall
A. Chapman
W. S. Goslee Law Office
Dr. H. C. Bunce
N. A. Turner
Gaines House
C. F. Gaines
C. F. Gaines
School No. 2.

T. Welles
T. Welles
Res.

T. W.

Dr W.
Thro Est.
L. Wright
G. L. Ford
Mrs. Richmond
Miss J. Price
P. O.
Store
Mrs.
Wm Taylor
B. Taylor
Mrs.
Gaines
Wm Reid
H. Hale
Wm Morley

H. Higgins
Wagon Sh.
A. J. Keeney

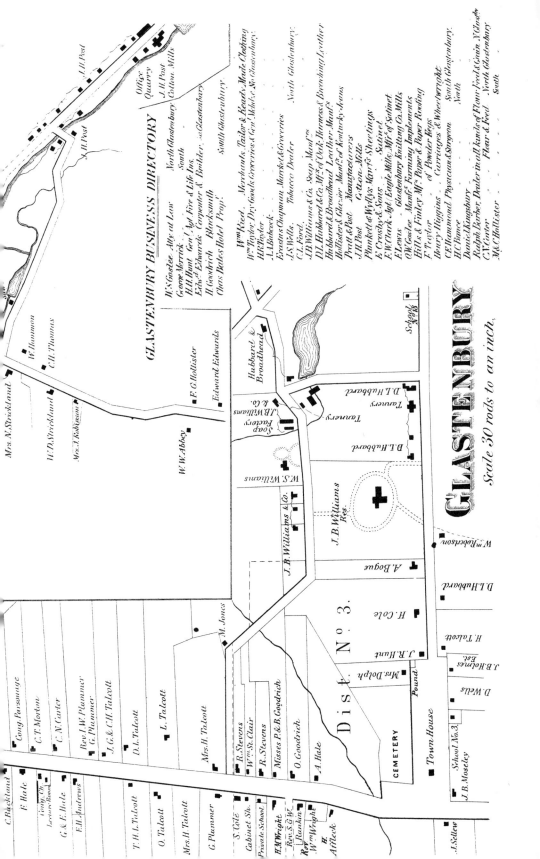

GLASTENBURY

Scale 30 rods to an inch.

GLASTENBURY BUSINESS DIRECTORY

W.S Goslee.	Att'y at Law
Geore Merrick.	
H.H. Hunt.	Gen.l Ag.t Fire & Life Ins.
Edw.d Edwards.	Carpenter & Builder. ..Glastenbury
H Goodrich	Blacksmith
Chas. Betes	Hotel Prop.r	South Glastenbury
W.m Reed.	Merchants, Tailor & Ready Made Clothing
W.m Taylor.	Dry Goods Groceries & Gen.l Mdse. No Glastenbury:
H.R.Taylor.	North Glastenbury
A.A.Babcock.	South
Erastus Chapman	Market & Groceries
J.S.Wells.	Tobacco Dealer ...... North Glastenbury
C.L.Ford.	
J.B.Williams & Co.	Soap Manf.rs
D.L.Hubbard & Co.	Mf.s of Oak Harness.(Breeching) Leather
Hobbard & Broadhead	Leather. Manf.s
Hollister & Glazier	Manf.s of Kentucky Jeans
Pratt & Post	Manufacturers
J.H.Post	Cotton Mills
Plunkett & Wellys	Manf.s Sheetings
E. Crosby & Sons.	Satinet
F.W.Clark-Ag.t	Eagle Mills, Mf.s of Satinet
E.Lewis	Glastenbury Knitting Co. Mills
O.W.Goslee	Manf.s Farming Implements
Hills & Finley	Mf.s Paper & Paper Roofing
F. Taylor	of Powder Kegs
Henry Higgins	Carriages. & Wheelwright
C.E Hammond	Physcican & Surgeon North
H.C Bunce	
Danl. Kingsbury	South Glastenbury
Ralph Barber	Dealer in all kinds of Flour Feed & Grain N.Glas.b
C.N Carter	Flour & Feed North Glastenbury
M.& C.Hollister	South